CHAMPIONS OF FREEDOM

The Ludwig von Mises Lecture Series

CHAMPIONS OF FREEDOM

Volume 27

HUMAN ACTION
A 50-YEAR TRIBUTE

Richard M. Ebeling, Editor

Hillsdale College Press
Hillsdale, Michigan 49242

Hillsdale College Press

The views expressed in this volume are not necessarily the views of Hillsdale College.

The Champions of Freedom series
HUMAN ACTION: A 50-YEAR TRIBUTE

Printed in the United States of America

Photo: Richard M. Ebeling

First printing 2000

Library of Congress Catalog Card Number 99-76146
ISBN 0-916308-59-6

Contents

Contributors

Richard M. Ebeling is the Ludwig von Mises Professor of Economics at Hillsdale College. A former professor at the University of Dallas, he joined the Hillsdale faculty in 1988. In addition, he has served on the editorial board of the *Review of Austrian Economics* and is vice president of the Future of Freedom Foundation, which regularly publishes his essays on political and economic issues. He edited *Money, Method, and the Market Process: Essays by Ludwig von Mises* (Norwell, MA: Kluwer Academic Press, 1990), and *The Case for Free Trade and Open Immigration* (Fairfield, VA: Future of Freedom Foundation, 1995), as well as a number of volumes in the Hillsdale College Press Champions of Freedom series. Professor Ebeling has also lectured extensively on privatization and monetary reform throughout the United States, Latin America, and the former Soviet Union, where he has consulted with the Lithuanian government, the city of Moscow, and the Russian parliament. Currently he is writing a biography of Ludwig von Mises and editing a series of volumes that will feature Mises' recently unearthed pre-World War II papers. The first, *The Political Economy of International Reform and Reconstruction,* was released by Liberty Fund, Inc., of Indianapolis, Indiana, in June 2000.

Gene Epstein brings an enviable combination of academic, professional, and journalistic experience to his work as *Barron's* economics editor, a position he has held since 1993, when he was promoted from commodities editor. Now the author of the weekly financial magazine's "Economic Beat" column, he previously worked for a decade as a senior economist at the New York Stock Exchange and taught economics for three years at St. John's University and New York City University. Mr. Epstein is a graduate of Brandeis University and holds a master's degree in economics from New School University.

Sanford Ikeda is an associate professor of economics at Purchase College, State University of New York, and a research associate in the Austrian Economics Program at New York University, where he earned his Ph.D. He currently serves on the executive committee of the Society for the Development of Austrian Economics and holds membership in the American Economic Association. His past accomplishments include fellowships from the Institute for Humane Studies and NYU and three F. A. Hayek Fund Awards. He has written one book, *Dynamics of the Mixed Economy: Toward a Theory of Interventionism* (London: Routledge, 1996), co-edited the fifth volume in a series titled *Advances in Austrian Economics* (London: JAI Press, 1998), and contributed chapters to five books, including Volume 17 of the Hillsdale College Press Champions of Freedom series. He also has been published in numerous scholarly journals, and his television and radio appearances have brought an Austrian School economist's perspective to such contemporary issues as technology, health-care reform, and the demise of communism.

After more than four decades as a New York University economics professor, **Israel M. Kirzner** is the "dean" of Austrian School economists in the United States. A *summa cum laude* graduate of Brooklyn College, Dr. Kirzner received prestigious Volker and Earhart fellowships while earning M.B.A. and Ph.D. degrees at NYU. He has written ten books, including *How Markets Work: Disequilibrium, Entrepreneurship and Discovery* (London: Institute of Economic Affairs, 1997); *Essays on Capital and Interest: An Austrian Perspective* (Lyme, NH: Edward Elgar Publishing, 1996); and *Discovery, Capitalism and Distributive Justice* (Malden, MA: Basil Blackwell, 1989). He has edited five books, including the three-volume series *Classics in Austrian Economics* (London: William Pickering, 1994). He also has written thirty book reviews and nearly one hundred articles and book chapters, including four for Hillsdale College Press publications.

Charles Murray is the Bradley Fellow at the American Enterprise Institute (AEI) and the author of four influential and controversial books: *Losing Ground: American Social Policy 1950–1980* (New York: Basic Books, 1984); *In Pursuit: Of Happiness and Good Government* (New York: Simon and Schuster, 1988); *The Bell Curve: Intelligence and Class Structure in American Life* (New York: Free Press, 1999); and *What It Means to Be a Libertarian: A Personal Interpretation* (New York: Broadway Books, 1997). With a B.A. from Harvard and a Ph.D. from MIT, Dr. Murray has been published in numerous academic journals, but his articles have also appeared in such lay periodicals as *Public Interest*, the *New Republic*, *Commentary*, the *New York Times*, the *Wall Street Journal*, *National Review*, and the *Washington Post*. Additionally he has been the subject of cover articles in *Newsweek*, the *New York Times Magazine*, and the *Los Angeles Times Magazine*, as well as segments on numerous network and cable television programs. Before joining AEI, Dr. Murray was a fellow with the Manhattan Institute, chief scientist at the American Institutes for Research, and a Peace Corps volunteer.

Robert W. Poole, Jr., is founder and president of the Reason Foundation, a nonprofit public policy research institute based in Los Angeles. A nationally recognized expert on privatization of government services and the author of dozens of published articles and policy studies, Mr. Poole founded the Local Government Center in the mid-1970s. He went on to consult for the Reagan administration's White House Office of Policy Development and to serve on several California state and local transportation and privatization commissions. He holds bachelor's and master's degrees from MIT.

George Roche served as president of Hillsdale College from 1971 until his retirement in 1999. Formerly the presidentially appointed chairman of the National Council on Education Research, the director of seminars at the Foundation for Economic Education, a professor of history at the Colorado School of Mines, and a U.S. Marine, he is the author of thirteen books, including six Conservative Book Club selections. In 1994, he wrote *The Fall of the Ivory Tower: Government Funding, Corruption, and the Bankrupting of American Higher Education* (Washington: Regnery Gateway, 1994), which was named "Book of the Year" in an *Insight* cover story and which earned coverage in *Forbes,* the *Wall Street Journal,* and *Reader's Digest.* In 1998, Regnery Publishing released his *Book of Heroes: Great Men and Women in American History,* a series of short biographies for students and interested laymen.

After earning a bachelor's degree in political economy from Hillsdale College and master's and Ph.D. degrees in philosophy from Purdue, **Roberto Salinas-León** returned to his native Mexico to conduct research and write on free market issues. Currently the executive director of Policy Analysis for TV Azteca in Mexico City, he has delivered more than five hundred lectures throughout the world and published more than eight hundred editorials in such prestigious outlets as the *Wall Street Journal,* the *Dallas Morning News,* the *Washington Times,* the *Journal of Commerce,* the *Miami Herald, Investor's Business Daily,* and *Barron's.* He also writes a weekly column for one English and three Spanish language publications and appears as an economic analyst on Mexican television. He is president of The Economist Conferences Mexico Business Forum and an adjunct scholar of the Cato Institute. He has held leadership positions with the Center for Free Enterprise Research, Chambers of Commerce, and policy organizations in the United States and Latin America.

Hans F. Sennholz was the first Ph.D. student to write his dissertation under Ludwig von Mises at New York University. He quickly rose through the academic ranks to become chairman of Grove City College's economics department, a position he held for thirty-six years before retiring in 1992 to begin a five-year tenure as president of the Foundation for Economic Education. During his career, he also has served as a member of the Economists' National Committee on Monetary Policy, director and vice president of the Committee for Monetary Research and Education, and a member of several corporate boards. He has written fifteen books and booklets, including *Age of Inflation* (Belmont, MA: Western Islands, 1977, 1979); *Money and Freedom* (Spring Mills, PA: Libertarian Press, 1985); and *Reflection and Remembrance* (Irvington, NY: Foundation for Economic Education, 1997). Several of those works have also appeared in Spanish, and one has been translated into Polish. He has contributed thirty-six articles to German journals and newspapers and more than five hundred to American publications.

Karen I. Vaughn is professor of economics at George Mason University, where she has taught since 1978. She is the founding president of the Society for the Development of Austrian Economics and has held the presidency of the Southern Economic Association and the History of Economics Society. The recipient of numerous faculty research fellowships, Dr. Vaughn has written two books, edited a third, contributed chapters to fifteen, and reviewed twenty. More than two dozen of her articles have been published in scholarly journals, on topics ranging from John Locke to feminist economic theory to Austrian welfare economics.

Gleaves Whitney is the senior speechwriter for Michigan Governor John Engler, a position he has held since 1992. In 1993, he served on the governor's education task force, which recommended reforms described by the *New York Times* as "the most dramatic in the nation." Since 1995, Mr. Whitney has served as the first senior fellow of the Russell Kirk Center for Cultural Renewal and as a member of the Intercollegiate Studies Institute's colloquium faculty. A member of Phi Beta Kappa and the recipient of a Fulbright Scholarship and Weaver and H. B. Earhart fellowships, the Colorado State University graduate completed graduate courses at Universität Konstanz and Exeter College, Oxford University. He earned a master's degree from the University of Michigan, where he is currently a Ph.D. candidate. He has written one book, *Colorado Front Range* (1983), and has contributed to four others, including Volume 23 in the Hillsdale College Press Champions of Freedom series.

Leland B. Yeager is the Ludwig von Mises Distinguished Professor Emeritus of Economics at Auburn University. After serving in the U.S. Army as a Japanese cryptanalytic translator during World War II, Dr. Yeager went on to graduate Phi Beta Kappa from Oberlin College and earn M.A. and Ph.D. degrees from Columbia University. He has also taught at Texas A&M, the University of Maryland, the University of Virginia, Southern Methodist University, UCLA,

New York University, and George Mason University. He has served as president of the Southern Economic Association and the Atlantic Economic Society. An adjunct scholar of the Cato Institute and the American Enterprise Institute, he is on the editorial boards of several professional journals. He has written fourteen books and pamphlets and translated Ludwig von Mises' *Nation, State, and Economy* from German. Among his dozens of articles and book chapters are three contributions to the Hillsdale College Press Champions of Freedom series.

Foreword

Hillsdale College was built under the influence of the American Revolution. In that revolution there was much talk of property rights. These are rights, said Madison, to the material things that we have made and earned. These are also rights to every natural property that belongs to the human being. This means his ability to think and to speak. It means his capacity to worship the Almighty, and his individual responsibility to that highest Being. Property rights are a kind of summation of all of our rights.

In modern times, many great economists have worked to recover the full force of this powerful view, which has been the chief foundation of liberty in the modern world. Among these economists, none is more important than the great Ludwig von Mises.

Hillsdale College has a special connection to Mises. He gave us his personal library, and in making this splendid gift he said these fine words: "Hillsdale, more than any other educational institution, most strongly represents the free market ideas to which I have given my life."

LARRY P. ARNN
President
Hillsdale College

Introduction

Shortly after the publication of Ludwig von Mises' treatise *Nationalökonomie* (the German-language forerunner of *Human Action*) in Geneva, Switzerland, in May of 1940, Mises' friend and fellow Austrian economist Friedrich A. Hayek said in a review of the book:

> There appears to be a width of view and an intellectual spaciousness about the whole book which are much more like that of an eighteenth-century philosopher than that of a modern specialist. And yet, or perhaps because of this, one feels throughout much nearer reality, and is constantly recalled from the discussion of technicalities to the consideration of the great problems of our time. . . . It ranges from the most general philosophical problems raised by all scientific study of human action to the major problems of economic policy of our own time.[1]

A few months later another review appeared, this one by Walter Sulzbach, a prominent free market German economist then in exile in the United States, a refugee from the ravages of war in Europe. Sulzbach, too, emphasized the uniqueness of the man and the work:

> Mises has written a remarkable book. Few economists of our generation can boast of a similar achievement. It is the work of a man who combines an immense knowledge of economic history, economic theories and present-day facts with a thoroughly logical mind. . . . It is the tragedy of Mises', as of the

> published and unpublished works of other Central European authors, that the vast majority of the people who speak German are no longer able to read and understand scholarly books and that the people who are able to do so, are not able or willing to read German. It would be highly desirable if an American publisher would sponsor an English translation of *Nationalökonomie.* So vigorous a statement of the case of economic theory against historicism would be valuable at the present moment also for other than German scholars.[2]

Two months after *Nationalökonomie* had been published, Ludwig von Mises came to the United States, also as a refugee from Nazi-occupied Europe. And nine years later, on September 14, 1949, the book appeared in a revised and enlarged form in English under the title *Human Action: A Treatise on Economics.*[3] Just a few days after its publication, free market economist Henry Hazlitt reviewed it in his regular "Business Tides" column in *Newsweek* magazine:

> There has just been published by the Yale University Press a book that is destined to become a landmark in the progress of economics. Its title is *Human Action,* and its author is Ludwig von Mises. It is the consummation of half a century of experience, study, and rigorous thought. No living writer has a more thorough knowledge of the history and literature of economics than Mises. . . . The result is a work of great originality written in a great tradition. . . . [I]t extends beyond any previous work the logical unity and precision of modern economic analysis. I know of no other work, in fact, which conveys to the reader so clear an insight into the intimate interconnectedness of all economic phenomena. . . . The book is, in fact, as the publishers declare, the counterweight of Marx's *Das Kapital,* of Lord Keynes's *General Theory,* and of countless other books recommending socialization, collectivist planning, credit expansion, and similar panaceas. . . . *Human Action* is, in short, at once the most uncompromising and the most rigorously reasoned statement of the case for capitalism that has yet appeared. If a single book can turn the ideological tide that has been running in recent years so heavily toward statism, socialism, and totalitar-

ianism, *Human Action* is that book. It should become the leading text of everyone who believes in freedom, in individualism, and in the ability of a free market economy not only to outdistance any government-planned system in the production of goods and services for the masses, but to promote and safeguard, as no collectivist tyranny can ever do, those intellectual, cultural, and moral values upon which all civilization ultimately rests.[4]

And as Mises' American student and friend Murray N. Rothbard once pointed out:

> *Human Action* is it: Mises' greatest achievement and one of the finest products of the human mind in our century. It is economics whole . . . and provided a way out for the discipline of economics, which had fragmented into uncoordinated and clashing subspecialties. In addition to providing this comprehensive and integrated economic theory, *Human Action* defended sound, Austrian economics against all its methodological opponents, against historicists, positivists, and neo-classical practitioners of mathematical economics and econometrics. He also updated his critique of socialism and interventionism.[5]

Ludwig von Mises was born in Lemberg, Austria–Hungary, on September 29, 1881. Though originally interested in history, shortly after entering the University of Vienna in 1900 Mises turned to economics after reading *Principles of Economics* by Carl Menger, the founder of the Austrian School of Economics.[6] While at the university he studied with Eugen von Böhm-Bawerk, the person perhaps most responsible for establishing the internationally respected reputation of the Austrian School. In 1906 Mises was awarded a doctoral degree in jurisprudence (at that time economics was studied as part of the law faculty at the university).

Beginning in 1909, Mises was employed at the Vienna Chamber for Commerce, Trade and Industry, as an economic analyst within its department of finance. In this capacity he evaluated and made recommendations about various legislative proposals in the areas of banking, insurance, monetary and foreign exchange policy, and public finance. In the years between the two world wars, he was a senior secretary with the Chamber, enabling him to argue with some authority on the economic policy issues confronting the Austrian government.

The general consensus of economists and others who knew Mises during this time was that he was extremely influential in moderating collectivist and inflationary policies in the Austria of the interwar period. He was instrumental in preventing the full nationalization of the Austrian economy by a socialist government immediately after the end of the First World War. He successfully helped to redirect public and political opinion to bring the Great Austrian Inflation to an end in 1923. And in the aftermath of this monetary disaster, he played an important role in the writing of the statutes and bylaws of the reconstructed National Bank of Austria, under the auspices of the League of Nations in 1924.

In 1913 Mises had been given the right to teach at the University of Vienna as a *Privatdozent* (an unsalaried lecturer); in 1918 he was promoted to the title of "Professor Extraordinary." He taught a course at the University almost every semester until 1934 that influenced a new generation of young Viennese and foreign scholars. He also co-founded and served as vice-president of the Austrian Economic Society.

In 1920, Mises began a *Privatseminar* (private seminar) that normally met twice a month from October to June at his Chamber office. It brought together a group of Viennese scholars in economics, political science, philosophy, sociology and law, many of whom became world-renowned scholars in their respective fields. The participants, almost to a man, recalled the seminar as one of the most rigorous and rewarding experiences of their lives.

One other important activity of Mises' during this period was his founding of the Austrian Institute for Business Cycle Research in 1926. With a young, twenty-seven-year-old Friedrich A. Hayek as the first director, the Institute was soon internationally recognized as a leading center for economic forecasting and policy analysis in Central Europe.

In 1934, Mises was offered and accepted a position as Professor of International Economic Relations at the Graduate Institute of International Studies in Geneva, Switzerland. Shortly after arriving in Geneva he set about a project he long had in mind, the writing of a comprehensive treatise on economics that finally became *Nationalökonomie.* Most of his time from 1934 to 1940, outside of his light teaching responsibilities at the Graduate Institute, was devoted to writing this work.

In the summer of 1940, Mises resigned his position at the Graduate Institute and left for the United States. Mises' first years in the United States were not easy ones. He experienced great difficulty in finding a permanent teaching position, partly because of his age (he was fifty-nine years old when he arrived in America) and partly because of the intellectual climate prevailing in the country at that time. His was a voice for an older classical liberalism and free market capitalism that was out-of-step with the popular trends of socialism, interventionism, and Keynesian economics that were embraced by a large majority of American academics and policymakers of the time.

Not until 1945 was he able to receive an academic appointment as visiting professor in the Graduate School of Business at New York University, a position and status he retained until his retirement in 1969 at the age of eighty-eight. During this almost quarter-of-a-century of teaching in the United States, Mises trained a new generation of economists in the tradition of the Austrian School.

In Europe, Mises had already established an international reputation as one of the most original and controversial economists of his time. Before the First World War, in 1912, he had published *The Theory of Money and Credit,* in which he successfully applied the concept of marginal utility for explaining the demand for money, demonstrated the process by which the interaction of the demand and supply of money established the purchasing power of the monetary unit, and developed a theory of the business cycle that showed that government manipulations of the market rate of interest were the primary cause of economywide fluctuations in production, investment, and employment.[7]

In the early 1920s, Mises also challenged the most fundamental assumptions of a socialist planned economy. In his 1920 article "Economic Calculation in the Socialist Commonwealth" and in his 1922 treatise *Socialism: An Economic and Sociological Analysis,* he showed that socialism's abolition of private property, the market economy, and money prices for both consumer goods and the factors of production meant the end of any possibility for rational economic calculation. Rather than ushering in a utopian epoch of material plenty, socialist central planning would create economic waste, inefficiency, and stagnant or falling standards of living.[8]

In his later books, *Liberalism* (1927) and *Critique of Interventionism* (1929), Mises argued that only free market capitalism could create a social order of individual freedom, material prosperity, and domestic and international peace. A regulated and "hampered" market economy under a regime of government intervention could only produce an economy of distortions, imbalances, political corruption, and abuse.[9]

And in 1933, Mises published a series of essays under the title *Epistemological Problems of Economics*, in which he argued that economics was a distinct science derived from the insight that all social processes are derived from the choices and actions of the individual participants in the social and market order. Attempts to reduce conscious and intentional human conduct to the physicalist methods of the natural sciences would not merely distort any real understanding of human decisionmaking and activity, it would create a serious false impression that social and market processes could be manipulated and controlled in more or less the same manner as inanimate matter in a laboratory experiment.[10]

As both Hayek and Rothbard clearly understood, however, it was in *Human Action* that all of these themes were integrated into a systematic conception of man, the social order, the market economy, and its alternatives. Mises explained that our knowledge of the logic of human action is fundamentally different from the way scientists acquire knowledge about the physical world. The inanimate matter of the external world can be measured, quantified, and organized on the basis of various hypotheses concerning the nature and relationships between the physical objects and entities of the universe. But we have no way of determining the "real" or "true" causal reasons as to why the elements of nature have the properties and relational characteristics they seem to possess. We can only observe, hypothesize, quantitatively test, and draw tentative conclusions that may be falsified by some new conjecture that is tested tomorrow.

Human sciences like economics, however, have a radically different starting point. Here we have the ability to know the nature and properties of the causal factor that generates the complex relations of the social and economic processes. All of the social processes have their origin in and can be reduced to the actions and reactions of individual human beings. Being human, the social scientist can draw upon a source of knowledge unavailable to the natural scientist: Introspection. That is, the social scientist can look within and trace the logical and formal characteristics of his own mental processes.

As Mises expressed it, "action" is reason applied to purpose. By understanding the logic of our own reasoning processes, the social scientist can comprehend the essentials of human action: that man, as a conscious being, invariably finds some aspects of his human condition unsatisfactory; he imagines ends or goals that he would like to attain in place of his present or expected circumstances; and he perceives methods and means to try to achieve them. But he soon discovers that some of the means with which he could attain ends are limited in quantity and quality relative to their potential uses. Hence, man is confronted with the necessity to choose among desired ends and has to set some goals aside either for a day or forever, so those means can be used for the pursuit of other ends to which he has assigned greater importance. Few human decisions, however, are completely categorical, that is, either/or. Most are incremental, that is, giving up a little bit of one attainable end so as possibly to attain a little bit more of some other desired end; thus, most choices are made at the "margin."

From these elementary and self-evidently true foundations, all the complex theorems of economics can be traced. But the resulting "laws" of economics are not open to quantitative verification or prediction. The laws of economics, in other words, are logical, not empirical, relationships. Why? Because man has volition, free will, the ability to change his mind and imagine new possibilities that make his actions and responses in the future different in their concrete form from what they were yesterday or today. Hence, the search for a quantitative economics for deterministic prediction of what men and markets will do today, tomorrow, or a year from now is the pursuit of the unattainable.

For Mises, one of the greatest accomplishments of mankind was the discovery of the higher productivity arising from a division of labor. The classical economists' analysis of comparative advantage, under which specialization in production increased the quantities, qualities, and varieties of goods available to all participants in the network of exchange, was more than merely a sophisticated demonstration of the mutual gains from trade. In Mises' view, as he was later to express it, the law of comparative advantage was in fact "the law of human association." The mutual benefits resulting from the specialization of activities, he argued, were the origin of society and the starting point for the development of civilization.

The rationality of the market economy arises from its ability to allocate the scarce means of production in society for the most efficient satisfaction of consumer wants in a complex system of division of labor, that is, to see to it that the means at people's disposal are applied to their most highly valued uses as expressed in the free choices of the participants of the market. This requires some method through which alternative uses for those scarce means and their relative value in those competing applications can be discovered.

Competitively determined market prices, in an institutional setting of private ownership over the means of production, provide the means for solving this problem, he said. On the market for consumers' goods, demanders express their valuations for commodities in the form of the prices they are willing to pay for various quantities and qualities of finished goods. On the market for producers' goods, entrepreneurs express their appraisals of the relative future profitability of using factors of production in manufacturing various goods through the prices they are willing to pay for their purchase or hire.

These prices, expressed through the common denominator of money, make economic calculation possible. The relative costs and expected revenues from alternative productive activities can now be compared and contrasted with ease and efficiency. The competitive processes of the market tend to assure that none of the scarce factors of production are applied for any productive purpose for which there is a more highly valued use as expressed in a rival entrepreneur's bid for their use and hire. The value of the goods desired by consumers is imputed back to the scarce means of production through the competitive rivalry of entrepreneurs. Thus the means available in society are applied to serve people's ends. And the relative values assigned to those means in their alternative uses reflect the relative valuations of the consumers desiring the products that can be manufactured through their employment.

Mises concisely summarized the role and nature of competition and the competitive process in the market order:

> Competitors aim at excellence and preeminence in accomplishments within a system of mutual cooperation. The function of competition is to assign to every member of a social system that position in which he can best serve the whole of society and all its members. It is a method for selecting the most able man for each performance. . . . The pricing process is a social process. It is consummated by an interaction of all members of the society. All collaborate and cooperate, each in the particular role he has chosen for himself in the framework of the division of labor. Competing in cooperation and cooperating in competition all people are instrumental in bringing about the result, viz., the price structure of the market, the allocation of the factors of production to the various lines of want-satisfaction, and the determination of the share of each individual.[11]

Mises' crucial argument against both socialism and interventionism was that they prevented the effective operation of this market process and thus reduced the rationality of the social system. The triumph of socialism—with its nationalization of the means of production under government control and central planning—meant the irrationalization of the economic order. Without market-based prices to supply information about the actual opportunity costs of using those resources as estimated by the competing market actors themselves, decisionmaking by socialist central planners would be arbitrary and "irrational." The socialist economy, therefore, was fundamentally anti-economic.

Interventionism does not abolish the market economy. Instead, it introduces various forms of controls and regulations that necessarily deflect production from the paths that would have been followed if entrepreneurs had been left free to more fully follow their own judgments, to determine for themselves the use and disposal of the factors of production under their control, while searching for profits through the best satisfaction of consumer demand. Price controls, in particular, Mises argued, distort the competitively determined relationships between selling prices and cost-prices, resulting in severe misallocations of resources and misdirected production activities.

Mises also restated and refined the Austrian theory of money and the business cycle in *Human Action.* He developed a dynamic sequence analysis enabling him to explain the process by which changes in the quantity of money brought about redistributions of wealth, relative price changes that modified the allocation of real resources among various sectors of the market, and how monetary changes introduced through the banking system could distort interest rates in such a way as to generate business cycles. A central conclusion that he reached in his analysis of monetary processes was that the business cycle was not a phenomenon inherent in the market economy. Rather, they were caused by government mismanagement of the monetary and banking system. Only a separation of money and the banking system from all government control and influence could reduce, if not eliminate, the recurring patterns of inflations and depressions.[12]

In 1949, Mises' arguments were ignored or scorned as the reactionary misconceptions of a man out-of-step with the more enlightened ideas and economic policies of the postwar era. But now, fifty years after the publication of *Human Action,* it is evident that Mises understood the fundamental flaws in socialism, interventionism, and the welfare state far better than the vast majority of his contemporary economists and policy advocates.

Since Mises' death on October 10, 1973, at the age of 92, the world has seen the collapse of socialist central planning and the economic and ideological bankruptcy of the interventionist–welfare state. The superiority of the market economy, the competitive process, and private entrepreneurial creativity is widely admitted if, alas, still far from being allowed to function freely. But the clearest, most uncompromising voice for economic reason and respect for the freedom and dignity of the individual in our century has been Ludwig von Mises.

For half a century, *Human Action* has served as the medium through which tens of thousands have learned the lessons of a society of peace, freedom, and prosperity. It stands, like Adam Smith's *Wealth of Nations*, as one of the great works not only of economics but of human and social understanding. And like Smith's book, it will remain a timeless classic, as read and as influential in the twenty-first century as it is in our own time. It speaks to and about the most fundamental and universal truths of man and the human condition.

The twenty-seventh volume of *Champions of Freedom: The Ludwig von Mises Lecture Series* is devoted to commemorating the fiftieth anniversary of the publication of *Human Action*. The contributors, some of whom had been Mises' students and friends in the United States, take this opportunity to focus on various aspects of his many contributions to economic theory and policy. They emphasize the significance of Mises' contributions to the development of and the debates over economic ideas in the twentieth century, and have shown his continuing relevance and importance to the issues of today.

This volume is offered as a tribute on the fiftieth anniversary of its publication to the lasting value of the ideas that Ludwig von Mises formulated in *Human Action*.

RICHARD M. EBELING
Ludwig von Mises Professor
of Economics
Hillsdale College

Notes

[1]F. A. Hayek, review of "Nationalökonomie: Theorie des Handelns und des Wirtschaftens" in *The Economic Journal* (April 1941), pp. 125 & 127, reprinted in Peter G. Klein, ed., *The Collected Works of F. A. Hayek, Vol. 4: The Fortunes of Liberalism, Essays on Austrian Economics and the Ideal of Freedom* (Chicago: University of Chicago Press, 1992), pp. 149 &152.

[2]Walter Sulzbach, review of "Nationalökonomie: Theorie des Handelns und des Wirtschaftens" in *Journal of Social Philosophy* (October 1941): 77.

[3]Ludwig von Mises, *Human Action, Treatise on Economics* (New Haven, CT: Yale University Press, 1949). The story of the difficulties of arranging sponsorship for the translation and publication of the 889-page volume in English is told in the "Introduction to the Scholar's Edition" of the recent reprint of the first edition of *Human Action*, published by The Ludwig von Mises Institute of Auburn, Alabama, see pp. xii–xv.

[4]Henry Hazlitt, "The Case for Capitalism," *Newsweek* (September 19, 1949): 70, reprinted in Mary Sennholz, ed., *On Freedom and Free Enterprise: Essays in Honor of Ludwig von Mises* (Princeton, NJ: D. Van Nostrand, 1956), pp. 37–38.

[5]Murray N. Rothbard, *Ludwig von Mises: Scholar, Creator, Hero* (Auburn, AL: Ludwig von Mises Institute, 1988), p. 64.

[6]Ludwig von Mises, *Notes and Recollections* [1940] (South Holland, IL: Libertarian Press, 1978), p. 33. For an exposition of the ideas of the Austrian School of Economics, see Richard M. Ebeling, "The Significance of Austrian Economics in Twentieth-Century Economic Thought," in Richard M. Ebeling, ed., *Austrian Economics: Perspectives on the Past and Prospects for the Future,* Champions of Freedom, Vol. 17 (Hillsdale, MI: Hillsdale College Press, 1991), pp. 1–40; and, Ludwig M. Lachmann, "The Significance of the Austrian School of Economics in the History of Ideas," in Richard M. Ebeling, ed., *Austrian Economics: A Reader,* Champions of Freedom, Vol. 18 (Hillsdale, MI: Hillsdale College Press, 1991), pp. 17–39.

[7]Ludwig von Mises, *The Theory of Money and Credit* (Indianapolis: Liberty Classics, 1981). On Mises' contributions to monetary theory and policy, see Richard M. Ebeling, "Ludwig von Mises and the Gold Standard," in Llewellyn H. Rockwell, ed., *The Gold Standard: An Austrian Perspective* (Lexington, MA: Lexington Books, 1983), pp. 35–59.

[8]Ludwig von Mises, "Economic Calculation in the Socialist Commonwealth," [1920] reprinted in Israel M. Kirzner, ed., *Classics in Austrian Economics, Vol. 3: The Age of Mises and Hayek* (London: William Pickering, 1994), pp. 3–30; and *Socialism: An Economic and Sociological Analysis* (Indianapolis: Liberty Classics, 1981). On Mises' contribution to the theory of socialism and the planned economy, see Richard M. Ebeling, "Economic Calculation Under Socialism: Ludwig von Mises and His Predecessors," in Jeffrey M. Herberner, ed., *The Meaning of Ludwig von Mises* (Norwell, MA: Kluwer Academic Press, 1993), pp. 56–101.

[9]Ludwig von Mises, *Liberalism: the Classical Tradition* [1927] (Irvington-on-Hudson, NY: Foundation for Economic Education, 1996); and *Critique of Interventionism* [1929] (Irvington-on-Hudson, NY: Foundation for Economic Education, 1999); also *Interventionism: An Economic Analysis* [1940] (Irvington-on-Hudson, NY: Foundation for Economic Education, 1998).

[10]Ludwig von Mises, *Epistemological Problems of Economics* [1933] (New York: New York University Press, 1981). On Mises' conception of "human action" and his contributions to the theories of the market economy, socialism, and interventionism, see Richard M. Ebeling, "A Rational Economist in an Irrational Age: Ludwig von Mises," in Richard M. Ebeling, ed., *The Age of Economists: From Adam Smith to Milton Friedman,* Champions of Freedom, Vol. 26 (Hillsdale, MI: Hillsdale College Press, 1999), pp. 69–120; see also Richard M. Ebeling, "The Free Market and the Interventionist State," in Richard M. Ebeling, ed., *Between Power and Liberty: Economics and the Law,* Champions of Freedom, Vol. 25 (Hillsdale, MI: Hillsdale College Press, 1998), pp. 9–46.

[11]Ludwig von Mises, *Human Action: A Treatise on Economics* (Irvington-on-Hudson, NY: Foundation for Economic Education, 4th revised ed., 1996), pp. 117 & 338.

[12]For an exposition of the Austrian theory of money and the business cycle and its explanation of the causes and duration of the Great Depression of the 1930s, see Richard M. Ebeling, "The Austrian Economists and the Keynesian Revolution: The Great Depression and the Economics of the Short Run" in the present volume.

Richard M. Ebeling

The Austrian Economists and the Keynesian Revolution: The Great Depression and the Economics of the Short Run

The Fiftieth Anniversary of Human Action

On September 14, 1949, Yale University Press released a major new work—*Human Action* by the Austrian economist Ludwig von Mises. The following week, in his regular *Newsweek* column, Henry Hazlitt referred to this book as "a landmark in the progress of economics. . . . *Human Action* is, in short, at once the most uncompromising and the most rigorously reasoned statement of the case for capitalism that has yet appeared. If a single book can turn the ideological tide that has been running in recent years so heavily toward statism, socialism, and totalitarianism, *Human Action* is that book. It should become the leading text of everyone who believes in freedom, individualism, and . . . a free market economy."[1]

It is perhaps useful to recall the state of the world when *Human Action* first appeared in 1949. The Soviet system of central economic planning had been imposed by Stalin on all of eastern Europe. In Asia, Mao Tse-Tung's communist armies were just completing their conquest of the Chinese mainland. In western Europe, many of the major noncommunist governments were practicing what the German free market economist Wilhelm Röpke called "national

---

This chapter is partly based on a forty-part series, "Monetary Central Planning and the State," which appeared in *Freedom Daily* (January 1977–April 2000), published by The Future of Freedom Foundation in Fairfax, Virginia.

collectivism"—a "combination of repressed inflation, collectivist controls, 'full employment,' exchange control, state monopolies, bilateralism, subsidies, fiscal socialism [and] 'cheap money' policies." In the United States, government policy was guided by what Henry Hazlitt had referred to in his *Newsweek* column (a few weeks before his review of *Human Action*) as "ultra-Keynesian ideology."[2]

In *Human Action*, Ludwig von Mises opposed every one of these trends and policies, plus many others in contemporary social philosophy, philosophy of science, and in economic theory and method. He challenged the foundations, logic, and conclusions of every facet of twentieth-century collectivism. In 1949, Mises' arguments were ignored or scorned as the reactionary misconceptions of a man out-of-step with the more enlightened ideas and economic policies of the postwar era. In 1999, however, it is evident that it was Mises who understood far better than the vast majority of the contemporary economists and policy advocates the fundamental flaws in socialism, interventionism, and the welfare state.

The Legacy of Keynes's "Demand Management" Economics

But even as the twentieth century drew to a close, one legacy of the interventionist thinking of our time continued to dominate public policy thinking. It is the idea that government must manage and guide monetary and fiscal policy to assure full employment, and a stable price level and to foster economic growth. The terms of the debate have changed considerably over the last half-century, but the belief that it is the responsibility of government to control the supply of money and aggregate spending in the economy persisted in the 1990s as it had in the 1940s. As one example, leading free market economists Milton Friedman and Allen Meltzer have both argued recently that the solution to possible depression problems in the United States or Japan would be a dramatic increase in the supply of money to inflate prices and stimulate "aggregate demand" as a method to restore business profitability and create employment opportunities.[3]

The modern conception of "demand management" is a legacy of perhaps the most influential variation on the interventionist theme during the past one hundred years: the Keynesian Revolution that was born out of the Great Depression and the publication of John Maynard Keynes's 1936 book *The General Theory of Employment, Interest and Money*. The impact of Keynes's book and its message should not be underestimated. Its two central tenets were the claim that the market economy is inherently unstable and likely to generate prolonged periods of unemployment and underutilized productive capacity, and the argument that governments should take responsibility to counteract these periods of economic depression with the various monetary and fiscal policy tools at their disposal. This was bolstered by Keynes's belief that policy managers guided by the economic theory developed in his book could have the knowledge and ability to do so successfully.[4]

No less important in propagating his idea of demand management economic policy was Keynes's literary ability to persuade. As Leland Yeager expressed it, "Keynes saw and provided what would gain attention—harsh polemics, sardonic passages, bits of esoteric and shocking doctrine."[5] Keynes possessed an arrogant amount of self-confidence and belief in his ability to influence public opinion and policy. Austrian economist Friedrich A. Hayek, who knew Keynes fairly well, referred to his "supreme confidence . . . in his power to play on public opinion as a supreme master plays his instrument." On the last occasion he saw Keynes in early 1946 (shortly before the latter's death from a heart attack), Hayek asked if Keynes wasn't concerned that some of his followers were taking his ideas to extremes. Keynes replied that Hayek need not be worried. If it became necessary, Hayek could "rely upon him again quickly to swing round pubic opinion—and he indicated by a quick movement of his hand how rapidly that would be done. But three months later he was dead."[6]

Even today, respected economists argue that Keynesian-style macroeconomic intervention is needed as a balancing rod against instability in the market economy. One example is Robert Skidelsky, the author of a widely acclaimed multi-volume biography of Keynes and director of the London-based Social Market Foundation.[7] Professor Skidelsky has recently argued that capitalism has at its heart an instability of financial institutions and, "This insight by Keynes into the causes and consequences of financial crises remains supremely valuable." In any significant economic downturn, government should begin "pumping money into the economy, like pumping air into a deflating balloon."[8]

Mises and Keynes on Money and Monetary Policy in the 1920s and 1930s

In the 1920s, Ludwig von Mises and John Maynard Keynes were among the most influential economists in their respective countries of Austria and Great Britain. Shortly before the First World War Mises had published a major work on monetary theory, *The Theory of Money and Credit.* In the immediate aftermath of the Great War, Mises wrote *Nation, State and Economy,* in which he analyzed the causes and consequences of the First World War. Then in 1920, he published an article, "Economic Calculation in the Socialist Commonwealth," in which he argued that a fully centrally planned economy would be unable to allocate resources rationally because of the elimination of market-based prices following the nationalization of the means of production. He expanded this argument into the wider context of a comprehensive treatise in *Socialism: An Economic and Sociological Analysis* in 1922. In 1927, Mises published *Liberalism,* a forceful defense of economic and personal liberty. This was followed in 1929 by *Critique of Interventionism,* a collection of essays arguing that government regulation of prices and production in a market economy could only create imbalances and distortions that, if carried to their logical conclusion, threatened to lead to socialism via piecemeal extension of such controls. And in 1928, Mises published *Monetary Stabilization and Cyclical Policy,* in which he made the case for a gold standard, private competitive banking, and an end to inflationary policies.

During the Great Austrian Inflation of the early 1920s, Mises was a proponent of a noninflationary monetary policy. He was primarily responsible for writing the charter and bylaws of the reconstituted Austrian National Bank once inflation was brought to an end. In his role as economic advisor to the Austrian Chamber of Commerce, Trade, and Industry, he was also a prominent advocate of free market reforms in the Austrian economy.

In the early 1930s, Mises forcefully argued, in monographs and articles, that the Great Depression had been caused by the mismanagement of monetary policy in both the United States and

Europe. And its severity and duration was the result of misguided interventions and controls introduced by governments that prevented or delayed the normal self-correcting adjustments through which the market would have restored balance and coordination, resulting in a return to full employment and a rational market-directed use of capital, resources, and labor. He restated this case for the free market in the wider context of his 1940 treatise, *Nationalökonomie,* the forerunner of his 1949 magnum opus, *Human Action.*

Shortly before the First World War, Keynes, too, published a book on monetary policy, *Indian Currency and Finance.* During the Great War, he had worked in the British Treasury. In 1919 he served as an advisor to the British delegation in Versailles. But frustrated with the attitude of the Allied powers toward Germany in setting the terms of the peace, Keynes returned to Britain and published *The Economic Consequences of the Peace,* in which he severely criticized the peace settlement. In 1921, he published *A Treatise on Probability.* And in 1923, he published *A Tract on Monetary Reform,* in which he called for the end of the gold standard, suggesting a national managed paper currency in its place. He strongly opposed Great Britain's return to the gold standard in the mid-1920s at the prewar gold parity. He argued that governments should have discretionary power over the management of a nation's monetary system to assure a desired target level of employment, output, and prices.

In 1930 Keynes published *A Treatise on Money,* a two-volume work that he hoped would establish his reputation as a leading monetary theorist of his time instead of only an influential economic policy analyst. However, over the next two years a series of critical reviews appeared, written by some of the most respected economists of the day. The majority of them demonstrated serious problems with either the premises or the reasoning with which Keynes attempted to build his theory on the relationships between savings, investment, the interest rate, and the aggregate levels of output and prices. He devoted the next five years to reconstructing his argument, the result being his most famous and influential work, *The General Theory of Employment, Interest and Money,* published in 1936.

Keynes argued that the Great Depression was caused by inescapable irrationalities in the market economy that not only created the conditions for the severity of the economic downturn, but necessitated activist monetary and fiscal policies by government to restore and maintain full employment and maximum utilization of resource and output capabilities. For the next half-century Keynes's ideas, as presented in *The General Theory*, became the cornerstone of macroeconomic theorizing and policymaking throughout the Western world.

The Federal Reserve Policy and Price Level Stabilization in the 1920s

Contrary to Keynes' interpretation, the Great Depression was not the result of "reckless" and "unstable capitalism" combined with "passive, indifferent government." The Great Depression was caused by monetary mismanagement by America's central bank, the Federal Reserve System. The Depression's intensity and duration were the result of government interventionist and collectivist policies that prevented the required readjustments in the economy that would have enabled a normal recovery in a much shorter period of time.

The roots of the Great Depression were laid with the establishment of the Federal Reserve System in 1913. While the American monetary system had many serious flaws before 1913—practically all connected with federal and state regulations and controls over the banking industry—the Federal Reserve System became the mechanism for centralizing control over the monetary and banking structures in the United States. And those controls became the mechanism for monetary central planning that generated a large inflation during the First World War, the illusion of "stabilization" in the 1920s, and the reality of the Great Depression in the early 1930s.

In the first seven years after the Federal Reserve came into full operation in 1914, wholesale prices in the United States rose more than 240 percent. How had this come about? Between 1914 and 1920, the currency in circulation had increased 242.7 percent. Demand (or checking) deposits had gone up by 196.4 percent, and time deposits had increased by 240 percent.

With the establishment of the Fed, gold certificates began to be replaced with the new Federal Reserve Notes. Unlike the older gold certificates that had 100 percent gold backing, Federal Reserve Notes had only a 40 percent gold reserve behind them, enabling a dramatic expansion of currency. Member banks in the new system were required to transfer a portion of their gold reserves to the Fed to "economize" on gold in the system. At the same time, reserve requirements on deposit liabilities were lowered by 50 percent from the pre-1914 average level of 21 percent to 11.60 percent; and they were lowered even further in June 1917 to 9.67 percent. Reserve requirements on time deposits were set at only 5 percent and diminished further to 3 percent in June 1917.

The decreased reserve requirements on outstanding bank liabilities created a tidal wave of available funds for lending purposes in the banking industry. And, indeed, between 1914 and 1920, bank loans increased by 200 percent. Much of the additional lending ended up in U.S. government securities, especially after America's entry into the First World War in April 1917. Between March 1917 and June 1919, bank loans to the private sector increased by 70 percent, while investments in government securities went up by 450 percent.[9]

As C. A. Philips, T. F. McManus, and R. W. Nelson explained in their important work, *Banking and the Business Cycle: A Study of the Great Depression in the United States*:

> Had it not been for the creation of the Federal Reserve System, there would have been a [lower] limit to the expansion of bank credit during the War. . . . The establishment of the Federal Reserve System, with its pooling and economizing of reserves, thus permitted a greater credit expansion on a given reserve base. . . . It is in the operations of the Federal Reserve System, then, that the major explanation of the War-time rise in prices lies.[10]

The years 1920 to 1921 saw the postwar slump. Prices fell by about 40 percent during these two years, and unemployment rose to more than 10 percent. But the depression, though steep, was short-lived. Why? Because the American economy still had a great degree of wage and price flexibility. The imbalances in the market created by the preceding inflation were soon corrected with appropriate adjustments in the structure of wages and prices to more fully reflect the new postwar supply-and-demand conditions in the market.[11] But this postwar adjustment did not return prices to anything near prewar levels. Prices in the United States were still almost 40 percent higher in 1922 than they had been in 1913.

This was not surprising, since the money supply contracted by only about 9 percent to 13 percent during this period.[12]

Following the depression of 1921, the Federal Reserve System began a great experiment with price level stabilization under the influence of Yale University economist Irving Fisher, one of the most internationally respected economists of the time. Fisher argued that unexpected changes in the general level of prices can have disruptive effects on production and employment in the economy as a whole. This was a theme that he developed in his 1911 work, *The Purchasing Power of Money*, and that he popularized in a series of books, such as *Elementary Principles of Economics, Stabilizing the Dollar,* and *The Money Illusion*, as well as in the dozens of articles he published throughout the 1920s.[13]

Fisher said that during a period of unexpected price inflation or price deflation, prices for finished goods and services and the prices for resources and labor change at different times and to different degrees. As a result, profit margins between the prices for finished goods and the means of production can be artificially and temporarily increased or decreased, resulting in fluctuations in production and employment in the economy.

Prices for finished consumer goods, Fisher explained, tend to be fairly flexible and responsive to changes in the level of market demand. On the other hand, resource prices, including the wages for labor, tend to be fixed by contract.

During periods of unexpected price inflation, the profit margins between consumer-goods prices and resource prices are artificially widened, creating an incentive for employers to expand output to take advantage of the increased return from sales. This, he argued, is the cause of the "boom," or expansionist, phase of the business cycle.

But the boom inevitably comes to an end when resource prices, including wages, come up for contractual renegotiation. Resource owners and laborers, in a market environment of heated demand for their services, bargain for higher prices and money wages to compensate for the lost purchasing power they have suffered while their money incomes have been contractually fixed in the face of rising prices.

The "bust" or contractionist phase of the business cycle then sets in, as profit margins narrow in the face of the new higher costs of production and as employers discover that they have overexpanded and overextended themselves in the earlier boom period.

During periods of unexpected price deflation, profit margins between consumer-goods prices and resource prices are artificially narrowed or wiped out, as consumer-goods prices are declining while resource prices and wages temporarily remain fixed at their contractual levels. Employers have an incentive to reduce output to economize on costs and reduce losses, generating a general economic downturn. The diminished profits or losses are eliminated when resource prices (including wages) come up for contractual renegotiation. Rather than risk losing their businesses and jobs, resource owners and workers moderate their price and wage demands to reflect the lower prices in the marketplace for their products. Furthermore, since consumer-goods prices in general are declining, resource owners and workers can accept lower resource prices and money wages. In real buying terms, they will be no worse off than before the price deflation began.

If price inflations and price deflations could be perfectly anticipated, changes in the purchasing power of money could be incorporated into resource and labor contracts, with profit margins being neither artificially widened nor narrowed by the movements in the general level of prices. The business cycle of booms and busts would be mitigated or even eliminated.

Unfortunately, Fisher again argued, such perfect foresight is highly unlikely. And unless some external force is introduced to keep the price level stable—to eliminate both price inflations and price deflations—Fisher concluded that, given the monetary institutions prevailing in most modern societies during the time he was writing, the business cycle would remain an inherent part of a market economy.

Irving Fisher's solution was to advocate a stabilization of the price level. What was needed, he insisted, was a monetary policy that would ensure neither price inflation nor price deflation. In *Stabilizing the Dollar*, Fisher stated:

> What is needed is to stabilize, or standardize, the dollar just as we have already standardized the yardstick, the pound weight, the bushel basket, the pint cup, the horsepower, the volt, and

> indeed all the units of commerce except the dollar. . . . Am I proposing that some Government official should be authorized to mark the dollar up or down according to his own caprice? Most certainly not. A definite and simple criterion for the required adjustments is at hand—the familiar "index number" of prices. . . . For every one percent of deviation of the index number above or below par at any adjustment date, we would increase or decrease the dollar's weight (in terms of purchasing power) by one percent.[14]

How would the government do this? By changing the quantity of money and bank credit available in the economy for the purchase of goods and services. In his 1928 volume, *The Money Illusion,* Fisher praised the Federal Reserve Board—the American central bank's monetary managers—for following a policy since 1922 close to the one he was advocating. Though only a "crude" beginning, "stabilization ushers in a new era for our economic life . . . adding," he claimed, "much to the income of the nation."

> The dollar . . . has been partially safeguarded against wide fluctuations ever since the Federal Reserve System finally set up the Open Market Committee in 1922 to buy and sell securities, especially Government bonds, for the purpose of influencing the credit situation. . . . When they buy securities they thereby put money into circulation. . . . When they sell, they thereby withdraw money from circulation. [Along with the Federal Reserve's control over bank reserves and the discount rate at which it directly lends to banks, through Open Market Operations] the Federal Reserve does and should safeguard the country . . . against serious inflation and deflation. . . . This power, rightly used, makes the Federal Reserve System the greatest public service institution in the world.[15]

Through the power of the Federal Reserve System, Fisher happily pointed out, America had established a "managed currency," guided by the policy goal of a stable price level.[16] That this was the Fed's goal was confirmed by Benjamin Strong, chairman of the New York Federal Reserve Bank through most of the decade and the most influential member of the Federal Reserve Board of Governors during this period. In 1925, Strong said, "It was my belief . . . that our whole policy in the future, as in the past, would be directed toward the stability of prices so far as it was possible for us to influence prices." And in 1927, he once again emphasized, "I personally think that the administration of the Federal Reserve System since the [depression] of 1921 has been just as nearly directed as reasonable human wisdom could direct it toward that very policy [of price level stabilization]."[17]

Did the Federal Reserve succeed in its policy of price level stabilization? An index of wholesale prices, with 1913 as the base year of 100, shows that the average level of prices remained within a fairly narrow band: 1922—138.5; 1923—144.1; 1924—140.5; 1925—148.2; 1926—143.2; 1927—136.6; 1928—138.5; 1929—136.5. During the entire decade, wholesale prices on average were never more than about 7 percent higher than in 1922. And at the end of the decade, before the Great Depression set in (1929), wholesale prices, as measured by this index, were in fact about 1.5 percent lower than in 1922.

Like Irving Fisher in his praise of Federal Reserve policy in 1928, John Maynard Keynes, in his two-volume *Treatise on Money*, pointed to the Fed's record during the decade and said, "The successful management of the dollar by the Federal Reserve Board from 1923 to 1928 was a triumph . . . for the view that currency management is feasible."[18]

By how much had the Federal Reserve changed the supply of money and credit during the decade to bring about price level stabilization? The answer to this depends on how one defines the "money supply." Milton Friedman and Anna Schwartz, in their famous *Monetary History of the United States, 1867–1960,* estimate that between 1921 and 1929, the money supply increased about 45 percent, or approximately 4.6 percent a year. They used a definition of money that included currency in circulation and demand and time deposits (a definition known as "M–2").[19]

In *America's Great Depression*, Austrian economist Murray Rothbard used a broader measurement of the money supply that included currency, demand and time deposits, savings and loan shares, and the cash value of life-insurance policies. Using these figures, Rothbard estimated that the money supply had increased by 61.8 percent between 1921 and 1929, with an average annual increase of 7.7 percent.[20]

While shares owned in savings and loan banks increased by the largest percentage of any component of the money supply—318 percent between 1921 and 1929—it represented only 4 percent to 8 percent of the total money supply during the period, as measured by Rothbard. The cash value of life insurance policies increased by 213 percent during the period; and it represented between 12.5 percent and 16.5 percent of the money supply, as measured by Rothbard.

If the cash value of life insurance policies is subtracted from Rothbard's measure of the money supply, and if deposits at mutual savings banks, the postal savings system, and the shares at savings and loans are added to Friedman and Schwartz's definition (which, in fact, they do to calculate a broader money definition called "M–4"), the results practically coincide. The money supply, by both measurements, increased by about 54 percent for the period, with an average annual increase of approximately 5.5 percent.

During the decade, this monetary increase did not, however, occur at an even, annualized rate. Rather, it occurred in spurts, especially in 1922, 1924–1925, and 1927, with monetary slowdowns in 1923, 1926, and late 1928 and early 1929. These were not accidents, but rather represented the "fine-tuning" methods of the Federal Reserve Board of Governors in their attempt to counteract tendencies toward either price inflation or economic recession, with price-level stabilization as a crucial signpost of success.

The two main Federal Reserve policy tools for influencing the amount of money in the economy were open-market operations and the discount rate. When the Fed purchases government securities, it pays for them by creating new reserves on the basis of which banks can expand their lending. The sale of government securities by the Fed drains reserves from the banking system, reducing the ability of banks to extend loans.

The discount rate is the rate at which the Fed will directly lend reserves to member banks of the Federal Reserve System. Throughout most of the 1920s, the Fed kept the discount rate below the market rates of interest, creating a positive incentive for member banks to borrow from the Fed and lend the borrowed funds to the market at higher rates of interest, earning the banks a profit. Even when the Fed sold government securities at certain times during the 1920s, member banks were often able to reverse the resulting drains of reserves out of the banking system by borrowing them back from the Fed at the below-market discount rate.

Increases in currency in circulation were a negligible fraction of the monetary expansion, representing less than 1 percent of the increase. Demand deposits increased by 44.6 percent, and time deposits expanded by 76.8 percent. This fostered a major economic boom. As Philips, McManus, and Nelson explained in *Banking and the Business Cycle*:

> As a result of the plethora of bank credit funds and the utilization by banks of their excess reserve to swell their investment accounts, the long-term interest rate declined and it became increasingly profitable and popular to float new stock and bond issues. This favorable situation in the capital funds market was translated into a construction boom of previously unheard-of dimensions; a real estate boom developed, first in Florida, but soon was transferred to the urban real estate market on a nation-wide scale; and finally, the stock market became the recipient of the excessive credit expansion.[21]

Trying to rein in the stock market boom, the Fed all but froze the money supply in late 1928 and the first half of 1929. The monetary restraint finally caught up with the stock market in October 1929.

But why did the stock market downturn develop into the Great Depression? Other than the boom in the stock market, there were few outward signs of an unstable inflationary expansion that would have suggested a need for a recessionary adjustment period to reestablish certain fundamental balances in the economy. The wholesale price index, as we saw, had remained practically unchanged between 1922 and 1929.

Clearly, however, there were forces at work beneath the surface of a stable price level that were generating the conditions for a needed correction in the economy. But depressions had occurred before and recoveries had followed, usually not too long afterward. Why, then, did this downturn become the Great Depression?

The Austrian Economists on the Origin and Purchasing Power of Money

Even before the First World War, a number of prominent American economists had criticized Irving Fisher's proposal for price-level stabilization through monetary manipulation by the government. Frank Taussig of Harvard University, J. Laurence Laughlin of the University of Chicago, and David Kinley of the University of Illinois had forcefully argued that implementing Fisher's scheme would generate more, not less, economic instability.

But it was the Austrian economists who reasoned most persuasively against a price-level stabilization policy in the 1920s. To understand their criticisms, it is necessary to begin with Carl Menger, the founder of the Austrian school. In his *Principles of Economics* and in a monograph on "Money," Menger explained the origin of a medium of exchange.[22] Often there are insurmountable difficulties preventing people from trading one good for another. One of the potential trading partners may not want the good the other possesses. Perhaps one of the goods offered in exchange cannot readily be divided into portions reflecting possible terms of trade. Therefore, the transaction cannot be consummated.

As a result, individuals try to find ways to achieve their desired goals through indirect methods. An individual may first trade away the good in his possession for some other commodity for which he has no particular use. But he may believe that it would be more readily accepted by a person who has a good he actually wants to acquire. He uses the commodity for which he has no direct use as a medium of exchange. He trades commodity A for commodity B and then turns around and exchanges commodity B for commodity C. In this sequence of transactions, commodity B has served as a medium of exchange.

Menger went on to explain that over time transactors discover that certain commodities have qualities or marketable attributes that make them especially serviceable as media of exchange. Some commodities are in greater general demand among a wide circle of potential transactors. Some commodities are more readily transportable and more easily divisible into convenient amounts to reflect agreed-upon terms of exchange. Some are relatively more durable and scarce and difficult to reproduce. The commodities that possess the right combinations of these attributes and characteristics tend to become, over a long period of time, the most widely used and readily accepted media of exchange in an expanding arena of trade and commerce.

Therefore, those commodities historically became the money-goods of the market because the very definition of money is that it is a commodity that is most widely used and generally accepted as a medium of exchange in a market. Money, then, begins as an ordinary market commodity, but because of its particular marketable qualities, it slowly comes to be demanded for its usefulness as a medium of exchange. Over time, its use as a medium of exchange may supersede its other uses as an ordinary commodity. Gold and silver thus came to serve as the most widely accepted media of exchange—the money-goods of the market.

For Menger and later members of the Austrian school, this was a strong demonstration, both theoretically and historically, that money is not a creation or a creature of the state. In its origin, money naturally emerges from the processes of the market, as individuals search for better and easier ways to satisfy their wants through trade and exchange.

A second question that the Austrians asked was: Once a money is in use, how does one define its purchasing power or value in the market? First Menger and then Ludwig von Mises in his book *The Theory of Money and Credit* devoted careful attention to this question.[23]

In a state of barter, when every commodity directly trades for all the others, each good on the market has as many prices as the goods against which it exchanges. But in a money-using economy, goods no longer trade directly one for the other. Instead, each good is first sold for money; with the money earned from selling commodities, individuals then turn and purchase other goods. Each good comes to have only one price on the market—its money-price.

But money remains the one exception to this. Money is the one commodity that continues to trade directly for all the other goods offered on the market. As a result, money has no single price. Rather, money has as many prices as goods with which it trades on the market. The purchasing power of money, therefore, is the array or set of exchange ratios between money and each good. And the actual value of money at any moment in time is that set of specific exchange ratios that have emerged on the market.

By definition, the purchasing power or value of money is always subject to change. Anything that changes people's willingness and ability to sell goods for money or to sell money for goods will modify the exchange ratios between money and goods. If people change a preference, such as they now want to consume more chicken and less hamburger, the demand for chicken on the market would rise and the demand for hamburger would fall. This would change the relative price between chicken and hamburger: the price of chicken would tend to go up relative to the price of hamburger. But at the same time, it would also change the purchasing power or value of money, since now the money price of chicken would have increased and the money price of hamburger would have decreased. The array or set of exchange ratios between money and other goods on the market would, therefore, also now be different.

Suppose, instead, that people changed their preferences and decided to demand fewer goods and to hold a larger amount of the money they earned from selling goods as an available cash balance for some future exchange. The demand for goods would decrease and the demand for holding money as a cash balance would increase. The money prices of goods would tend to decline, raising the purchasing power or value of each unit of money, since at lower money prices, each unit of money would command a greater buying power over goods.

Unless people decreased their demand for goods proportionally at the same time that the value of money was rising the relative prices among goods would change as well. Why? Because if the demand for, say, chicken decreased more than the demand for hamburger, then even at the overall lower scale of money prices, the money price of chicken will have tended to decrease more than the money price of hamburger. The structure of relative prices would have changed as part of the same process that had changed the scale or level of money prices in general.

Irving Fisher's proposal, therefore, to "stabilize, or standardize, the dollar just as we have already standardized the yardstick, the pound weight, the pint cup. . . " was built on a false analogy. A yardstick is a multiple of a fixed unit of measurement—an inch. But the purchasing power or value of money is not a fixed unit of measurement. It is composed of a set of exchange ratios between money and other goods, reflecting the existing and changing valuations of the participants in the market about the desirability of and their demand for various commodities relative to the attractiveness of spending money or holding it as a cash balance of a certain amount.

In *The Theory of Money and Credit* and his later monograph "Monetary Stabilization and Cyclical Policy," Ludwig von Mises also challenged Irving Fisher's proposal for measuring changes in the purchasing power of money through the use of index numbers.[24] A consumer price index, for example, is constructed by selecting a group of commodities chosen as "representative" of the normal and usual types of goods bought by an average family within a particular community. The items in this representative basket of consumer purchases are then "weighted" in terms of the relative amounts of each good in the basket that this representative family is assumed to purchase during any normal period. The prices for these goods times the relative quantities of each bought is then defined as the cost of purchasing this representative basket of consumer items.

The prices of these goods, multiplied by the fixed relative amounts assumed to be bought, are tracked over time to determine whether the cost of living for this representative consumer-family has increased or decreased. Whether the sum of money originally required to buy the basket at the beginning of the series is able to buy a larger, smaller, or the same basket at a later period is then taken to be a measure of the extent to which the purchasing power or value of money has increased, decreased, or stayed the same.

Mises argued that the construction of index numbers, rather than being a supposedly precise method for measuring changes in the purchasing power of money, was in fact a statistical fiction built on arbitrary assumptions. The first of these arbitrary assumptions concerned the selection of goods to include in the basket and the relative weights to assign to them. Preferences for goods vary considerably among individuals, even among individuals in similar income and social groups or geographic locations. Which group of goods to include, therefore, can claim no scientific precision, nor can the judgment concerning the relative quantities be labeled "representative."

The second arbitrary assumption also concerns the "weights" assigned to the goods in the basket. It is assumed that over the periods compared, the same relative amounts purchased in the beginning period are purchased in future periods. But in the real world of actual market transactions, the relative amounts of various goods purchased are always changing. Preferences and desires for goods are constantly open to change. Even when people's basic preferences for goods have not changed, in the real world the relative prices of various goods are changing. People tend to buy less of goods that are rising in price and more of goods decreasing in price or more of those not rising in price as much as others.

The third arbitrary assumption is that new goods are not being offered on the market and that older goods are not being taken off the market. But both occurrences are common and modify the types and quantities of goods in a consumer's basket. The fourth arbitrary assumption concerns changes in the quality of the goods offered. A good that improves in quality but continues to be sold at the same price is now a cheaper good; that is, the consumer is receiving more for the same amount of money. However, the index records no increase in the value of the consumer's dollar. A good may rise in price and, at the same time, be improved, but there is no exact way to determine how much of the higher price can be attributed to the product's improvement and how much is due to market conditions.

Mises' conclusion, therefore, was that there is no scientific way of knowing whether and by how much the purchasing power or value of money may have changed over a given period of time. Thus, the statistical method considered by Irving Fisher to be the key for guiding monetary policy to stabilize price levels was fundamentally and irreparably flawed.

But whether the construction and application of index numbers was flawed or not, stabilization of the price level became a target for the Federal Reserve in the 1920s. And that policy was a prime ingredient in creating the market imbalances that resulted in the Great Depression.

Ludwig von Mises and the Non-Neutrality of Money

In the late 1850s, the British economist John E. Cairnes published a series of articles analyzing the sequence of events that followed the gold discoveries in Australia. He explained that the increase in gold had its initial impact on prices in coastal towns and cities, where the miners first spent their new supplies of gold as money. The increased money demand for goods and services stimulated additional imports into Australia. The Australian merchants paid for these increased stocks of goods with the new gold paid to them by the miners. As gold entered, and then was spent in, the European markets, prices for goods and services began to rise there as well. Manufacturers in Europe, in turn, increased their demand for resources and raw materials from Asia and Africa, paying for them with the new gold that had passed into their hands. Prices then began to rise in those other parts of the world.

The increase in gold supplies brought about a general rise in prices that followed a particular pattern. It began when the gold was introduced into the market, followed by a sequence of expenditures and receipts that reflect the increased demand for commodities and resources in the order of who received the new gold money first, second, third, and so on.

Changes in the quantity of money have long been understood as a primary influence on the rise or decline of prices in general. But the particular method of analysis used by different economists has not only affected the explanation of money's effects on an economy, it has influenced various policy conclusions drawn from this analysis as well.

In *The Purchasing Power of Money* and many of his other works, Irving Fisher presented a rather "aggregated" analysis. As we have already seen, Fisher argued that an increase in the supply of money tended to bring about a rise in selling prices in general, relative to the costs of production. The temporary increase in profit margins between selling prices and costs (due to input prices being fixed for a period of time by contract) acted as the stimulus for attempts to increase output. But when contracts came up for renewal and were revised upward, profit margins would return to "normal" and the "boom" phase of the business cycle would end. It would be followed by a period of correction, in the wake of businessmen's discovering that their overexpansive plans were unsustainable; this was the downturn or depression phase of the business cycle.

Fisher concluded that the cause and sequence of the business cycle were the result of unanticipated increases in the money supply that made selling prices rise relative to cost prices. His policy prescription was to keep the price level stable. If that were done, he argued, price–cost relationships would be kept in proper order, at least to the extent they were influenced by monetary forces. And that, in turn, would mitigate, if not eliminate, the primary cause behind the business cycle.

An alternative method of analysis for explaining money's influence on prices and production was in the tradition represented by John E. Cairnes. In this alternative approach, the analysis is "disaggregated" into a study of money's impact on the economy and traces the path by which changes in the money supply are introduced into the economy and the sequence of events by which this change in the money supply passes from one individual to another and from one sector of the economy to another.[25]

This alternative tradition of monetary analysis is the one followed by the Austrian economists, their leading expositor being Ludwig von Mises. He developed this approach in *The Theory of Money and Credit*, in *Monetary Stabilization and Cyclical Policy*, and in his comprehensive treatise on economics, *Human Action*.[26]

If increases or decreases in the quantity of money brought about simultaneous and proportional increases and decreases in all prices, changes in the supply of money would be neutral in their effects on the economy. That is, neither the structure of relative prices nor the patterns of relative income shares earned by individuals and groups in the society would be affected by changes in the quantity of money. Money's effect on the economy would be nominal and not real.

Mises and the Austrians argued that money's impact on the market was always non-neutral. Economists such as Irving Fisher reasoned that the non-neutrality of money was due only to the fact that changes in the money supply were less than fully anticipated, and as a result, resource and labor contracts did not completely incorporate the actual average rate of price changes into resource prices and wage negotiations. Hence, cost prices would temporarily lag behind selling prices, creating temporary profit differentials.

The Austrians, on the other hand, insisted that money would be non-neutral in its effects even if resource prices and wages were as flexible as selling prices and even if market participants were to fully anticipate the average rate of change in the general price level as measured by a price index. The reason for that was the Austrians' method of analysis. Mises pointed out that any change in market conditions must ultimately have its beginning in the circumstances of one or more individuals. Nothing happens in the market that does not start with the decisions and choices of acting individuals.

If there is an increase in the supply of money, it must necessarily take the form of an increase in the cash holdings of particular people, who are at the starting point of the resulting social consequences of a change in the quantity of money. Finding themselves with a greater amount of cash than they normally hold, they proceed to spend the "surplus" cash on the goods and services they find attractive and profitable to buy.

The demand for goods and services begins to rise because of this increase in the money supply. But it is not all demands that initially increase—only the particular demands for the particular goods that the individuals with the additional cash purchase in greater quantities. In this "first round" of the process, the prices of only those goods for which there has been an increased demand begin to rise. As the money is spent on those goods, the resulting sales become additional money receipts for the sellers. Those sellers, finding their cash positions improved, increase their demands for various goods and services. This is the "second round" of price increases, but again the prices affected are only of those goods which this second group of recipients of new money wishes to purchase.

The money spent in the second round becomes additional money receipts for another group of sellers, who likewise find their cash position improved and who, in turn, increase their demands for various goods and services. That results in a "third round" increase in prices. The process will continue until the demand for all goods and services in the economy, in principle, have been affected, with all prices to one extent or another changed by the monetary expansion. Prices in general will be higher, but each will have been affected by the monetary increase in a particular sequence, to a different degree, and at different times in the process.

The fact that monetary change works its way through the economy in a particular temporal sequence means that relative price relationships in the market will have been modified. The sequential price-increase differentials modify the relative profitabilities of producing various goods, which in turn influence the demand for and the allocation of resources and labor among the various sectors of the economy. As long as the inflationary process is working its way through the market, the patterns of demand for goods and services and the distribution of the factors of production are different from what they were before the inflationary process began, and they are different from what they will be when the inflationary process has come to an end.

At the same time, the very fact that the prices for those goods and resources (including labor) are changing in a non-neutral manner means that income and wealth are redistributed among individuals and groups as an integral part of the monetary process. Those who receive increases in the money supply earlier in the inflationary process are able to purchase more goods and services before the full price effect on the economy has materialized. On the other hand, those whose demands and incomes are impacted much later in the process find themselves paying higher prices for many of the goods they buy, while their own prices and wages have either not increased at all or not to an extent equal to the general rise in prices. That inevitably creates groups of net gainers and net losers during the sequential–temporal process following changes in the money supply.

Any anticipation by the participants in the market of the increase in the average level of prices remains just that: a statistically calculated average of the individual price changes. Both during an inflationary (or deflationary) process and at its end, some prices will have increased (or decreased) more than the average and some less than the average. For money to be neutral during an inflationary (or deflationary) process, it would be necessary for each participant in the market to anticipate correctly when and to what extent the demand and the price for his particular resource (including labor services) would be affected by the monetary expansion (or contraction) in the particular temporal sequence of that historically distinct timeframe. This clearly involves a greater degree of knowledge than can ever be possessed by agents in the market.

Nor is the non-neutrality of money dependent on the fact that the prices for many resources and labor services are fixed by contract for various periods of time. Even if they were not, in the temporal–sequential stages of an inflationary (or deflationary) process, the prices for different goods are affected at different times, necessarily modifying the relative profitabilities of producing those goods. It is those price-differential effects that influence producers to change their production decisions during an inflation (or deflation) and not merely the fact that some prices and wages are fixed.

Likewise, it is not the unanticipated changes in the money supply per se that cause money to be non-neutral and, therefore, to have real output and employment effects on the economy. Rather it is the fact that monetary changes work their way through the economy in a manner that necessarily cannot be fully anticipated and that actually modifies the relative prices of goods and the relative income positions among individuals and groups as an inherent part of any inflationary or deflationary process.

If any monetary change is always non-neutral in its effect on the market, then changes in the money supply made by the government's monetary authority in an attempt to maintain a "stable" price level can themselves be destabilizing. This, in fact, was the argument made by Mises' fellow Austrian economist Friedrich A. Hayek.

Friedrich A. Hayek and the Destabilizing Influence of a Stable Price Level

One indication of rising standards of living are increases in the quantity and quality of goods available to the consuming public. For example, during the twenty-year period from 1880 to the turn of the century a dramatic increase in the productive capacity of the United States economy occurred, matched by an equally significant expansion of goods and services. In their *Monetary History of the United States, 1867–1960,* Milton Friedman and Anna Schwartz pointed out: "The two final decades of the nineteenth century saw a growth of population of over 2 per cent per year, rapid extension of the railway network, essential completion of continental settlement, and an extraordinary increase both in the acreage of land in farms and output of farm products. . . . [A]t the same time, manufacturing industries were growing even more rapidly."[27]

As a result, between 1879 and 1897, real net national product increased at an average annual rate of about 3.7 percent, with per capita net national product increasing at a 1.5-percent annual average rate during this period. The improvements in productive capacity and output, of course, did not occur evenly year-by-year. During this period the United States experienced several severe economic downturns, sometimes related to the uncertainties surrounding the political battles of the time concerning whether America would remain on a gold standard or shift to a bimetallic standard of gold and silver.

But what is also interesting about this period of rapid industrial growth and rising standards of living is that it occurred during a time when prices in general were falling. Between 1865 and 1899 the average level of prices declined more than 45 percent. From 1880 to 1897 prices in general declined by more than 22 percent, or 2 to 3 percent each year. "Economic growth," as Milton Friedman later observed, "was entirely consistent with falling prices."[28]

Assuming that there is neither an increase in the supply of money nor a decrease in the demand for money, it is inevitable that increases in productivity, output, and, therefore, the quantities of goods and services offered on the market will result in the prices of those goods and services decreasing. Given the demand for any commodity, an increase in its supply will result in a decrease in its price, if all that is offered for sale is to attract enough buyers to take the good off the market.

If improvements in productivity and increases in output are occurring in many sectors of the economy more or less at the same time, then many prices will be decreasing, each one sufficiently to bring supply and demand into balance in its respective market. If statistical averages of market prices are calculated before and after these greater supplies of goods have been placed on the market, they will show that a decline in the general "price level" of goods and services has occurred. The market will have experienced "price deflation."

But it should be clear that there is nothing inherently harmful in this type of deflationary process. If an entrepreneur introduces a technological innovation to lower his costs of production, it is because he hopes to be able to make a commodity for less, so he can offer it for a lower price, yet still reap larger profits. The price decline is part of his plans. Even if competition forces him to fully lower the price to reflect his now lower costs of production, there are no negative consequences for the economy. Competition will have done its job, which is to compete prices down to the lowest level consistent with the most efficient costs of manufacturing.

It is, of course, possible that an entrepreneur may have overestimated the quantity that will be demanded at the lower price. As a consequence, his total revenue might be less than before the cost efficiencies were introduced into the operation. This means that consumers value other goods on the market more. For example, suppose that the old price was $10 and he had been selling 100 units each month. His total monthly revenues would have been $1,000. Suppose the new price is $9 but he sells 105 units per month; his total revenue would now be $945. Consumers would be buying more and economizing while doing so.

These consumers would shift those saved dollars toward other purchases. Suppose that an entrepreneur in another market has also introduced cost efficiencies into his line of production. Previously he sold 200 units of his commodity each month at a price of $16 apiece, for a total revenue of $3,200. Now he prices the good at $15 and sells 217 units each month for total revenues of $3,255. Consumers will be buying more of this second good as well, paying for the additional quantities with the $55 saved on the first good. Previously consumers spent a total of $4,200 on the two goods and obtained 100 units of the first good and 200 units of the second. After cost-efficiencies in production have lowered prices, they still spend a total of $4,200 on these two goods, but now they are able to buy 105 units of the first and 217 units of the second. Their standard of living has improved through an increase in the real buying power of their dollars. In the jargon of the economist, the demand for the first good was inelastic (at the lower price total revenue was less), while the demand for the second good was elastic (at the lower price total revenue was more). As a result, it may be necessary for some of the resources, including labor, to be let go in the manufacture of the first good and reemployed in the market where the second good is produced. There is simply no way to get around this in the long run. Changes in demand or supply always carry the need to modify what goods are produced, where they are manufactured, or with what resources. It is part of the price people must pay in a free society for improvements in the quantities and qualities of the goods and services offered on the free market.

If there is an attempt to prevent prices from adjusting to their market-clearing levels in the face of cost-efficiencies and greater supply, the result can only be imbalances and distortions in the market. Eventually adjustments must be made to the reality of supply and demand. Delaying them only builds a backlog of needed market changes that will be more severe in their effects than had the necessary incremental adjustments been allowed to occur as they slowly manifested themselves.[29]

In the late 1920s and early 1930s, Austrian economist Friedrich A. Hayek argued that the policy of price-level stabilization was creating such imbalances in the market by preventing a fall in prices in the face of cost-efficiencies and greater supplies of goods. He made this case in an essay, "Intertemporal Price Equilibrium and Movements in the Value of Money," and in two books, *Monetary Theory and the Trade Cycle* and *Prices and Production*.[30]

Hayek said that if a proper balance between supplies and demands was to be maintained, then the price of each good had to reflect the actual supply and demand conditions in existence in the various markets during each time period. Any attempt to "stabilize" the price of a good or a set of goods at some given "level," in spite of differing market conditions that might arise, would set in motion market responses that would be "destabilizing."

If, for example, the supply of a good would be greater in the future than today because of some innovation introduced that would lower costs, and if equilibrium existed in that future period as well as in the present period, the price of that good in the future (assuming given demand conditions) would have to be lower than the price in the present period. If this good's future price was "stabilized" at the "level" that prevailed in the present, this would result in future expected profit margins being greater than if natural market forces were at work, competing the price down to reflect the now lower costs of production. The "stabilized" higher price in the future would tend to induce an excess production of the good in comparison to what the "real" supply and demand conditions would dictate; this "surplus" would eventually have a destabilizing effect on the market.

What was true for any particular good would be true during a general expansion of output due to falling costs across markets. If each price in this situation was permitted to find its proper equilibrium level, then, as measured by some statistical averaging, the general "price level" would have declined. But the structure of relative prices will have kept the various supplies and demands in balance.

However, through most of the 1920s the Federal Reserve expanded the money supply in an attempt to prevent prices from falling in the face of increasing supplies of goods resulting from cost-efficiencies in the methods of production. The monetary expansion created a situation in which the prices for various goods and services were above what they would have been if not for the increase in the money supply.

Suppose, using our previous example, that our two entrepreneurs had each lowered their costs by $1 a unit, enabling them to lower their respective prices from $10 and $16 to $9 and $15. But now suppose that the government monetary authority increased the money supply by $322 and distributed this sum among consumers in a manner that enabled them to buy five more units of the first good and seventeen more of the second at the original prices of $10 and $16, respectively. The first entrepreneur would earn total revenues of $1,050 instead of $945, and the second would earn total revenues of $3,472 instead of $3,255. Our two entrepreneurs would be earning additional profits of $105 and $272, respectively, with total spending on the two goods being $4,522 instead of $4,200.

The artificially maintained selling prices and the larger earned profits would stimulate these entrepreneurs to expand their outputs to, say, 110 and 225 units. But for consumers to be able to buy these larger quantities at the original prices of $10 and $16, total consumer spending would have to be $4,700 ($1,100 for the first good and $3,600 on the second). If the money supply was not expanded by another $178 when the additional quantities were offered on the market, these entrepreneurs would discover that they had increased their supplies in excess of the consumers' ability to buy them at the original prices of $10 and $16.

Furthermore, in the process of attempting to expand their outputs due to the stimulus of greater profits, these entrepreneurs would have to attract resources and labor from other sectors of the economy to increase their levels of production. Part of the additional profits earned, therefore, would have to be expended as higher resource prices and wages to bid them away from their alternative employments in other parts of the economy.

But unless there were to be a change in the patterns of consumer demand, when these resource owners and workers earned these higher input prices and wages, they would spend them not on the larger quantities of these two goods that were now available, but on other goods they preferred instead. As result, it would be discovered that too much of these two goods were on the market, and too little of the other commodities.

The market would then have to go through a "correction," in which output was cut back in the two sectors of the economy that had originally experienced the cost efficiencies, and resources and labor would have to be reallocated to sectors of the economy that had greater consumer demand. The false appearance of economic stability with a stabilized "price level" would be hiding the fact that the monetary expansion that stabilized the price level was in fact distorting profit margins and creating imbalances in the relative supplies of various goods offered.

Austrian economists such as Mises and Hayek then combined their theory of money with the Austrian theory of capital and interest to develop what is known as the Austrian theory of the business cycle.

The Austrian Theory of Capital and Interest

Time is an element inseparable from the human condition. Everything we do involves time. Reading this essay takes time. And the time taken by reading is not available for other things. The importance of time in the processes of production and in the evaluation of choices has been emphasized by many members of the Austrian School of Economics, beginning with Carl Menger, the founder of the School.

But among the early members of the Austrian School it was Eugen von Böhm-Bawerk who developed the first detailed analysis of the role of time in the processes of production and the process of human choice. The first two volumes of his master work on this theme, *Capital and Interest*, were published in the 1880s. The third volume, which mostly replied to his critics, appeared in its final edition in 1914, shortly before his death.[31]

The other major contributor to the Austrian theory of time in the early years of the twentieth century was the American economist Frank A. Fetter. His analysis of the process of "time-valuation" was presented in two treatises, *The Principles of Economics* and *Economic Principles*.[32] During the 1930s and 1940s, additional contributions to the theory of capital and interest were made by the Austrian economists Richard von Strigl in *Capital and Production*,[33] Friedrich A. Hayek in *Prices and Production* and *The Pure Theory of Capital*,[34] and Ludwig von Mises in *Nationalökonomie*[35] and *Human Action*.

Every one of our actions requires us to think about time and act through time. Whether it is boiling an egg or constructing a spaceship, we are confronted with the necessity of waiting for the desired result. We apply the means at our disposal to the tasks at hand, and we try to bring about the desired ends. But the cause (the application of the means) always precedes the effect (the resulting end or goal); and between the initiation (cause) and its conclusion (effect), there is always a period of time, be it merely a few minutes or many, many years. Each one of our plans, therefore, contains within it a *period of production*.

Rarely, however, can our production plans be completed in one step. Usually the resources must go through various transformations in a number of *stages of production* before the consumer good is ready for use. A tree must be chopped down in the forest. The wood must be transported to the lumber mill and processed. The cut wood must be taken to the pulp factory and manufactured into paper. The paper must be boxed and shipped to the print shop. The paper must be printed and trimmed to size to produce the volume that is in your hands. What is expressed in this simple example has its analog in every line of production for the manufacture of every conceivable good.

To undertake these processes of production, however, requires a certain amount of savings. Resources and raw materials that might otherwise have been used to satisfy a more immediate want must be freed up for more time-consuming production activities. First, some resources must be available for transformation into capital goods—tools, machinery, and equipment—with which workers who are not employed in the more direct manufacture of consumer goods can combine their efforts in more time-consuming, or "roundabout," production processes. Second, resources and consumer goods must be available for use by those employed during the production processes leading up to the completion of other finished goods.

The more savings, the more and longer are the processes of production that can be undertaken and, as a result, the greater the quantities and the qualities of the goods that will be available in the future. Why? Because other things held even, the more time-consuming, or "roundabout," the production process, the more productive are the resulting methods of production.

However, the longer the periods of production, the longer we have to wait for the goods we desire. Therefore, we have to evaluate the sacrifice, in terms of time spent waiting, that we are willing to make to get a potentially greater and more desired effect.

The sacrifices of time people are willing to make differ among individuals. And these differing evaluations of time open up opportunities for potential gains from trade. Those who are willing to defer consumption and the uses of resources in the present may find individuals who desire access to larger quantities of goods than they can afford. And this group may be willing to *pay a price in the future* for the use of those resources in the present.

An intertemporal price emerges in the market as transactors evaluate and "haggle" over the value of time and the use of resources. The rate of interest is that intertemporal price. It reflects the time preferences of the market actors regarding the value of resources and commodities in the present compared to their future value.

As the price of time, the rate of interest balances the willingness by some to save with the desire by others to borrow. But the rate of interest not only coordinates the plans of savers and investors, it also acts as a "brake" or "regulator" on the length of the time of production undertaken with the available savings. For example, what are the respective present values of $100 invested for one year, two years, or three years, with a market rate of interest of, say, 10 percent? They would be, respectively, $90.91, $82.64, and $75.13. Suppose that people changed their time preferences and now chose to save more, and the resulting greater supply of savings available for lending decreased the rate of interest to 7 percent. What would be the present values of $100 invested for one, two, or three years? The present values would be, respectively, $93.46, $87.74, and $81.97.

The present value will have increased for all three potential investments, with their different time horizons. But the percentage increases in the present values of these three possible investment horizons would not be the same. On the one-year investment project, its present value will have increased by 2.8 percent. On the two-year project, its present value will have increased by 5.7 percent. And on the three-year, its present value will have increased by 8.6 percent. Clearly, the tendency from a fall in the rate of interest would be an increase in investments with longer periods of production.

If time preferences were to move in the opposite direction, with people choosing to save less, the resulting increase in the rate of interest would make longer-term investments relatively less attractive. If the rate of interest were to rise from 7 percent to 10 percent, the present values on $100 invested for one, two, or three years would decrease, respectively, by 2.7 percent, 5.4 percent, and 8 percent. This would make investments with shorter periods of production appear relatively more attractive.

In an economy experiencing increases in real income, decisions by income-earners to save a larger proportion of their income need not require an absolute decrease in consumption. Suppose income-earners' time preferences were such that they normally saved 25 percent of their income. On an income of $1,000, they would save $250. If their preference for saving were to rise to 30 percent, with a given income of $1,000, their consumption would have to decrease from $750 to $700 to increase their savings from $250 to $300. However, if income earners were to have an increase in real income to $1,100 and their savings preference were to increase to 30 percent, they would now save $330. But consumption would also rise to $770. This is why savings can increase for new capital formation and investments in even longer periods of production without any absolute sacrifice of consumption in a growing economy. Consumption increases with higher real income, it just increases less than it could have had income-earners not chosen to save a greater percentage.

But if there were a decline in the demand for consumer goods and an increase in savings, what would be the incentive for producers to invest in more capital and productive capacity? This criticism was leveled against Böhm-Bawerk at the turn of the century by an economist named L. G. Bostedo. He argued that since market demand stimulates manufacturers to produce goods for the market, a decision by income-earners to save more and consume less destroys the very incentive for undertaking the new capital projects that greater savings are supposed to facilitate. Bostedo concluded that greater savings, rather than being an engine for increased investment, served to retard investment and capital formation.[36]

In 1901, in "The Function of Savings," Böhm-Bawerk replied to this criticism.[37] "There is lacking from one of his premises a single but very important word," Böhm-Bawerk pointed out. "Mr. Bostedo assumes . . . that savings signifies necessarily a curtailment in the demand for consumption goods." But, Böhm-Bawerk continued:

> Here he has omitted the little word "present." The man who saves curtails his demand for present goods but by no means his desire for pleasure-affording goods generally. . . . For the principle motive of those who save is precisely to provide for their own futures or for the futures of their heirs. This means nothing else than that they wish to secure and make certain their command over the means to the satisfaction of their future needs, that is over consumption goods in a future time. In other words, those who save curtail their demand for consumption

goods in the present merely to increase proportionally their demand for consumption goods in the future.[38]

But even if there is a potential future demand for consumer goods, how shall entrepreneurs know what type of capital investments to undertake and what types of greater quantities of goods to offer in preparation for that higher future demand?

Böhm-Bawerk's reply was to point out that production is always forward-looking—a process of applying productive means today with a plan to have finished consumer goods for sale tomorrow. The very purpose of entrepreneurial competitiveness is to constantly test the market, so as to better anticipate and correct for existing and changing patterns of consumer demand. Competition is the market method through which supplies are brought into balance with consumer demands. And if errors are made, the resulting losses or less than the anticipated profits act as the stimuli for appropriate adjustments in production and reallocations of labor and resources among alternative lines of production.

When left to itself, Böhm-Bawerk argued, the market successfully assures that demands are tending to equal supply, and that the time horizons of investments match the available savings needed to maintain the society's existing and expanding structure of capital in the long run.

The Austrian Theory of the Business Cycle

The Austrian theory of the business cycle was first developed by Ludwig von Mises. He built the theory on the earlier contributions of his Austrian teacher Eugen von Böhm-Bawerk and the writings of the Swedish economist Knut Wicksell.

We saw that the Austrian economists, especially beginning with Böhm-Bawerk, had emphasized that all production takes time. The Austrians also explained that for time-consuming processes of production to be undertaken, savings were needed to free up resources from more direct consumption uses for investment in the formation and maintenance of capital and for supplying goods and resources to sustain the "roundabout" production processes.

Savings come from the time preferences of market participants who are willing to forgo present uses and consumption of goods and resources and transfer them to those who wish to utilize those goods and resources in the processes of production. The market interactions of suppliers and demanders of those resources generated market rates of interest that balanced savings with investment. At the same time, the available savings resulting from these intertemporal market exchanges set the limits on the periods of production that could successfully be undertaken and maintained given the fund of savings available to sustain them in the long run.

In 1898, the Swedish economist Knut Wicksell published *Interest and Prices.*[39] He adapted Böhm-Bawerk's theory of capital and time-consuming processes of production and took it a step further. Wicksell explained that in the actual market goods do not trade directly one for the other. Rather, money serves as the intermediary in all transactions, including the transfer of savings to potential borrowers and investors. Individuals save in the form of money income not spent on consumption. They then leave that money savings on deposit with banks, which serve as the financial intermediaries in the market's intertemporal transactions.

These banks pool the money savings of numerous people and lend those savings to creditworthy borrowers at the prevailing market rates of interest, and which balance the supply of savings with the investment demand for it. The borrowers then use that money savings to enter the market and demand the use of resources, capital, and labor by offering money prices for their purchase and hire. Thus, the decrease in the money demand and the lower prices for consumer goods (the results of savings) and the increased demand and the higher money prices for producer goods (the results of investment borrowing) act as the market's method to shift and reallocate resources and labor from consumption purposes to capital-using production purposes.

But Wicksell pointed out that precisely because money served as the intermediary link in connecting savings decisions with investment decisions, a peculiar and perverse imbalance in the savings-investment process could result. Suppose that the savings in society were just enough to sustain the undertaking and completion of one-year periods of production. Now suppose that the government monetary authority were to increase the amount of money available to the banks for lending. To attract borrowers to take these additional funds, the banks would lower the rates of interest.

The lowered market rates of interest created by the monetary expansion would raise the present value of investment projects with longer time horizons to their completion. As a consequence, suppose that borrowers were to undertake investment projects with a two-year period of production. Because of the increased money demands for resources and labor of these two-year investment projects, some factors of production would be drawn from one-year projects. Thus, at the end of the first year fewer consumer goods would be available. With fewer goods on the market at the end of this first year, consumers' goods prices would rise and consumers would have to cut back their purchases. Consumers, Wicksell said, would be forced to save—that is, they would have to consume less in the present and wait for the two-year investment projects to be completed to enjoy a greater supply of goods.

At the same time, the greater supply of money would tend to increase prices, and, as a consequence, society would experience a general price inflation. If the government monetary authority were to repeat its increase of the money supply time-period after time-period, it would set in motion what Wicksell called an unending "cumulative process" of rising prices.

In writing *The Theory of Money and Credit*, Ludwig von Mises accepted the general outline of Wicksell's analysis of the effect of monetary expansion on production and prices. But he took Wicksell's idea further and demonstrated the process by which a monetary expansion of this type eventually created an "economic crisis" and generated the sequence of events known as the business cycle.[40]

Mises distinguished between two types of credit offered on the market: "commodity credit" and "circulation credit." Mises' student and early follower in applying the Austrian theory of the business cycle, Fritz Machlup, called these types of credit "transfer credit" and "created credit."[41] And it is this latter terminology that we will use because it more clearly states the distinction that Mises was trying to make.

If there were no increase in the money supply, any money savings out of income would represent a real transfer of market control over resources and labor from income-earners to potential investors. Savers will have loaned a quantity of real resources represented by the monetary value of those real resources in investment activities instead of using them in the more direct and immediate manufacture of consumer goods. This "transfer credit" of real resources for investment purposes would be returned to savers when the money loans were paid off with the agreed-upon rate of interest, and that returned sum of money would then have the capacity to purchase a greater quantity of real goods and services for consumption purposes. And the investment projects undertaken with this transfer credit would have time horizons consistent with the available savings and the period over which the loans were made.

However, the government monetary authority has the capacity to disrupt this fairly tight fit between savings and investment that is kept in balance by the market-determined rates of interest. Through its ability to expand the money supply, the monetary authority has the power to create credit for lending purposes. The "created credit" is indistinguishable from transfer credit for market transactions. It represents additional units of the medium of exchange that are interchangeable with all other units of money. Thus they are as readily accepted in market transactions as the units of money in existence before the monetary expansion.

Yet, Mises argued, there is an important difference: There is no compensating decrease in consumer demand for goods, services, and resources, which normally follows from the decision to save more, to counterbalance the increased demand for the use of resources and labor by the investment borrowers who took the created credit offered on the loan market.

At this point, Mises applied his theory of the non-neutrality of money to explain the sequence of events likely to follow. With newly created credit, the investment borrowers would bid resources and labor away from the production of consumer goods and investment projects with shorter time-horizons to begin investment projects with lengthier periods of production.

To attract resources and labor to these time-consuming activities, the investment borrowers would have to bid up the prices of the required factors of production to draw them away from their alternative uses in the economy. The newly created credit now passes to these factors of production as higher money incomes. They become the "second-round" recipients of the newly created money. Unless these factors of production change their time-preferences, and therefore their willingness to save, their real demand for consumer goods would be the same as before the increase in the money supply. They would, therefore, increase their money demand for finished goods and services in the same proportion of income as before.

As a result, the prices for consumer goods would now start to rise as well. But because of the reallocation of resources away from consumer goods production, the quantities of such goods available on the market are less than before, which intensifies the rise in the prices of consumer goods. As the "second-round" factors of production expend their higher money incomes on desired consumer goods, the sellers and producers of these goods become the "third-round" recipients of the newly created money. Producers of consumer goods now increase their demand for the same scarce factors of production to draw them back into the consumer goods sectors of the economy and into investment projects with shorter time-horizons to satisfy more quickly the greater money demand for consumer goods. The factors of production drawn back into these activities closer to the final consumer stage of production become the "fourth-round" recipients of the newly created money.

Those who initially had taken the created credit from the loan market now find it increasingly difficult to continue and complete their longer-term investment projects. A "crisis" begins to emerge as a growing number of these longer-term investment projects cannot be financially continued. The demand for additional loanable funds from banks pushes market rates of interest up, creating an even greater crisis in the investment sector. The expansionary or "boom" phase of the business cycle now turns into the contractionary or "depression" phase as a growing number of these lengthier investment projects collapse.

The only way to temporarily save some of these investment activities would be for the government monetary authority to increase the money supply again in the form of more created credit. But this would merely set the same process in motion again with the same inevitable result. And if the monetary authority were to try to prevent this inevitable result through greater and greater increases in the money supply, the end-result would be a higher and higher rate of price inflation, which would threaten destruction and collapse of the society's monetary system.

Mises' conclusion from this analysis was that the causes of the business cycle in modern society were not to be found in some fundamental flaw in the market economy. Rather its basic cause was to be found in government manipulation and mismanagement of money and credit.

Austrian Business Cycle Theory and the Causes of the Great Depression

In June 1931, British economist Lionel Robbins wrote a foreword for Friedrich A. Hayek's *Prices and Production.* Professor Robbins explained the "marvelous renaissance" that the Austrian School of Economics had experienced since the end of the First World War under the leadership of such economists as Ludwig von Mises. Among the Austrian School's most important recent contributions, he said, was its theory of the business cycle, which Hayek's small volume was meant to introduce to the English-speaking world. Professor Robbins pointed out:

> Most monetary theorists seem to have failed utterly to apprehend correctly the nature of the forces operative in America before the coming of the [great] depression, thinking apparently that the relative stability of the price level indicated a state of affairs necessarily free from injurious monetary influences. The Austrian theory, of which Dr. Hayek is such a distinguished exponent, can claim at least this merit, that no one who really understood its principle tenets could have cherished for a moment such vain delusions.[42]

History is never the result of one influencing factor, even a strongly dominating one. And this was no less true in the case of the political and economic influences at work before the Great Depression began in 1929. The First World War had disrupted normal economic and political relationships around the globe.

Vast quantities of physical capital and human labor were consumed and destroyed in the four years of war. Wartime and postwar inflations tore apart the social and cultural fabrics of several major countries in Europe, especially those of Germany and Austria. The institutions of civil and liberal society were severely weakened and replaced with interventionist and socialist political regimes that limited or abolished civil and economic liberties.

New nations rose up in central and eastern Europe with the collapse of the German, Austrian, and Russian empires. To one degree or another, all followed the path of economic nationalism, imposing protectionist trade barriers, subsidizing agriculture and various privileged industries, nationalizing entire sectors of the economy, instituting artificial foreign exchange rates and exchange controls, and establishing welfare statist programs. Germany's reparations payments were a peculiar mechanism of financial musical chairs, with the U.S. lending money to the Germans so that they could meet their payments to the Allied powers, including America. American and European trade barriers made it difficult for the Germans to earn the needed sums through exports to fulfill all their financial obligations under the terms of the peace treaty that had ended the war.

The monetary system of the world—the international gold standard—was fatally weakened by inflationary policies during and after the war. In spite of the weaknesses of the gold standard and in spite of the abuses of the gold standard by the governments that had managed it before 1914, it had brought about the high degree of monetary stability that fostered a global economic environment conducive to savings, investment, international trade, and capital formation. In the 1920s, however, the monetary systems of the major nations of Europe were increasingly fiat currencies more directly controlled and manipulated by government, even when they remained nominally "linked" to gold. In the United States, the establishment of the Federal Reserve System in 1913 created a new centralized engine for monetary expansion. In this setting, the American Federal Reserve System undertook its experiment in the monetary stabilization of the price level.[43]

In the 1920s, as we have seen, Ludwig von Mises had demonstrated the fundamental weakness in all attempts to stabilize an economy through price-level stabilization by explaining the inherent non-neutrality of money. Changes in the money supply necessarily originate through the injection of additional sums into the market. These additions to the money supply then have an impact on the rest of the economy through the particular temporal–sequential process through which the new money is spent. The result would be a change in the general purchasing power or value of money, but in the process of bringing this about the structure of relative prices, wages, and income, as well as the allocation of resources, would also have been changed. And if the monetary injections occurred through the banking system, a business cycle might very well be set in motion.

But it was Mises' young Austrian colleague Friedrich A. Hayek who detailed why stabilizing the price level could distort the structure of relative prices into setting a business cycle in motion. In *Monetary Theory and the Trade Cycle*, Hayek argued that the role of the interest rate in a market economy was to assure that the amount and the time-horizons of investment activities were kept in balance with the available savings.

In an economy experiencing increases in productivity and capital formation, cost efficiencies and increased productive capacities would, over time, put downward pressure on prices due to the increased supplies of goods offered. The price of each good would decrease to the extent required to assure that the market was kept in balance. In the markets in which consumer demand was fairly responsive (or "elastic") to the increase in available supplies, the individual prices might decline only moderately. While in other markets in which consumer demand was noticeably less responsive (or "inelastic") to such an increase, the individual prices would have to decrease to a greater extent to keep the greater supply in balance with the demand.

Over time, the average level of prices as measured by some statistical price index would record that a "deflation" of prices had occurred. But this "price deflation" was not harmful—it was essential if the market-determined structure of relative prices was to keep supplies and demands in balance.

Instead of allowing this secular downward trend in prices to occur naturally, the Federal Reserve increased the supply of money in the American economy to counteract this normal process of price deflation. In aggregate terms, the amount of money demanded for goods and services was increased just enough to match the increase in the quantity of goods and services to maintain the general statistical average of prices at a fairly "stable" level throughout most of the 1920s (as measured by the wholesale price index).

But, argued Hayek:

> [T]he rate of interest which equilibrates the supply of real savings and the demand for capital cannot be a rate of interest which also prevents changes in the price level. In this case, stability of the price level presupposes change in the supply of money: but these changes must always lead to a discrepancy between the amount of real savings and the volume of investment. The rate of interest at which, in an expanding economy, the amount of new money entering circulation is just sufficient to keep the price-level stable, is always lower than the rate which would keep the amount of available loan-capital equal to the amount simultaneously saved by the public: and thus, despite the stability of the price-level, it makes possible a development leading away from the equilibrium position.[44]

Increases in the money supply, institutionally, are introduced in the form of increased reserves supplied to the banking system by the Federal Reserve, on the basis of which additional loans may be extended. But the only way banks can induce potential borrowers to take up these increased loanable funds is to lower the rate of interest and so decrease the cost of borrowing relative to the expected rate of return. But the rate of interest is not only the measure of the cost of a loan; it is also the factor by which the prospective value of a investment is capitalized in terms of its present value. The lower rate of interest also acts, therefore, as a stimulus for undertaking longer-term investment projects.[45]

Thus in the 1920s, beneath the apparent calm of a stable price level, Federal Reserve policy was creating a structure of relative price and profit relationships that induced an amount of longer-term investments that were in excess of actual savings to sustain them in the long run. Why were they unsustainable in the long run? Because as new money was spent on new and expanded investment projects, it eventually passed as higher money incomes into the hands of factors of production drawn into these employments. As these higher money incomes were then spent, the demands for consumer goods increased as well, attracting resources back to consumer goods production and investment projects with shorter time-horizons. Only through further injections of additional quantities of money into the banking system was the Federal Reserve able to keep market rates of interest below their proper equilibrium levels and thus temporarily maintain the profitabilities of the longer-term investment projects set into motion by the attempt to keep price level stable.

Finally, in late 1928, under the pressure of this monetary expansion, the price level began to rise. The Federal Reserve, fearful of creating an absolute inflationary rise in prices, reined in the money supply. But with the end of monetary expansion, interest rates began to rise to their real market levels. Some longer-term investment projects were now unprofitable at the higher rates of interest. The investment "boom" collapsed, its first major indication being the "break" in the stock market in October 1929.

In 1932, Hayek summarized the lessons of the 1920s in "The Fate of the Gold Standard":

> Instead of prices being allowed to fall slowly, to the full extent that would have been possible without inflicting damage on production, such volumes of additional credit were pumped into circulation that the level of prices was roughly stabilized. . . . Whether such inflation merely serves to keep prices stable, or whether it leads to an increase in prices, makes little difference. Experience has now confirmed what theory was already aware of; that such inflation can also lead to production being misdirected to such an extent that, in the end, a breakdown in the form of a crisis becomes inevitable. This, however, also proves the impossibility of achieving in practice an absolute maintenance of the level of prices in a dynamic economy.[46]

The inherent limitations in focusing upon any index of prices in general was pointed out by another of Mises' students, Gottfried

Haberler, in 1928, before the beginning of the Great Depression. Haberler emphasized, "The general price level is not a given, self-evident fact, but a theoretical abstraction. . . . For each purpose a separate concept of price level must be established. . . . An economically relevant definition of price level cannot be independent of the purpose in mind, and for each purpose a separate index must be computed." Indices are constructed on the basis of selecting a particular group of prices for purposes of tracing the path of some average price trend, depending on whether one was interested in tracking changes in real income, for example, shifts in the real value of deferred payments, or in the general movements in consumer or producer prices. Furthermore, regardless of the particular purpose for which a price index may be statistically constructed, any such average necessarily hid changes that might occur between the individual prices subsumed under the average. "The relative position and change of different groups of prices are not revealed, but are hidden and submerged in a general [price] index," Haberler emphasized. And he pointed out, "It may happen, and it would be by no means inexplicable, that a period will come when prosperity is correlated with a downward movement of the price level and depression with an upward movement."[47]

Corrective forces in the market were now set in motion in 1929, once the monetary expansion had come to an end. But the depth and duration of the Great Depression turned out to be far greater and longer than would have normally seemed to be required for economywide balance to be restored. The reasons for the Great Depression's severity, however, were not to be found in any inherent failing in the market economy, but in the political ideologies and government policies of the 1930s.

The Great Depression and the Crisis of Government Intervention

The Great Depression of the early 1930s was the most severe in modern history. In terms of the usual statistical figures alone, its magnitude was catastrophic. Between 1929 and 1933, the gross national product in the United States decreased by 54 percent, with industrial production declining 36 percent. Between 1929 and 1933, investment spending decreased by 80 percent, while consumer spending declined by 40 percent; expenditures on residential housing declined by 80 percent. In 1929, unemployment had been 3.2 percent of the civilian work force; by 1932 unemployment had gone up to 24.1 percent, and it rose even further, to 25.2 percent, in 1933.

The wholesale price index decreased by 32 percent from 1929 to 1933, and the consumer price index decreased by 23 percent. American agriculture saw the prices paid by farmers for raw materials, wages, and interest decrease by 32 percent, while the amounts farmers received for their output decreased by 52 percent.

Between 1930 and 1933, 9,000 banks failed in the United States, and tens of thousands of people lost their savings. The money supply (measured as currency in circulation and demand and time deposits, or "M–2") decreased by more than 30 percent between 1929 and 1933. Even if a larger measurement of the money supply is calculated ("M–2" plus deposits at mutual savings banks, the postal savings system, and the shares at savings and loans, a measurement known as "M–4"), the supply of money still decreased by about 25 percent between 1929 and 1933.

Internationally, the Great Depression was also devastating. The value of global imports and exports decreased by almost 60 percent, while the real volume of goods and services traded across borders declined by almost 30 percent. The gross domestic product fell by 5 and 7 percent, respectively, in Great Britain and France between 1929 and 1933. From 1929 to 1932, industrial production fell 12, 22, and 40 percent, respectively, in Great Britain, France, and Germany. Wholesale prices fell, on average, 25, 38, and 32 percent, respectively, in Great Britain, France, and Germany. Declines in consumer prices were 15 percent on average in both Great Britain and France, and 23 percent in Germany during this period.[48]

After the 1930s, most historians and many economists interpreted these numbers as a demonstration that the capitalist system had inherent flaws and tendencies toward cumulative instability that would prevent a return to a normal economic balance within any reasonable period of time. The Great Depression, therefore, came to be viewed as a "crisis of capitalism" and proof of the failure of (classical) liberal society.

This was not how the free market economists of the time viewed the early 1930s. For example, when German economist Moritz J. Bonn delivered the third Richard Cobden lecture in London on April 29, 1931, his topic was "The World Crisis and the Teaching of the Manchester School." Professor Bonn told his audience:

> The free play of economic forces have been replaced everywhere, at least in part, by private monopoly or by Government monopoly, by tariffs, and by all sorts of price control, from wage fixing by arbitration boards to valorization by farm boards. . . . There is intervention now on a big scale, based on forecasting and bent on planning, and there is a crisis much bigger than any crisis the world has seen so far. . . . For in the present economic situation of the world half of its institutions are [politically] manipulated whilst the other half are supposed to be free. The prices of the goods subject to the play of free competition have fallen all over the world. . . . The other prices have remained fairly rigid. They are maintained by economic and political coercion, by combines of labor and capital, supported by tariffs and other manipulating legislation. . . . If selected prices and sheltered wages can be maintained whilst all other prices are declining, a new satisfactory level [of equilibrium] cannot be attained. . . . The conflict between the free play of economic forces and the manipulation by Governments and monopolies is the main cause of the long continuation of the crisis.[49]

It was for this reason that a year later, in 1932, Mises concluded, "The crisis under which the world is presently suffering is the crisis of interventionism and of state and municipal socialism, in short the crisis of anticapitalist policies."[50]

In the United States, the crisis of anticapitalist policies arose from the interventions of the Hoover administration. In November 1929, President Herbert Hoover met with leading American business and labor leaders; he told them that in this period of crisis purchasing power had to be maintained to keep the demand for goods and services high. He argued that wage rates should not be cut, that the work week should be shortened to "spread the work" among the labor force, and that governments at all levels should expand public works projects to increase employment.

Under the persuasion of the president and then through the power of trade unions, the money wage rates for many workers were kept artificially high. But this merely created the conditions for more, rather than less, unemployment. In 1930, consumer prices fell by 2.5 percent, while money wages declined on average by 2 percent. In 1931, consumer prices fell by 8.8 percent, while money wages decreased by only 3 percent. In 1932, consumer prices declined by 10.3 percent, while money wages decreased by only 7 percent. In 1933, consumer prices fell by 5.1 percent, and money wages decreased by 7.9 percent. While consumer prices fell almost 25 percent between 1929 and 1933, money wages on average only decreased 15 percent. Besides money wages lagging behind the fall in the selling prices of consumer goods through most of these years, labor productivity was also falling—by 8.5 percent. As a result, the real cost of hiring labor actually increased by 22.8 percent. The "high-wage" policy of the Hoover administration and the trade unions, therefore, only succeeded in pricing workers out the labor market, generating an increasing circle of unemployment.[51]

American agriculture was also thrown out of balance by government intervention. During the First World War the demand for American farm output had increased dramatically. But after 1918 European demand for our agricultural goods decreased. This was partly due to a normal reexpansion of European agricultural production in peacetime, but also because of the growth in agricultural protectionism in central and eastern Europe that closed off part of the European market to American exports.

In the 1920s, the U.S. government attempted to prop up American farm production and income through subsidies and federally sponsored farm cooperative programs. In June 1929, the Hoover administration established the Federal Farm Board (FFB). Once the Depression began, the FFB started to extend cheap loans to the farming community to keep output off the market and prevent prices from falling. First wheat, then cotton and wool, and then dairy products came within the orbit of government intervention. The artificially high prices merely generated increasingly larger surpluses. Then the government attempted to restrict farm output to prevent prices from falling due to the very surpluses the government's farm price support programs had helped to create.

As Austrian economist Murray Rothbard explained:

> [T]he grandiose stabilization effort of the FFB failed ignominiously. Its loans encouraged greater production, adding to the farm surplus, which overhung the market, driving prices down both on direct and psychological grounds. The FFB thus aggravated the very farm depression that it was supposed to solve. With the FFB generally acknowledged a failure, President Hoover began to pursue the inexorable logic of government intervention to the next step: recommending that productive land be withdrawn from cultivation, that crops be plowed under, and that immature farm animals be slaughtered—all to reduce the very surpluses that government's prior intervention had brought into being.[52]

In a further attempt to protect American agriculture from adjusting prices and production to the real supply and demand conditions of the world market, Congress passed and Herbert Hoover signed the Hawley-Smoot Tariff in June 1930. Benjamin Anderson, in his financial and economic history of the U.S., *Economics and the Public Welfare,* scathingly criticized this act of aggressive protectionism:

> In a world staggering under a load of international debt which could be carried only if countries under pressure could produce goods and export them to their creditors, we, the greatest creditor nation of the world, with tariffs already far too high, raised our tariffs again. The Hawley-Smoot Tariff Bill of June, 1930, was the crowning financial folly of the whole period from 1920 to 1933. . . . [O]nce we raised our tariffs, an irresistible movement all over the world to raise tariffs and to erect other trade barriers, including quotas, began. Protectionism ran wild over the world. Markets were cut off. Trade lines were narrowed. Unemployment in the export industries all over the world grew with great rapidity, and prices of export commodities, notably farm commodities in the United States, dropped with ominous rapidity.[53]

U.S. farm exports as a percentage of farm income fell from 16.7 percent in the late 1920s to 11.2 in the early 1930s. U.S. exports of farm commodities fell by 68 percent between 1929 and 1933. Never was there a clearer case of government intervention resulting in consequences that were exactly contrary to its stated purpose!

After the British government abandoned the Gold Standard in September 1931, the Abnormal Importation Act was passed, giving the British Board of Trade authority to impose duties of up to 100 percent of the value of imported goods. The very day the Act was passed, a 50-percent import duty was imposed on 23 classes of goods, and importation of these goods practically ceased. On March 1, 1932, a 10-percent general tariff increase was established by the British government. And in July 1932, the British government introduced preferential tariffs for countries belonging to its empire at the expense of all other nations, including the U.S.

Germany instituted import licensing and bilateral trading arrangements supervised by the government in November 1931. By 1934, with the advent of the Nazis coming to power in Germany, exchange controls and import licenses were reinforced as part of the new National Socialist system of economic planning.

In 1928, the French government had lowered the import tariff rate to 15 percent, and lowered it once more to 12 percent in 1930. But in November 1931, a foreign exchange surcharge of 15 percent was imposed on British goods. And beginning in mid-1931, the French government established quotas on many imported goods. Indeed, by 1936, 65 percent of goods imported into France were entering the country under the quota system.

Christian Saint-Etienne, in his book *The Great Depression, 1929–1938*, concluded:

> [T]ariff restrictions were increasingly complemented by administrative measures, such as prohibitions, quotas, licensing systems, and clearing agreements. . . . Protectionism only led to a reduction in international trade, affecting all trading nations to a comparable extent, whether they initiated the trade war or merely retaliated. . . . It is clear that the collapse of international trade in the Depression made international recovery virtually impossible for a decade.[54]

What, then, was the way out of the Great Depression? The Austrians argued that there was only one successful route: a return to free, competitive markets.

The "Austrian" Analysis and Solution for the Great Depression

In February 1931, Ludwig von Mises delivered a lecture before a group of German industrialists on "The Causes of the Economic Crisis."[55] He explained that the economic depression through which they were living had its origin in the misguided monetary policies of the 1920s. The leading central banks of the major industrial countries had followed a policy of monetary expansion that had created an artificial boom that came to an end in 1929.

But after the downturn began, the depression was much more severe and prolonged than similar business cycles in the past. A unique circumstance was present that prevented the normal process of economic recovery. The unique circumstance was the pervasiveness of government interventionist policies:

> If everything possible is done to prevent the market from fulfilling its function of bringing supply and demand into balance, it should come as no surprise that a serious disproportionality between supply and demand persists, that commodities remain unsold, factories stand idle, many millions are unemployed, destitution and misery are growing and that finally, in the wake of all these, destructive radicalism is rampant in politics. . . . With the economic crisis, the breakdown of interventionist policy—the policy being followed today by all governments, irrespective of whether they are responsible to parliaments or rule openly as dictatorships—becomes apparent. . . . Hampering the functions of the market and the formation of prices does not create order. Instead it leads to chaos, to economic crisis.[56]

To the Austrian economists, the Great Depression had been caused in the United States by the attempt to stabilize price levels through monetary expansion. The monetary expansion had artificially lowered interest rates and this, in turn, had induced an investment boom in excess of real savings in the economy. Capital, resources, and labor had been misdirected into longer-term investment projects that, with the end of monetary inflation, were found to be unprofitable and economically unsustainable. Capital had been malinvested, labor had been misdirected, and the structure of relative prices and wages had been distorted.

Governments in the major industrial countries, including the United States, responded to the economic crisis by introducing a vast spider's web of interventionist regulations, controls, and restrictions on both domestic and international trade, as well as numerous public works projects. Rather than alleviating the depression, the interventionist measures had only made the situation worse. Governmental attempts to maintain prices and wages at levels inconsistent with real market conditions resulted in falling production and rising unemployment as goods went unsold and workers were released from their jobs.

These imbalances soon spread. The reason for this can be found in the fundamental truth of what economists since Jean-Baptiste Say in the early nineteenth century have called "the law of markets." No one can demand what others have for sale in the market unless they have something to supply in exchange. Each potential demander, therefore, has to offer in trade some good or service that others are interested in buying and at a price they are willing to pay. Doing otherwise limits the money income that can be earned from sales; and this in turn limits the amount of goods and services that can be bought from others.

Wrong prices—"disequilibrium" prices in the jargon of the economist—resulted in products and workers being priced out of the market once the Depression began in 1929. The resulting decreased revenues from the sale of goods and the resulting falling income from loss of employment meant that both businessmen and workers had to cut back their purchases of goods and services. These others, when unwilling to lower their prices and wages sufficiently in the face of falling demand, also saw, in turn, a decrease in sales and employment. The failure of prices and wages to adjust downward in the face of changing market conditions generated a "cumulative contraction" of output and employment, which, in turn, put further downward pressure on prices and wages in a widening circle of related markets. As the famous English economist Edwin Cannan concisely put it in 1932, "general unemployment is the result of a general asking too much."[57]

In 1933, Mises summarized the nature of the problem:

> [T]he duration of the present crisis is caused primarily by the fact that wage rates and certain prices have become inflexible, as a result of union wage policy and various [government] price support activities. Thus, the rigid wage rates and prices do not fully participate in the downward movement of most prices, or do so only after a protracted delay. . . . [T]he continuing mass unemployment is a necessary consequence of the attempts to maintain wage rates above those that would prevail on the unhampered market.[58]

Mises explained that now that interventionist policies had resulted in mass unemployment, governments proposed to get around the consequences of their own policies by resorting to a policy of reflation. Governments hoped that if prices were raised through a new monetary expansion, unions would not immediately demand higher money wages to compensate for any purchasing power lost due to the resulting increase in the cost of living. If money wages remained relatively unchanged while the prices of goods and services were rising, this would mean that real wages would be cut, and employers might find it once again profitable to hire the unemployed. But, Mises argued, even if money wages did not immediately increase, the new monetary expansion merely would set the stage for another "bust" after a temporary "boom."

The inevitability of this result was explained by the British "Austrian" Lionel Robbins in the pages of *Lloyd's Bank Review* in 1932:

> [I]t is perhaps natural that the wish should arise to meet deflation by a counter inflation: to get around cost rigidities by acting on prices. And no doubt if inflation simply meant the simultaneous and definitive marking up of prices, as by a Government decree, there would be much to be said for this procedure. Unfortunately, inflation does not work this way. It

> is the essence of inflation that it affects some prices before others, that its final effects are different from its impact effects, and that production is affected differently at different stages of the process. In an inflationary boom, it is this unequal incidence of the inflation which gives rise to the maladjustments, which eventually produce the slump. Entrepreneurs are encouraged by artificially cheap money to embark on enterprises which can only be profitable provided costs do not rise. As the new money works through the system, costs do rise, and their enterprise is thus rendered unprofitable. For the time being, trade seems good but when the full effects of the inflation have manifested themselves there comes a crisis and subsequently depression.[59]

What then was the way out of the Great Depression? For the Austrian economists it required the reversal of the interventionist policies that had exacerbated the economic crisis, and the forgoing of any monetary manipulation as a method to overcome the dilemma of unemployment. On the latter point, Friedrich Hayek, writing in 1932, was clear:

> To combat the depression by a forced credit expansion is to attempt to cure the evil by the very means which brought it about; because we are suffering from a misdirection of production, we want to create further misdirection—a procedure which can only lead to a much more severe crisis as soon as the credit expansion comes to an end.[60]

On the issue of interventionist policies that were preventing the market from normally and competitively functioning to restore economic balance, Lionel Robbins was also clear in 1932:

> It is impossible to get back to a state of true prosperity until the real underlying causes of the present stagnation are removed—barriers to international trade, in the shape of tariffs, quota systems, exchange restrictions and the like obstacles to internal adjustments in the shape of cost rigidities and bad debts which should be written off. . . . But, above all, policy must be directed to restoring the freedom of the market in the widest sense of the term. By this I mean not only the

> lowering of tariffs and the abolition of trade restrictions but also the removal of all those causes which produce internal rigidity—rigid wages, rigid prices, rigid systems of production. . . . It is this inflexibility of the economic system at the present day which is at the root of most of our troubles.[61]

For Austrian economists such as Mises, Hayek, and Robbins, the Great Depression was the fruit of the interventionist state. Beginning with the First World War, throughout the 1920s and into the Depression years of the early 1930s, the classical liberal world of free markets, free trade, and sound money under the gold standard had been undermined, weakened, and finally broken. In its place had arisen government-imposed systems of domestic regulation, nationalistic trade protectionism, price and wage rigidities, production subsidies, and state-sponsored monopolies and cartels.

The pre-World War I gold standard, though operated by government central banks, had more or less kept monetary and artificial credit expansions within narrow bounds. By the early and mid-1930s, the monetary systems of most countries were paper money systems, or monetary systems nominally gold-based but manipulated and abused by governments to serve interventionist domestic policies.

The Austrian economists attempted to show the deadend to which these policies had led. Unfortunately, their logical arguments and reasoned appeal fell on deaf ears. Instead, the United States and the European nations moved further down the interventionist road. And a major force for moving the intellectual climate in that direction was John Maynard Keynes.

John Maynard Keynes and the "New Liberalism"

In 1925, John Maynard Keynes delivered a lecture at Cambridge titled "Am I a Liberal?"[62] He rejected any thought of considering himself a conservative because conservatism "leads nowhere; it satisfies no ideal; it conforms to no intellectual standard; it is not even safe, or calculated to preserve from spoilers that degree of civilization which we have already attained."

Keynes then asked whether he should consider joining the Labour Party. He admitted, "Superficially that is more attractive," but rejected it as well. "To begin with, it is a class party, and the class is not my class," Keynes argued. "When it comes to the class struggle as such, my local and personal patriotism, like those of everyone else, except certain unpleasant zealous ones, are attached to my own surroundings. . . . [T]he Class war will find me on the side of the educated bourgeoisie." Furthermore, he doubted the intellectual ability of those controlling the Labour Party, believing that it was dominated by "those who do not know at all what they are talking about."

This led Keynes to conclude that all things considered, "the Liberal Party is still the best instrument of future progress—if only it has strong leadership and the right programme." But the Liberal Party of Great Britain could serve a positive role in society only if it gave up "old-fashioned individualism and laissez-faire," which he considered "the dead-wood of the past." Instead, what was needed was a "New Liberalism" that would involve "new wisdom for a new age." What this entailed, in Keynes's view, was "the transition from economic anarchy to a regime which deliberately aims at controlling and directing economic forces in the interests of social justice and social stability."

In 1926, Keynes published a lecture, "The End of Laissez-Faire," in which he argued, "It is *not* true that individuals possess a prescriptive 'natural liberty' in their economic activities. There is *no compact* conferring perpetual rights on those who Have or on those who Acquire." Nor could it be presumed that private individuals pursuing their enlightened self-interest would always serve the common good.[63]

In a period in which industry was becoming concentrated and controlled by handfuls of industrial managers, Keynes proposed "a return, it may be said, towards mediaeval conceptions of separate [corporate] autonomies." But instead of these corporate entities being left to their own profit-making purposes, Keynes's proposed semimonopolistic structures that would operate under government approval and clearly with government supervision.

In a world of "uncertainty and ignorance" that sometimes resulted in periods of unemployment, Keynes suggested "the cure for these things is partly to be sought in the deliberate control of the currency and of credit by a central institution." It also required the government's centralized collection of statistics and data about "the business situation" so the government could exercise "directive intelligence through some appropriate organ of action over many of the inner intricacies of private business." And he believed that "some coordinated act of intelligent judgment" by the government was required to determine the amount of savings in the society and how much of the nation's savings should be permitted to be invested in foreign markets as well as the relative distribution of that domestic savings among "the most nationally productive channels."

And, finally, Keynes argued that government had to undertake a "national policy" concerning the most appropriate size of the country's population, "and having settled this policy, we must take steps to carry it into operation." Furthermore, Keynes proposed serious consideration of adopting a policy of eugenics: "The time may arrive a little later when the community as a whole must pay attention to the innate quality as well as to the mere numbers of its future members."

This did not make Keynes a socialist or a communist in any strict sense of these words. Indeed, after a visit to Soviet Russia he published an essay in 1925 strongly critical of the Bolshevik regime.[64] "For me, brought up in a free air undarkened by the horrors of religion, with nothing to be afraid of, Red Russia holds too much which is detestable. . . . I am not ready for a creed which does not care how much it destroys the liberty and security of daily life, which uses deliberately the weapons of persecution, destruction, and international strife. . . . It is hard for an educated, decent, intelligent son of Western Europe to find his ideals here."

But where Soviet Russia had an advantage over the West, Keynes argued, was in its almost religious revolutionary fervor, in its romanticism of the common working man, and its condemnation of money-making. Indeed, the Soviet attempt to stamp out the "money-making mentality" was, in Keynes's mind, "a tremendous innovation." Capitalist society, too, in Keynes's view, had to find a moral foundation above self-interested "love of money." What Keynes considered Soviet Russia's superiority over capitalist society, therefore, was its moral high-ground in opposition to capitalist individualism. And he also believed that "any piece of useful economic technique" developed in Soviet Russia could easily be grafted onto a Western economy following his model of a New Liberalism "with equal or greater success" than in the Soviet Union.

By the time John Maynard Keynes wrote these essays in the mid-1920s, he was already one of the most acclaimed economists in the world. His international notoriety had been established in 1919 when he published his criticism of the Treaty of Versailles, *The Economic Consequences of the Peace.*[65] In 1924 Keynes published *A Tract on Monetary Reform,* in which he called for abandoning the traditional gold standard and establishing a government-managed currency.[66] The gold standard meant that the value of a country's money was determined by international market forces to which each country had to conform in terms of appropriate adjustments in its domestic structure of prices and wages. If trade unions were strong and would not conform their wage demands to market conditions, then adherence to a market-guided gold standard could result in unemployment if the money wages that trade unions insisted upon were above what the global market determined those wages should be.

Instead, Keynes advocated abandoning the fixed exchange rate between gold and the British pound; the foreign exchange value of the British pound should be raised or lowered by the central bank to maintain domestic prices and wages at the politically determined desired level. Or as Keynes expressed it, "When stability of the internal price level and stability of the external exchanges are incompatible, the former is generally preferable.[67] As far as Keynes was concerned "there is no escape from a 'managed' currency, whether we wish it or not. . . . In truth, the gold standard is already a barbaric relic."[68]

In 1930, Keynes published a massive two-volume work that he hoped would establish his reputation as one of the great economists of the twentieth century, *A Treatise on Money.* But over the next two years many of the leading economists in Europe and North America wrote reviews that demonstrated the fundamental flaws in both the assumptions and the logic of his argument. But the most devastating criticisms were made by a young Friedrich A. Hayek in a two-part review essay that appeared in 1931–1932.[69]

Hayek showed that Keynes understood neither the nature of a market economy in general nor the significance and role of the rate of interest in maintaining a proper balance between savings and investment for economic stability. At the most fundamental level Hayek argued that Keynes's method of aggregating the individual supplies and demands for a multitude of goods into a small number of macroeconomic "totals" distorted any real understanding of the actual relationships in and between actual markets. "Mr. Keynes's aggregates conceal the most fundamental mechanisms of change," Hayek said.[70]

In a complex market economy, it was one function of the rate of interest—as the price for the exchange of goods across time—to bring the supply of savings into balance with the demand to borrow funds for investment purposes. Changes in the rate of interest (reflecting a change in savings) assured such a proper balance and guided potential investors into using those funds for investment projects involving a period of time consistent with the available savings needed to sustain them. Keynes's argument that this was not the case led Hayek to state:

> Mr. Keynes's assertion that there is no automatic mechanism in the economic system to keep the rate of saving and the rate of investing equal might with equal justification be extended to the more general contention that there is no automatic mechanism in the economic system to adapt production to any shift in demand. I begin to wonder whether Mr. Keynes has ever reflected upon the function of the rate of interest in . . . society.[71]

If there occurred prolonged unemployment and industrial depression, Hayek argued, then the cause was to be found in prices for goods and resources (including labor) being kept too high relative to actual supply and demand conditions in various markets. The solution was a free, competitive process to bring prices and costs into proper balance, and with this a return to full employment. Keynes's emphasis on aggregates and averages hid the actual pricing problems under the cover of macro "totals."

With the coming of the Great Depression, however, Keynes once again rejected the idea of a free market solution to the rising unemployment and idled industry that intensified following the crash of 1929. His remedy was outlined in two "open letters" to Franklin D. Roosevelt in December 1933 and June 1934, as well as in some addresses and speeches he delivered in England evaluating the possibilities and results of the New Deal.[72]

Keynes considered FDR "the trustee for those in every country who seek to mend the evils of our conditions by reasoned experiment within the framework of the existing social system," and he was the leader for whom Keynes was "the most sympathetic in the world." In Keynes's view, the New Deal contained two elements: "recovery and reform." The National Recovery Administration (NRA) represented one of the reform aspects of the New Deal. While considering this a desirable shift in American industrial policy for the long run, Keynes was critical of it as a short-run policy. First, the forced cartelization of American industry would "upset the confidence of the business world and weaken its existing motives to action before you have had time to put other motives in their place" and "[i]t may overtask your bureaucratic machine." Second, by coercively restricting production and pushing up industrial prices and wages by decree, it was decreasing the demand for labor and thus doing nothing to stimulate employment.

Instead, Keynes recommended monetary expansion and federal deficit spending as the avenues for overcoming the mass unemployment of the Great Depression:

> [P]ublic authority must . . . create additional current incomes through the expenditure of borrowed or printed money. . . . When more purchasing power is spent, one expects rising output at rising prices. Since there cannot be rising output without rising prices, it is essential to insure that the recovery shall not be held back by the insufficiency of the supply of money to support the increased monetary turnover. . . . The increased stimulation of output by increased aggregate purchasing power is the right way to get prices up. . . . I put in the forefront, for the reasons given above, a large volume of loan expenditure under government auspices. . . . [P]reference should be given to those which can be made to mature quickly on a large scale. . . . The object is to get the ball rolling. . . . I put in the

> second place the maintenance of cheap and abundant credit, in particular the reduction of the long-term rate of interest.[73]

In his writings of the 1920s and early 1930s, advocating a "New Liberalism" and a deficit-spending government to "solve" the Great Depression, were the premises for the Keynesian Revolution that would be officially inaugurated with the publication of *The General Theory of Employment, Interest and Money* in 1936. With those ideas, Keynes produced one of the greatest challenges to the free market economy in the twentieth century.

Keynes and Keynesian Economics

The General Theory of Employment, Interest and Money by John Maynard Keynes was published on February 4, 1936. Its influence on the economics profession was astonishing. And its impact on economic theory and policy over the last sixty years has been immense. Paul Samuelson of MIT, the 1970 recipient of the Nobel Prize in Economics and one of the most influential expositors of Keynesian Economics in the post-World War II period, contributed an essay to *The New Economics,* edited by Seymour Harris in 1948, two years after Keynes's death. In an often-quoted passage, Samuelson explained:

> It is quite impossible for modern students to realize the full effect of what has been advisably called "The Keynesian Revolution" upon those of us brought up in the [pre-Keynesian] orthodox tradition. To have been born as an economist before 1936 was a boon—yes. But not to have been born too long before! . . . *The General Theory* caught most economists under the age of 35 with the unexpected virulence of a disease first attacking and decimating an isolated tribe of south seas islanders. Economists beyond fifty turned out to be quite immune to the ailment. With time, most economists in-between began to run the fever, often without knowing or admitting the condition. . . . This impression was confirmed by the rapidity with which English economists, other than those at Cambridge took up the new Gospel . . . at Oxford; and still more surprisingly, the young blades at the London School [of

> Economics] . . . threw off their Hayekian garments and joined in the swim. In this country [the United States] it was pretty much the same story. . . . Finally, and perhaps most important from the long-run standpoint, the Keynesian analysis has begun to filter down into the elementary textbooks; and, as everybody knows, once an idea gets into these, however bad it may be, it becomes practically immortal.[74]

Even today, when the traditional Keynesian analysis has been challenged and set aside by many economists, the Keynesian framework still haunts most macroeconomic textbooks, demonstrating Samuelson's point that "however bad it may be" it has become "practically immortal."

The essence of Keynes's theory was to show that a market economy, when left to its own devices, possessed no inherent self-correcting mechanism to return to "full employment" once the economic system has fallen into a depression. At the heart of his approach was the belief that he had demonstrated an error in Say's Law. Named after the nineteenth-century French economist Jean-Baptiste Say, the fundamental idea is that individuals produce so they can consume. An individual produces either to consume what he has manufactured himself or to sell on the market to acquire the means to purchase what others have for sale. Or as the classical economist David Ricardo expressed it, "By producing, then, he necessarily becomes either the consumer of his own goods, or the purchaser and consumer of the goods of some other person. . . . Productions are always bought by productions, or by services; money is only the medium by which the exchange is effected."[75]

Keynes argued that there was no certainty that those who had sold goods or their labor services on the market will necessarily turn around and spend the full amount that they had earned on the goods and services offered by others. Hence, total expenditures on goods could be less than total income previously earned in the manufacture of those goods. This, in turn, meant that the total receipts received by firms selling goods in the market could be less than the expenses incurred in bringing those goods to market. With total sales receipts being less than total business expenses, businessmen would have no recourse other than to cut back on both output and the number of workers employed to minimize losses during this period of "bad business."

But, Keynes argued, this would merely intensify the problem of unemployment and falling output. As workers were laid off, their incomes would necessarily go down. With less income to spend, the unemployed would cut back on their consumption expenditures. This would result in an additional falling off of demand for goods and services offered on the market, widening the circle of businesses that find their sales receipts declining relative to their costs of production. And this would set off a new round of cuts in output and employment, setting in motion a cumulative contraction in production and jobs.

Why wouldn't workers accept lower money wages to make themselves more attractive to rehire when market demand falls? Because, Keynes said, workers suffer from money illusion. If prices for goods and services decrease because consumer demand is falling off, then workers could accept a lower money wage and be no worse off in real buying terms (that is, if the cut in wages was on average no greater than the decrease in the average level of prices). But workers, Keynes argued, generally think only in terms of money wages, not real wages (that is, what their money income represents in real purchasing power on the market). Thus, workers often would rather accept unemployment than a cut in their money wage.

If consumers demand fewer final goods and services on the market, this necessarily means that they are saving more. Why wouldn't this unconsumed income merely be spent hiring labor and purchasing resources in a different way, in the form of greater investment, as savers have more to lend to potential borrowers at a lower rate of interest? Keynes's response was to insist that the motives of savers and investors were not the same. Income-earners might very well desire to consume a smaller fraction of their income, save more, and offer it out to borrowers at interest. But there was no certainty, he insisted, that businessmen would be willing to borrow that greater savings and use it to hire labor to make goods for sale in the future.

Since the future is uncertain and tomorrow can be radically different from today, Keynes stated, businessmen easily fall under the spell of unpredictable waves of optimism and pessimism that raise and lower their interest and willingness to borrow and invest. A decrease in the demand to consume today by income-earners may be motivated by a desire to increase their consumption in the future out of their savings. But businessmen cannot know when those income-earners will want to increase their consumption, nor what particular goods will be in greater demand when that day comes. As a result, the decrease in consumer demand for present production merely serves to decrease the businessman's current incentives for investment activity today as well.

If for some reason there were to be a wave of business pessimism resulting in a decrease in the demand for investment borrowing, this should result in a decrease in the rate of interest. Such a decrease because of a fall in investment demand should make savings less attractive, since less interest income is now to be earned by lending a part of one's income. As a result, consumer spending should rise as savings goes down. Thus, while investment spending may be slackening off, greater consumer spending should make up the difference to assure a "full employment" demand for society's labor and resources.

But Keynes doesn't allow this to happen because of what he calls the "fundamental psychological law" of the "propensity to consume." As income rises, he says, consumption spending out of income also tends to rise, but less than the increase in income. Over time, therefore, as incomes rise a larger and larger percentage is saved.

In *The General Theory*, Keynes listed a variety of what he called the "objective" and "subjective" factors which he thought influenced people's decisions to consume out of income. On the "objective" side: a windfall profit; a change in the rate of interest; a change in expectations about future income. On the "subjective" side, he listed "Enjoyment, Shortsightedness, Generosity, Miscalculation, Ostentation and Extravagance." He merely asserts that the "objective" factors have little influence on how much to consume out of a given amount of income—including a change in the rate of interest. And the "subjective" factors are basically invariant, being "habits formed by race, education, convention, religion and current morals . . . and the established standards of life."[76]

Indeed, Keynes reaches the peculiar conclusion that because men's wants are basically determined and fixed by their social and cultural environment and only change very slowly, "The greater . . . the consumption for which we have provided in advance, the more difficult it is to find something further to provide for in advance."[77] In other words, men run out of wants for which they would wish investment to be undertaken; the resources in the society—including labor—are threatening to become greater than the demand for their employment.

Keynes, in other words, turns the most fundamental concept in economics on its head. Instead of our wants and desires always tending to exceed the means at our disposal to satisfy them, man is confronting a "post-scarcity" world in which the means at our disposal are becoming greater than the ends for which they could be applied. The crisis of society is a crisis of abundance! The richer we become, the less work we have for people to do because, in Keynes's vision, man's capacity and desire for imagining new and different ways to improve his life is finite. The economic problem is that we are too well-off.

As a consequence, unspent income can pile up as unused and uninvested savings; and what investment is undertaken can erratically fluctuate due to what Keynes called the "animal spirits" of businessmen's irrational psychology concerning an uncertain future.[78] The free market economy, therefore, is plagued with the constant danger of waves of booms and busts, with prolonged periods of high unemployment and idle factories. The society's problem stems from the fact that people consume too little and save too much to assure jobs for all who desire to work at the money wages that have come to prevail in the market and which workers refuse to adjust downward in the face of any decline in the demand for their services.

Only one institution can step in and serve as the stabilizing mechanism to maintain full employment and steady production: the government, through various activist monetary and fiscal policies.

This is the essence of Keynesian economics.

Keynesian Economic Policy and Its Consequences

In a famous lecture, "National Self-Sufficiency," delivered in Dublin, Ireland, in April 1933, John Maynard Keynes renounced his previous belief in the benefits of free trade. He declared, "I sympathize . . . with those who would minimize rather than those who would maximize economic entanglement between nations. . . . Let goods be homespun whenever it is reasonably and conveniently possible; and above all, let finance be primarily national."[79] He remained loyal to economic protectionism in *The General Theory*. In one of the concluding chapters he discovered new value in the seventeenth- and eighteenth-century writings of the Mercantilists and their rationales for government control over and manipulation of international trade and domestic investment.[80]

But Keynes expressed another sentiment in that 1933 lecture:

> We each have our own fancy. Not believing we are saved already, we each would like to have a try at working out our salvation. We do not wish, therefore, to be at the mercy of world forces working out, or trying to work out, some uniform equilibrium according to the ideal principles of laissez-faire capitalism. . . . We wish . . . to be our own masters, and to be free as we can make ourselves from the interference of the outside world.[81]

Keynes was convinced that left to itself, the market economy could not be trusted to assure either stable or full employment. Instead, an activist government program of monetary and fiscal intervention was needed for continuing economic prosperity. If this also required a degree of state planning, Keynes was open to that kind of direct social engineering as well. In an often-quoted 1944 letter to Austrian economist Friedrich A. Hayek, Keynes said that he found himself "in a deeply moved agreement" with Hayek's arguments in *The Road to Serfdom*. But less frequently mentioned is what Keynes went on to say in that same letter:

> I should say that what we want is not no planning, or even less planning, indeed I should say that what we almost certainly want is more. . . . Moderate planning will be safe if those carrying it out are rightly oriented in their own minds and hearts to the moral issue. . . . Dangerous acts can be done safely in a community which thinks and feels rightly, which would be the way to hell if they were executed by those who think and feel wrongly.[82]

Of course, the question is who determines which members of society think and feel "rightly" enough to qualify for the power and authority to plan for the rest of us? And how is it to be assured that such power does not fall into the hands of "those who think and feel wrongly"? Furthermore, on what basis can it be presumed that even those who claim to be "rightly oriented in their own minds and hearts" could ever possess the knowledge and ability to plan some desirable economic outcome for society?

Yet, as a number of commentators have pointed out, Keynes had no doubts about either his "rightness" or competency in claiming such authority or ability. He belonged to a British elite that viewed itself as superior to the other members of the society in practically every way. As Keynes's sympathetic biographer Roy Harrod explained, "he was strongly imbued with . . . the idea that the government of Britain was and could continue to be in the hands of an intellectual aristocracy using the method of persuasion."[83] And as the American Keynesian Arthur Smithies also pointed out, "Keynes hoped for a world where monetary and fiscal policy, carried out by *wise men* in authority, could ensure conditions of prosperity, equity, freedom, and possibly peace."[84]

As we have seen, Keynes argued that the fundamental problem with a laissez-faire market economy was that as incomes went up over time the saved part of that income would grow proportionally.

Individuals were habituated and socialized into having certain types and amounts of consumer wants. When these tended to be satisfied, consumers ran out of things to demand, both in the present and the future. As a result, this would limit the amount of that growing fund of savings for which there would be private investment demand.

With a psychological limit on the propensity to consume, and with investment demand restrained by limited investment opportunities for future profits, savings would accumulate and go to waste. Since workers were presumed to be unwilling to accept any significant downward adjustment in their money wage demands because of "money illusion," aggregate demand for goods and services in the economy would be insufficient to profitably employ those willing to work at the rigid money wages prevailing on the market.

In Keynes's mind the only remedy was for government to step in and put those unused savings to work through deficit spending to stimulate investment activity. How the government spent those borrowed funds did not matter. Even "public works of doubtful utility," Keynes said, were useful: "Pyramid-building, earthquakes, even wars may serve to increase wealth," as long as they create employment. "It would, indeed, be more sensible to build houses and the like," said Keynes, "but if there are political or practical difficulties in the way of this, the above would be better than nothing."[85]

Nor could the private sector be trusted to maintain any reasonable level of investment activity to provide employment. The uncertainties of the future, as we saw, created "animal spirits" among businessmen which produced unpredictable waves of optimism and pessimism that generated fluctuations in the level of production and employment. Luckily, government could fill the gap. Furthermore, while businessmen were emotional and shortsighted, the State had the ability to calmly calculate the long-run, true value and worth of investment opportunities "on the basis of the general social advantage."[86]

Indeed, Keynes expected the government would "take on ever greater responsibility for directly organizing investment." In the future, said Keynes, "I conceive, therefore, that a somewhat comprehensive socialization of investment will prove the only means of securing an approximation to full employment." As the profitability of private investment dried up over time, society would see "the euthanasia of the rentier" and "the euthanasia of the cumulative oppressive power of the capitalist" to exploit for his own benefit the scarcity of capital. This "assisted suicide" of the interest-earning and capitalist groups would not require any revolutionary upheaval. No, "the necessary measures of socialization can be introduced gradually and without a break in the general traditions of the society."[87]

This did not mean that the private sector would be completely done away with. Through its monetary and fiscal policies, the government would determine the aggregate level of spending in the economy, and then private enterprise would be allowed to operate in directing resources for the manufacture of the various individual goods to be sold on the market.

The role of fiscal policy was for the government to run deficits and inject a net increase of spending into the economy by borrowing the unused savings that accumulated as idle cash or unspent hoards of money. The key, in Keynes's view, was for the government to increase spending so that prices in general would rise. "The expectation of a fall in the value of money [a rise in prices] stimulates investment, and hence employment" because it would raise the profitability of prospective investments.

Why would rising prices stimulate investment profitability? Because, in Keynes's view, workers' "money illusion" worked both ways. Just as workers would not accept cuts in their money wages with a fall in prices, workers would not generally demand an increase in their money wages when there was a rise in prices. "[A] movement by employers to revise money-wage bargains downward," said Keynes, "will be much more strongly resisted than a gradual and automatic lowering of real wages as a result of rising prices."[88] Thus, the government's fiscal stimulus would raise prices in general relative to costs ofproduction (especially the money-wage costs of labor), thus increasing profit margins and creating the incentives for private employers and investors to expand output and rehire the unemployed.

Matching the fiscal stimulus, government was to introduce any required monetary expansion to keep interest rates low. If the government's fiscal stimulus succeeded in generating greater investment spending in the private sector, this would increase the private sector's demand to borrow for the financing of expanding production activities. This increased demand to borrow would push interest rates up and dampen some of the private sector business activity that the government would be trying to stimulate. Thus, the government's monetary authority was to create enough money to satisfy both the government's and the private sector's demands to borrow, while keeping interest rates unchanged (or even lowered).

While Keynes was suspicious of attempts to construct statistical models of the economy (indeed, in a 1939 article he forcefully criticized a leading developer of econometric techniques),[89] he clearly believed that it was within the capacity of the government to determine just the right amount of fiscal and monetary stimulus to establish and maintain a fully employed economy.

He also argued that government had to regulate and control a country's imports and exports to secure a desired level of domestic production and employment. "It will be essential for the maintenance of prosperity that the authorities should pay close attention to the state of the balance of trade. . . . For a favorable balance, provided it is not too large, will be extremely stimulating," Keynes said. As for the effects this would have on international trade, he stated that "the classical school [of economists] greatly overstressed . . . the advantages of the international division of labor."[90]

For Keynes no aspect of economic life would remain unaffected by the activist hand of government. After all, he had said, "We each have our fancy," and his purpose was to devise the rationale and tools for government "to have a try working out our salvation."

Keynesian Economics and Say's Law of Markets

In the preface to *The General Theory of Employment, Interest and Money,* John Maynard Keynes stated that "the composition of this book has been for the author a long struggle of escape . . . a struggle of escape from habitual modes of thought and expression."[91] What Keynes struggled to escape from was the common-sense foundations of economics.

From Adam Smith in the eighteenth century to the Austrian economists of the twentieth century, economics has developed and been refined into the study of human action and the logic of human choice. After more than two hundred years economists came to understand more clearly that nothing happens in "society" or "the market" that does not first begin with the actions and decisions of individuals. Indeed, "the market" is nothing more than a summarizing term to express the arena in which multitudes of individuals meet and interact as suppliers and demanders for the purpose of mutual gains through trade.

Each individual has various goals he would like to achieve. To attain them he must apply various means to bring those desired ends into existence through production. But man finds that, unfortunately, the means at his disposal are often insufficient to satisfy all the uses he has for them. He faces the reality of scarcity. He is confronted with the necessity to choose; he must decide which desired ends he prefers more. And then he must apply the means to achieve the more highly valued ends, while leaving the other, less valued, ends unfulfilled.

In his state of disappointment, man looks to see if there are ways to improve his situation. He discovers that others face the same frustration of unsatisfied ends. Sometimes he finds that those others have things that he values more highly than his possessions, and they in turn value his possessions more highly than their own. A potential gain from trade arises, in which each party can be better off if they trade away what they respectively have for what the other has. But how much of one thing will be exchanged for another? This will be determined through their bargaining in the market. Finally, they may agree upon terms of trade, and will establish a price at which they exchange one thing for another: so many apples for so many pears; so many bushels of wheat for so many pounds of meat; so many pairs of shoes for a suit of clothes.

Trade becomes a regular event through which men improve their circumstances through the process of buying and selling. Appreciating the value of these trading opportunities, men begin to specialize their productive activities and create a system of division of labor, with each trying to find that niche in the growing arena of exchange in which they have a comparative production advantage over their trading partners. As the market expands, a growing competition arises between buyers and sellers, with each trying to get the best deal possible as a producer and a consumer. The prices at which goods are traded come more and more to reflect the contributing and competing bids and offers of many buyers and sellers on both sides of the market.

The more complex the network of exchange, the more difficult the direct barter of goods one for another. Rather than be frustrated and disappointed in not being able to directly find trading partners who want the goods they have for sale, individuals start using some commodity as a medium of exchange. They first trade what they have produced for a particular commodity and then use that commodity to buy from others the things they desire. When that commodity becomes widely accepted and generally used by most, if not all, transactors in the market, it becomes the money-good.

It should be clear that even though all transactions are carried out through the medium of money, it is still, ultimately, goods that trade for goods. The cobbler makes shoes and sells them for money to those who desire footwear. The cobbler then uses the money he has earned from selling shoes to buy the food he wants to eat. But he cannot buy that food unless he has first earned a certain sum of money by selling a particular quantity of shoes on the market. In the end, his supply of shoes has been the means for him to demand a certain amount of food.

This, in essence, is the meaning of Say's Law. Say called it "the law of markets": that is, unless we first produce we cannot consume; unless we first supply we cannot demand.[92] But how much others are willing to take of our supply is dependent on the price at which we offer it to them. The higher we price our commodity, other things held equal, the less of it others will be willing to buy. The less we sell, the smaller the money income we earn; and the smaller the money income we earn, the smaller our financial means to demand and purchase what others offer for sale. Thus, if we want to sell all that we choose to produce we must price it correctly, that is, at a price sufficiently low that all we offer is cleared off the market by demanders. Pricing our goods or labor services too high, given other people's demands for them, will leave part of the supply of the good unsold and part of the labor services offered unhired.

On the other hand, lowering the price at which we are willing to sell our commodity or services will, other things held equal, create a greater willingness on the part of others to buy more of our commodity or hire more of our labor services. By selling more, our money income can increase; and by increasing our money income, through correctly pricing our commodity or labor services, we increase our ability to demand what others have for sale.

Sometimes, admittedly, even lowering our price may not generate a large enough increase in the quantity demanded by others for our income to go up. Lowering the price may, in fact, result in our revenue or income going down. But this, too, is a law of the market: what we chose to supply is worth no more than what consumers are willing to pay for it. This is the market's way of telling us that the commodity or particular labor skills we are offering are not in very great demand. It is the market's way of telling us that consumers value others things more highly. It is the market's way of telling us that the particular niche we have chosen in the division of labor is one in which our productive abilities or labor services are not worth as much as we had hoped. It is the market's way of telling us that we need to move our productive activities in other directions, where consumer demand is greater and our productive abilities may be valued more highly.

Can it happen that consumers may not spend all they have earned? Can it be the case that some of the money earned will be "hoarded," so there will be no greater demand for other goods, and hence no alternative line of production in which we might find remunerative employment? Would this be a case in which "aggregate demand" for goods in general would not be sufficient to buy all of the "aggregate supply" of goods and labor services offered?

The answers had already been suggested in the middle of the nineteenth century by the English classical economist John Stuart Mill in a restatement and refinement of Say's law of markets. In an essay titled "Of the Influence of Consumption on Production," Mill argued that as long as there are ends or wants that have not yet been satisfied, there is more work to be done.[93] As long as producers adjust their supplies to reflect the actual demand for the particular goods that consumers wish to purchase, and as long as they price their supplies at prices consumers are willing to pay, there need be no unemployment of resources or labor. Thus, there can never be an excess supply of all things relative to the total demand for all things.

But Mill admits that there may be times when individuals, for various reasons, may choose to "hoard," or leave unspent in their cash holding, a greater proportion of their money income than is the usual practice. In this case, Mill argued, what is "called a general superabundance" of all goods is in reality "a superabundance of all commodities relative to money." In other words, if we accept that money, too, is a commodity like all other goods on the market for which there is a supply and demand, then there can appear a situation in which the demand to hold money increases relative to the demand for all the other things that money could buy. This means that all other goods are now in relative oversupply in comparison to that greater demand to hold money.

To bring those other goods offered on the market into balance with the lower demands for them (i.e., given that increased demand to hold money and the decreased demand for other things), the prices of many of those other goods may have to decrease. Prices in general, in other words, must go down, until that point at which all the supplies of goods and labor services people wish to sell find buyers willing to purchase them. Sufficient flexibility and adjustability in prices to the actual demands for things on the market always assure that all those willing to sell and desiring to be employed can find work. And this, also, is a law of the market.

Free market economists, both before and after Keynes, have never denied that the market economy can face a situation in which mass unemployment could exist and a sizable portion of the society's productive capacity could be left idle. But if such a situation were to arise, they argued that its cause was to be found in a failure of suppliers to price their goods and labor services to reflect what consumers considered them to be worth, given the demand for various other things, including money. Correct prices always assure full employment; correct prices always assure that supplies create a demand for them; correct prices always assure the harmony of the market.[94]

This was the reality of the law of markets from which Keynes struggled so hard to escape.

Keynesian Economics and Savings, Investment, and Interest

In the 1939 foreword to the French edition of *The General Theory*, John Maynard Keynes said that in writing the book he had broken out of the prevailing economic orthodoxy, "to be in strong reaction against it, to be escaping from something, to be gaining an emancipation.[95]

The freedom that Keynes wanted to gain was from the laws of economics, the logic of human choice, and the relationships between savings, investment, and interest. For Keynes, spending out of income was determined by his "psychological law" of people's "propensity to consume" out of any given level of income. This, we saw, was dependent on various cultural, racial, class, and religious habits that change very slowly. One thing Keynes was certain did not significantly influence people's willingness to consume was a change in the rate of interest; a rise or a fall in the rate of interest had no significant effect on people's willingness to save or spend more or less out of income earned.

What did the rate of interest influence? According to Keynes, it influenced people's willingness or "propensity" to hoard money. Given that propensity to consume out of income, the amount of income saved could either be invested in interest-earning securities or bonds or held as an idle cash balance. All the rate of interest influenced was the relative attractiveness of holding bonds or cash. No matter how low the rate of interest might go, individuals would not consume more; their consumption was determined by the "psychological law." They would merely hold more and more of their savings in idle cash.[96]

In Keynes's system, the rate of interest also had no appreciable effect on the willingness to invest. People's willingness to invest was based on their estimates of likely profitability from a possible investment relative to the rate of interest paid to borrow the sums needed to undertake the project. But in Keynes's view there is no way to determine precisely what the future holds or what the prospective return from an investment will be. Since we all must try to make some estimate of the probable results from present actions undertaken toward a radically uncertain future, Keynes believed that people fall back on "conventional wisdom." That is, we model our beliefs about the future on the basis of what we think the majority of other people think at any point in time. "[B]eing based on so flimsy a foundation," Keynes argued, "it is subject to sudden and violent changes. . . . New fears and hopes will, without warning, take charge of human conduct." Being based on nothing but what each thinks the other person believes, investor expectations about investment possibilities and profitabilities are open to dramatic and unpredictable fluctuations that are far more important in influencing investment demand than any changes in the rate of interest, Keynes insisted.[97]

The great demon in the Keynesian system, therefore, was the "propensity" to save some portion of additional income earned, rather than consume it all. Savings diminished spending in the economy; diminished consumption spending decreased expected revenues from sales; lowered sales expectations made businessmen want to cut back production; lowered production meant fewer jobs; fewer jobs decreased total income earned in the economy; a decline in total income created a further falling off in consumer spending; and this additional falling off in consumer spending set the process of economic contraction in motion once again. If only everything that was earned was consumed, Keynes argued, then full employment and high production would be assured.

In explaining the fundamental error in Keynes's conception of the evils of savings, I can do no better than to quote the insightful response given by the German free market economist H. Albert Hahn, from his 1946 article, "Is Saving a Virtue or a Sin?":

> According to the classical [economic] concept of the problem of savings . . . the interests of the individual and of the community are in full harmony. He who saves serves his own as well as the nation's welfare.
>
> He improves his own welfare because savings implies the transfer of means of consumption from the present, where his earnings are ample, to the future where his earnings may become scarce through old age and sickness. Furthermore, savings will increase his means through the interest he receives.
>
> The nation as a whole, on the other hand, benefits from savings since these savings are paid into a bank or some other reservoir of money from which an employer may borrow for productive purposes, for instance to buy machinery. This means a change in the direction of productive activity.
>
> Through saving, production is diverted from goods for immediate consumption to goods which cannot themselves be consumed but with which consumer goods can be produced. Production is diverted, as one puts it, from a direct to a roundabout way of production. . . . The roundabout way of production has the advantage of greater productivity. . . . The high productivity of the more capitalistic production methods has further favorable effects. Because [of the greater cost-efficient productivity] employers can—and by competition are forced to—pay interest on the capital borrowed, to raise wages, and lower costs. The standard of living of the nation rises.
>
> This process is renewed over and over again, because increased savings permit primitive direct methods of production

requiring small amounts of capital to be replaced by roundabout indirect methods requiring large amounts of capital.[98]

But doesn't the falling off of consumption from the act of saving reduce the demand for goods and thus decrease the profitability from production? Why would businessmen undertake new and time-consuming investment projects to increase production capacity in the future when demand for consumer goods shows itself to be less in the present?

The answer to this Keynesian argument, as we saw, was given by the Austrian economist Eugen von Böhm-Bawerk thirty-five years before Keynes wrote *The General Theory*. In his 1901 essay, "The Function of Savings," Böhm-Bawerk pointed out that the error in such an argument arises from the failure to remember that what people do in an act of savings is defer present consumption, not forgo consumption permanently. Income earners shift a portion of their demand for goods from the present to the future, at which point they plan to utilize what they have saved and additionally earned as interest income for some desired purposes.

The savings set aside free the resources and labor to be applied to those different, roundabout productive ways, so greater and improved quantities of the goods can be produced for some future demand. The task of the entrepreneur, as Ludwig von Mises cogently emphasized in his theory of the market process, is to anticipate the direction and timing of future consumer demand, as well as the prices those future consumers might be willing to pay for goods offered in certain quantities and qualities. The market rewards those entrepreneurs who more correctly anticipate these future market conditions with earned profits and punishes the less competent with no profits, or even losses.[99]

The market system of profit and loss through competition for the use of resources and the selling of products assures a greater rationality to investment decisionmaking than suggested by Keynes's references to "animal spirits" and "conventional wisdom." In the market economy, control over the investment decisionmaking process always tends to shift into those entrepreneurial hands that, in the division of labor, demonstrate the most ability to direct production into the avenues most consistent with present and future patterns of consumer demand.[100]

The market rates of interest are meant to bring into balance the individual plans of savers with the individual plans of borrowers and investors. They serve the same function as all other prices in the market: to coordinate the activities of multitudes of people for purposes of mutual benefit through opportunities for gains from trade. Changes in market rates of interest potentially modify consumption, saving, and investment decisions just as any other change in price may modify the amount of a good consumers find attractive to buy and sellers to offer for sale.[101]

In a developed market, with numerous consumers and producers, changes in price will, at some point, modify people's response. Each of us has a threshold that leads to what economists call "marginal decisionmaking." Some incremental change in price will result in some incremental increase or decrease in the amount of a good that some people are willing to purchase or sell.

By arguing that a mystical "psychological law" makes people consume a certain amount of their income independent of changes in the interest rate, Keynes was rejecting the fundamental logic of human action and choice upon which economic understanding is based. The rate of interest not only influences the attractiveness, at the margin, of investing in bonds and securities versus holding a portion of one's income as a cash balance, the interest income to be earned from savings is also the cost of not consuming. And as with price, as the rate of interest rises or falls, some people will find it more or less attractive to consume. It is the logic of these changes in people's willingness to consume or save in the face of a change in the rate of interest that assures that the supplies and demands for consumer goods, savings, and investment projects of particular types and durations are kept in balance.

It was this logic of human choice and the rationality of market relationships between savings, investment, and interest that Keynes said he was "reacting strongly against" and from which he wanted to gain his "freedom."

Keynesian Economics and the Hubris of the Social Engineer

In September 1936, John Maynard Keynes prepared a preface for the German translation of *The General Theory of Employment, Interest and Money*. Addressing himself to German economists, Keynes hoped that his theory would "meet with less resistance on the part of German readers than from English, when I submit to them a theory of employment and production as a whole," because the German economists had long before rejected the teachings of both the classical economists and the more recent Austrian School of Economics. And, said Keynes, "if I can contribute a single morsel to a full meal prepared by German economists, particularly adjusted to German conditions, I will be satisfied."

What were those particular "German conditions"? For more than three years, Germany had been under the rule of Hitler's National Socialist regime; in 1936, the Nazis had instituted their own version of four-year central planning.

Toward the end of this preface Keynes pointed out to his Nazi economist readers:

> The theory of aggregate production, which is the point of the following book, nevertheless can be much easier adapted to the conditions of a totalitarian state, than . . . under conditions of free competition and a large degree of laissez-faire. This is one of the reasons that justifies the fact that I call my theory a *general* theory. . . . Although I have, after all, worked it out with a view to the conditions prevailing in the Anglo-Saxon countries where a large degree of laissez-faire still prevails, nevertheless it remains applicable to situations in which state management is more pronounced.[102]

It would be historically inaccurate to accuse Keynes of explicitly being either a Nazi sympathizer or an advocate of Soviet or fascist-type totalitarianism.[103] But Keynes clearly understood that the greater the degree of state control over any economy, the easier it would be for the government to manage the levers of monetary and fiscal policy to manipulate macroeconomic aggregates of "total output," "total employment," and "the general price and wage levels" for purposes of moving the overall economy into directions more to the economic policy analyst's liking.

On what moral or philosophical basis did Keynes believe that policy advocates such as himself had either the right or the ability to manage or direct the economic interactions of multitudes of peoples in the marketplace? Keynes explained his own moral foundations in *Two Memoirs,* published posthumously in 1949, three years after his death. One memoir, written in 1938, examined the formation of his "early beliefs" as a young man in his twenties at Cambridge University in the first decade of the twentieth-century.

He, and many other young intellectuals at Cambridge, had been influenced by the writings of philosopher G.E. Moore. Separate from Moore's argument, what is of interest are the conclusions reached by Keynes from reading Moore's work. Keynes said:

> Indeed, in our opinion, one of the greatest advantages of his [Moore's] religion was that it made morals unnecessary. . . . Nothing mattered except states of mind, our own and other people's of course, but chiefly our own. These states of mind were not associated with action or achievement or consequences. They consisted of timeless, passionate states of contemplation and communion, largely unattached to "before" and "after."[104]

In this setting, traditional or established ethical or moral codes of conduct meant nothing. Said Keynes:

> We entirely repudiated a personal liability on us to obey general rules. We claimed the right to judge every individual case on its own merits, and the wisdom, experience and self-control to do so successfully. This was a very important part of our faith, violently and aggressively held. . . . We repudiated entirely customary morals, conventions and traditional wisdoms. We were, that is to say, in the strict sense of the term immoralists. . . . [W]e recognized no moral obligation upon us, no inner sanction to conform or obey. Before heaven we claimed to be our own judge in our own case.[105]

Keynes declared that he and those like him were "left, from now onwards, to their own sensible devices, pure motives and reliable intuitions of the good." Then in his mid-fifties, Keynes declared in 1938, "Yet so far as I am concerned, it is too late to change. I remain, and always will remain, an immoralist." As for the social order in which he still claimed the right to act in such unrestrained ways, Keynes said that "civilization was a thin and precarious crust erected by the personality and the will of a very few, and only maintained by rules and conventions skillfully put across and guilely preserved."[106]

On matters of social and economic policy two assumptions guided Keynes, and they also dated from his Cambridge years as a student near the beginning of the century; they are stated clearly in a 1904 paper, "The Political Doctrines of Edmund Burke." First, "Our power of prediction is so slight, our knowledge of remote consequences so uncertain that it is seldom wise to sacrifice a present benefit for a doubtful advantage in the future. . . . We can never know enough to make the chance worth taking." And second, "What we ought to do is a matter of circumstances. . . . [W]hile the good is changeless and apart, the ought shifts and fades and grows new shapes and forms."[107]

Classical liberalism and the economics of the classical economists had been founded on two insights about man and society. First, there is an invariant quality to man's nature that makes him what he is; and if society is to be harmonious, peaceful, and prosperous, men must reform their social institutions in a way that directs the inevitable self-interests of individual men into those avenues of action that benefit not only themselves but others in society as well. They therefore advocated the institutions of private property, voluntary exchange, and peaceful, open competition. Then, as Adam Smith had concisely expressed, men would live in a system of natural liberty in which each individual would be free to pursue his own ends, but would be guided as if by an invisible hand to serve the interests of others in society as the means to his own self-improvement.[108]

Second, it is insufficient in any judgment concerning the desirability of a social or economic policy to focus only upon its seemingly short-run benefits. The laws of the market always bring about certain effects in the long run from any shift in supply and demand or from any government intervention in the market order. Thus, as French economist Frederic Bastiat emphasized, it behooves us always to try to determine not merely "what is seen" from a government policy in the short run, but also to discern as best we can "what is unseen," that is, the longer-run consequences of our actions and policies.[109]

The reason it is desirable to take the less immediate consequences into consideration is that longer-run effects may not only not improve the ill the policy was meant to cure, but can make the social situation even worse than had it been left alone. Even though the specific details of the future always remain beyond our ability to predict fully, one use of economics is to assist us to at least qualitatively anticipate the likely contours and shape of that future aided by an understanding of the laws of the market.

Keynes's assumptions deny the wisdom and the insights of the classical liberals and the classical economists. The biased emphasis is toward the benefits and pleasures of the moment, the short run, with an almost total disregard of the consequences. It led F. A. Hayek to lament in 1941:

> I cannot help regarding the increasing concentration on short-run effects . . . not only as a serious and dangerous intellectual error, but as a betrayal of the main duty of the economist and a grave menace to our civilization. . . . It used, however, to be regarded as the duty and the privilege of the economist to study and to stress the long effects which are apt to be hidden to the untrained eye, and to leave the concern about the more immediate effects to the practical man, who in any event would see only the latter and nothing else. . . . It is not surprising that Mr. Keynes finds his views anticipated by the mercantilist writers and gifted amateurs; concern with the surface phenomena has always marked the first stage of the scientific approach to our subject. . . . Are we not even told that, "since in the long run we all are dead," policy should be guided entirely by short-run considerations. I fear that these believers in the principle of *apres nous le deluge* may get what they have bargained for sooner than they wish.[110]

But if every action and policy decision is to be decided in the context of shifting circumstances, as Keynes insisted, on what basis shall such decisions be made, and by whom? Such decisions are to be made on the basis of the self-centered "state of mind" of the policymakers, with total disregard of traditions, customs, moral codes, rules, or the long-run laws of the market. Their rightness or wrongness was not bound by any independent standard of "achievement and consequence." Instead it was to be guided by "timeless, passionate states of contemplation and communion, largely unattached to 'before' and 'after.'" The decisionmaker's own "intuitions of the good," for himself and for others, were to serve as his compass. And let no ordinary man claim to criticize such actions or their results. "Before heaven," said Keynes, "we claimed to be our own judge in our own case."

Here was an elitist ideology of nihilism. The members of this elite were self-appointed and shown to belong to this elect precisely through mutual self-congratulations of having broken out of the straightjacket of conformity, custom, and law. For Keynes in his fifties, civilization was this thin, precarious crust overlaying the animal spirits and irrationality of ordinary men. Its existence, for whatever it was worth, was the product of "the personality and the will of a very few," like himself, naturally, and maintained through "rules and conventions skillfully put across and guilely preserved."

Society's shape and changing form were to be left in the hands of "the chosen" who stood above the passive conventions of the masses. Here was the hubris of the social engineer, the self-selected philosopher-king, who through manipulative skill and guile directed and experimented on society and its multitudes of individuals. It is what made Keynes feel comfortable in recommending his "general theory" to a Nazi readership. His conception of a society maintained by "the personality and the will of a very few," after all, had its family resemblance in the Fuehrer's principle of the unrestrained "one" who would command the Volk.

The rapidity with which Keynes's ideas captured the minds of economists was astounding. American economist Dudley Dillard began his 1948 book, *The Economics of John Maynard Keynes,* by pointing out, "Within the first dozen years following its publication, John Maynard Keynes's *The General Theory of Employment, Interest and Money* (1936) has had more influence upon the thinking of professional economists and public policy makers than any other book in the whole history of economic thought in a comparable number of years."[111]

Indeed, by the mid-1940s, especially in England and the United States, Keynes's *General Theory* had practically become a "new testament" for the economics profession. Soon after the Second World War, textbooks began incorporating its teachings to instruct the young, and nontechnical, readable expositions of Keynes's ideas were published to indoctrinate the general public with the "wisdom" of its policy proposals.

One of the most clearly written of these expositions was *The Keynesian Revolution* by Lawrence R. Klein (who was awarded the Nobel Prize in Economics in 1980).[112] Published in 1947, it represented the growing consensus of the time among economists and government policy advocates. The final chapter outlined what should be expected from government if the Keynesian "insights" were to be fully applied for the "social good."

In the brave new world guided by the ideas of Keynes, Americans would have to accept a greater degree of government regimentation than they had in the past. Should they be afraid of this? No, Dr. Klein assured his readers: "The regimentation of unemployment and poverty is infinitely more severe than the regimentation of economic planning." He was sure that the American people would "quickly come forth with support" for the regimentation of economic planning.[113]

The government "economic planners" would have to have "complete control over government fiscal policy so that they can spend when and where spending is needed to stimulate employment and tax when and where taxation is needed to halt upward price movements." The slow, cumbersome congressional budgetary process would have to be put aside. In its place:

> We must have a planning agency always ready with a backlog of socially useful public works to fill any deflationary gap that may arise [through discretionary government deficit spending powers]; similarly, we must have a price-control board always ready with directives and enforcement officers to wipe out any inflationary gap that may arise. . . . Government spending should be very flexible and subject to immediate release or curtailment, in just the precise amount which will maintain full employment, no more and no less. . . . This is the road to the kind of full employment that we need.[114]

At the same time, government would have to see to it that the members of society were kept from saving too much and spending too little, since excessive savings would diminish the "aggregate demand" upon which "full employment" was dependent. This would require, Dr. Klein argued, an active and conscious policy of redistribution of income:

> If we redistribute income from the rich, who have a relatively high marginal propensity to save, to the poor [whose marginal propensity to save is generally lower], we will decrease the community's marginal propensity to save. Such policies of income redistribution can be carried out by taxing the rich and paying a dole or other types of contributions to the poor.[115]

Also, the motives for people privately desiring to save would have to be undermined by the government taking greater responsibility for such things as retirement planning. Dr. Klein argued:

> Most children are raised on the virtues of thrift, and high spenders are usually considered to be unworthy citizens. It is difficult to change these fundamental habits. . . . The people acting on individualistic principles do not know their own best interests. They must be taught to look at the system as a whole [in which consumption rather than savings is the "socially" desirable conduct]. . . . We must resort to indirect methods such as social-security programs which wipe out the need for savings.[116]

Here was Keynes's ideal formulated for a new American future. The constitutional procedure for legislative approval for taxation and expenditures would be thrown away; economic planners would have discretionary control over taxing and spending. Taxation would be a redistributive tool for macroeconomic policy manipulation. And since individuals "do not know their own best interests," the Keynesian planners would have to teach people to give up their old bad habits of self-reliance and savings, with the state becoming the paternalistic provider.

Keynes had understood the implications of his own ideas, after all: "customary morals, conventions and traditional wisdoms" would have to be set aside—including the American tradition of constitutional government and individual financial self-responsibility. The Keynesian planners claimed, as Keynes had expressed in his memoir, "the right to judge every individual case on its own merits, and the wisdom, experience and self-control to do so successfully," in their role as macroeconomic managers. And Keynes had clearly appreciated that, as he had told the German economists of the 1930s, his "theory of aggregate production . . . nevertheless can be much easier adapted to the conditions of a totalitarian state." Thus did the Keynesian revolutionaries demand vast economic control over the private affairs and market activities of the population.

Ludwig von Mises and the Economics of the Long Run

This was the state of Keynesian economics when Ludwig von Mises' *Human Action* was published over fifty years ago. Mises devoted little space to directly challenging or refuting Keynes and his ideas. He did not consider Keynes to be the father of a "new economics." Instead, he viewed Keynes as the most successful modern defender of the interventionist and inflationist ideas of the time:

> Keynes was not an innovator and champion of new methods of managing economic affairs. His contribution consisted rather in providing an apparent justification for the policies which were popular with those in power in spite of the fact that all economists viewed them as disastrous. His achievement was a rationalization of the policies already practiced. He was not a "revolutionary," as some of his adepts called him. The "Keynesian revolution" took place long before Keynes approved of it and fabricated a pseudo-scientific justification for it. What he really did was to write an apology for the prevailing policies of governments. This explains the quick success of his book. It was greeted enthusiastically by the governments and the ruling political parties. Especially enraptured were a new type of intellectual, the "government economists." They had had a bad conscience. They were aware of the fact that they were carrying out policies which all economists condemned as contrary to purpose and disastrous.

> Now they felt relieved. The "new economics" reestablished their moral equilibrium.[117]

And as for Keynes's wit and literary style, Mises considered them to be "cheap rhetorical tricks" used to confuse, ignore, or distort the ideas of the classical economists and those of contemporary economists who opposed Keynes's policy proposals.[118]

He considered Keynes's emphasis on workers' "money illusion" to be nothing more than a rationale for not resisting the power of the unions to set money wages too high to assure full employment. In 1931, in his monograph "The Causes of the Economic Crisis" and his article "The Crisis and Capitalism," Mises argued that massive unemployment was the direct consequence of wage rates being set by trade unions at a height above the market value of the workers' labor, given the available capital supply and the resulting marginal productivity of the workers desiring employment. Government funding of the unemployed in the form of the dole reduced union violence and prevented those desiring work from underbidding union wages levels, which reduced the pressure on the trade unions to modify their money wage demands. As a consequence, unemployment became a widespread and long-term phenomenon.[119]

And in 1933 Mises had already criticized Keynes's idea that workers would be less resistant to a cut in their real wage if it occurred through a rise in the general price level while their money wages remained constant than if their real wage was lowered through a fall in their money wage. Said Mises:

> [I]t is no longer denied, as it generally was a few years ago, that the duration of the present crisis is caused primarily by the fact that wage rates and certain prices have become inflexible, as a result of union wage policy and various price support activities. Thus, the rigid wage rates and prices do not fully participate in the downward movement of most prices, or do so only after a protracted delay. . . . [I]t is also admitted that the continuing mass unemployment is a necessary consequence of the attempts to maintain wage rates above those that would prevail on the unhampered market.

> . . . Almost all who propose priming the pump through credit expansion consider it self-evident that money wages will not follow the upward movement of prices until their relative excess has disappeared. Inflationary projects of all kinds are agreed to because no one openly dares to attack the union wage policy, which is approved by public opinion and promoted by government. Therefore, so long as today's prevailing view, concerning the maintenance of higher than unhampered market wage rates and the interventionist measures supporting them, exists, there is no reason to assume that money wage rates can be held steady in a period of rising prices.[120]

Mises' point was that with unions knowing that none of their money wage demands would be opposed, any attempt to reduce the real value of those money wages through an inflationary rise in the price level would be met by new and higher money wage demands to make up for any lost ground in real income. Or as Mises expressed it in *Human Action*, "However, the success of such a cunning plan would require an unlikely degree of ignorance and stupidity on the part of the wage earners. As long as workers believe that minimum wage rates benefit them, they will not let themselves be cheated by such clever tricks."[121]

The only way the real wages and the standard of living of the general workforce could be raised in the long run was through capital formation, that is, through the processes of savings and investment to increase the marginal productivity of those employed in the production processes of the market.[122] This required secure property rights, low taxes, and a sound noninflationary political–economic environment, not one dominated and manipulated by an "activist" government.

A recurring theme in most of Mises' writings was the idea that there does not exist any inherent conflict between the interests of the individual and that of society, and that the market process is an arena of mutually beneficial cooperation through participation in the social system of division of labor. Guided by the principle of comparative advantage—what Mises termed the universal social Law of Association—each man finds his most profitable niche in the collaborative activities of production and exchange. Through participation in the division of labor, each man increases the quantities, qualities, and varieties of goods that are at his disposal in comparison to isolated, self-sufficient production.[123]

The social system of division of labor requires a number of institutions. Private property is paramount, along with money prices generated through the competitive processes of buying and selling both finished goods and the factors of production. Market prices enable the intellectual exercise of economic calculation, through which the relative value and cost of all market-traded goods and services can be established so as to assure their rational and efficient use.

The competitive interaction of market supplies and demands, the structure of relative prices for goods and resources, the presence of entrepreneurial creativity and alertness induced through the potential for market-based profits, and a relative flexibility in the mobility and adaptability of the factors of production to changing circumstances are what assure the effective functioning of the social order.

Without them the social system of competitive cooperation is weakened and, in the extreme, threatened with collapse. Preserving the functioning of market order, therefore, was the guiding principle for any social philosophy. This necessarily meant that the economist's and the social philosopher's task, in Mises' view, was never to lose sight of "the long run" interest of maintaining this system of human association.[124] "All that good government can do," Mises said, "to improve the material well-being of the masses is to establish and to preserve an institutional setting in which there are no obstacles to the progressive accumulation of new capital and its utilization for the improvement of technical methods of production. . . . Hence, the [classical] liberals conclude that the economic policy best fitted to serve the interests of all strata of a nation is free trade both in domestic business and international relations."[125]

This was the real basis for Ludwig von Mises' conflict with John Maynard Keynes. For Keynes, "in the long run we are all dead." The danger in the alternative "short-run" orientation of social and economic policy was that it was likely to undermine those institutions without which a free and prosperous society could not endure. Mises reasoned:

> In the short run an individual or group may profit from violating the interests of other groups or individuals. But in the long run, in indulging in such actions, they damage their own selfish interest no less than that of the people they have injured. The sacrifice that a man or a group makes in renouncing some short-run gains, lest they endanger the peaceful operation of the apparatus of social co-operation, is merely temporary. It amounts to an abandonment of a small immediate profit for the sake of incomparably greater advantages in the long run.[126]

That is why Mises so forcefully opposed Keynes and his New Economics. Keynesianism was an economics of the short run that meant the end of the market economy by validating inflexible wages and prices, undermining the incentives for private saving and capital formation, threatening inflation-induced malinvestment, and weakening the institution of private property and market-guided decisionmaking. Thus, in Mises' view, Keynesian policy was the implementation of an economic irrationality, because "unfortunately nearly all of us outlive the short run" and thus must bear the longer-run consequences.[127]

Unfortunately, many Keynesian presuppositions continue to dominate economic theory and policy. But if there ever was a voice that continues to warn of the temptations and dangers of an economics of the short run, it is Ludwig von Mises in his masterwork *Human Action.*

Notes

[1]Henry Hazlitt, "The Case for Capitalism," *Newsweek* (September 19, 1949).

[2]Henry Hazlitt, "Wrong Diagnosis, Wrong Remedy," *Newsweek* (August 15, 1949).

[3]Allan Meltzer, "Time to Print Money," *Financial Times* (July 17, 1998), where he argued, "Monetary expansion and devaluation is a much better solution" to Japan's economic difficulties; and Milton Friedman, "Bubble Trouble," *National Review* (September 28, 1998):16. "We know how to stop deflation—print money. The Fed [Federal Reserve System] has plenty of ability to print money."

[4]James Buchanan and Richard E. Wagner, *The Consequences of Mr. Keynes* (London: Institute of Economic Affairs, 1978), p. 14.

[5]Leland B. Yeager, "The Keynesian Heritage in Economics," in John Burton, ed., *Keynes's General Theory: Fifty Years On: Its Relevance and Irrelevance to Modern Times* (London: Institute of Economics Affairs, 1986), p. 27.

[6]F. A. Hayek, review of Roy Harrod's *Life of J. M. Keynes* [1952], reprinted in Bruce Caldwell, ed., *The Collected Works of F. A. Hayek, Vol. 9: Contra Keynes and Cambridge* (Chicago: University of Chicago Press, 1995), p. 232.

[7]Robert Skidelsky, *John Maynard Keynes: Hopes Betrayed, 1883–1920* (New York: MacMillan, 1983); and *John Maynard Keynes: The Economist as Savior, 1920–1937* (New York: MacMillan, 1992).

[8]Robert Skidelsky, "The Real Problem with Capitalism Is the Markets," *The Independent* (October 24, 1998).

[9]The figures on the money supply, required reserves, and bank loans are primarily derived from the monumental studies by Milton Friedman and Anna Schwartz, *A Monetary History of the United States, 1867–1960* (Princeton, NJ: Princeton University Press, 1963) and *Monetary Statistics of the United States: Estimates, Sources, Methods* (New York: Columbia University Press, 1970).

[10]C. A. Phillips, T. F. McManus and R. W. Nelson, *Banking and the Business Cycle: A Study of the Great Depression in the United States* [1937] (New York: Arena Press, 1972), pp. 22–23.

[11]Benjamin M. Anderson, *Economics and the Public Welfare* (Princeton, NJ: D. Van Nostrand, 1949), p. 77: "The rally in business production and employment that started in August of 1921 was soundly based on a drastic cleaning up of credit weakness, a drastic reduction in the costs of production, and the free play of private enterprise. It was not based on Government policy designed to make business good. . . . The depression [of 1920–1921] was, however, much less severe than that of the 1930s. This was primarily because of the very rapidity of the break in prices and the general readjustment of costs."

[12]Again, these figures are drawn from Friedman and Schwartz, *Monetary Statistics of the United States.*

[13]Irving Fisher, *The Purchasing Power of Money* [1911] (New York: MacMillan, revised ed., 1920); *Elementary Principles of Economics* (New York: MacMillan, 1912); *Stabilizing the Dollar* (New York: MacMillan, 1920); and *The Money Illusion* (New York: The Adelphi Co., 1928).

[14]Fisher, *Stabilizing the Dollar,* pp. 82 & 95–96.

[15]Fisher, *The Money Illusion,* pp. 132–33.

[16]Even on the eve of the great stock market crash that occurred during the last two weeks of October 1929, Irving Fisher declared on September 5, 1929, "There may be a recession in stock prices, but not anything in the nature of a crash." And on October 16, 1929, Fisher insisted: "Stock prices have reached what looks like a permanently high plateau. I do not feel that there will soon, if ever, be a fifty or sixty point break below present

levels. . . . I expect to see the stock market a good deal higher than it is today within a few months."

[17]Quoted in Murray N. Rothbard, *America's Great Depression* [1963] (Los Angeles: Nash Publishing, 1972), pp. 155–56.

[18]John Maynard Keynes, *A Treatise on Money, Vol. II: The Applied Theory of Money* (New York: Harcourt, Brace, 1930), p. 258.

[19]Friedman and Schwartz, *A Monetary History of the United States,* pp. 273–74.

[20]Rothbard, *America's Great Depression,* pp. 83–89.

[21]Phillips, McManus, and Nelson, *Banking and the Business Cycle,* p. 81.

[22]Carl Menger, *Principles of Economics* [1871] (Glencoe, IL: The Free Press, 1950), pp. 259–85; "On the Origin of Money," [1892] reprinted in Richard M. Ebeling, ed., *Austrian Economics: A Reader* (Hillsdale, MI: Hillsdale College Press, 1991), pp. 483–504.

[23]Ludwig von Mises, *The Theory of Money and Credit* [1912, 2nd revised ed., 1924] (Indianapolis, IN: Liberty Classics, 1981), pp. 117–246; see also Murray N. Rothbard, *Man, Economy and State: A Treatise on Economic Principles,* Vol. I [1962] (Los Angeles: Nash Publishing, 1970), pp. 201–15.

[24]Mises, *The Theory of Money and Credit,* pp. 215–23; "Monetary Stabilization and Cyclical Policy," [1928] in Israel M. Kirzner, ed., *Classics in Austrian Economics, Vol. III: The Age of Mises and Hayek* (London: William Pickering, 1994), pp. 48–52; and *Human Action: A Treatise on Economics* (Irvington-on-Hudson, NY: Foundation for Economic Education, 4th revised ed., 1996), pp. 219–23.

[25]John E. Cairnes, *Essays in Political Economy: Theoretical and Applied* [1873] (New York: Augustus M. Kelley, 1965), pp. 1–108.

[26]Mises, *The Theory of Money and Credit,* pp. 160–68 & 237–43; "Monetary Stabilization and Cyclical Policy," pp. 52–58; *Human Action,* pp. 416–22; and "The Non-Neutrality of Money," [1940] in Richard M. Ebeling ed., *Austrian Economics: A Reader,* pp. 505–17.

[27]Friedman and Schwartz, *A Monetary History of the United States,* p. 93.

[28]Milton Friedman, "Inflation: Causes and Consequences" [1963] in *Dollar and Deficits* (Englewood Cliffs, NJ: Prentice-Hall, 1968), p. 26.

[29]Gottfried Haberler, *The Different Meanings Attached to the Term "Fluctuations in the Purchasing Power of Gold" and the Best Instrument or Instruments for Measuring Such Fluctuations* (Geneva: League of Nations, F/Gold/74, 1931); Moritz J. Bonn and Alfred Tismer, *The Effect of Fluctuations in the Purchasing Power of Gold on the Economic Life of the Nations* (Geneva: League of Nations, F/Gold/80, 1931); Alexander Loveday, *The Instrument for the Measurement of the Purchasing Power of Gold* (Geneva: League of Nations, F/Gold/22, 1930); Fritz Machlup, "Inflation and Decreasing Costs of Production" in H. Parker Willis and John M. Chapman, eds., *The Economics of Inflation: The Basis of Contemporary American Monetary Policy* (New York: Columbia University Press, 1935), pp. 280–87; Allan G. B. Fisher, "The Significance

of Stable Prices in a Progressive Economy," *Economic Record* (March 1935): 49–64, and "Does an Increase in Volume of Production Call for a Corresponding Increase in Volume of Money?" *American Economic Review* (June 1935): 197–211; and George Selgin, "The 'Productivity Norm' Versus Zero Inflation in the History of Economic Thought," [1995] in *Bank Deregulation and Monetary Order* (London/New York: Routledge, 1996), pp. 163–89 and *Less Than Zero: The Case for a Falling Price Level in a Growing Economy* (London: Institute of Economic Affairs, 1997).

[30]Friedrich A. Hayek, "Intertemporal Price Equilibrium and Movements in the Value of Money," [1928] in Israel M. Kirzner, *Classics in Austrian Economics*, Vol. III, pp. 161–98; *Monetary Theory and the Trade Cycle* [1929] (New York: Augustus M. Kelley, [1933] 1966); *Prices and Production* [1932; revised ed., 1935] (New York: Augustus M. Kelley, 1967).

[31]Eugen von Böhm-Bawerk, *Capital and Interest* (South Holland, IL: Libertarian Press, 1959).

[32]Frank A. Fetter, *The Principles of Economics* (New York: The Century Co., 1910); *Economic Principles* (New York: The Century Co., 1915).

[33]Richard von Strigl, *Capital and Production* [1934] (Auburn, AL: Ludwig von Mises Institute, 1995).

[34]Friedrich A. Hayek, *The Pure Theory of Capital* (New York: MacMillan, 1941); and "The Mythology of Capital," [1936] reprinted in Stephen Littlechild, ed., *Austrian Economics*, Vol. II (Brookfield, VT: Edward Elgar, 1990), pp. 63–92; also, Fritz Machlup, "Professor Knight and the 'Period of Production,'" [1935] reprinted in Israel M. Kirzner, ed., *Classics in Austrian Economics, Vol. II: The Interwar Period* (London: William Pickering, 1994), pp. 275–315.

[35]Ludwig von Mises, *Nationalökonomie: Theorie des Handelns und Wirtschaftens* [1940] (Munich: Philosophia Verlag, 1980).

[36]L. G. Bostedo, "The Function of Savings," [1900] reprinted in Richard M. Ebeling, ed., *Austrian Economics: A Reader*, pp. 393–400.

[37]Eugen von Böhm-Bawerk, "The Function of Savings," [1901] reprinted in Richard M. Ebeling, ed., *Austrian Economics: A Reader*, pp. 401–13.

[38]Ibid., pp. 406–7.

[39]Knut Wicksell, *Interest and Prices: A Study of the Causes Regulating the Value of Money* [1898] (New York: Augustus M. Kelley, 1965).

[40]Mises, *The Theory of Money and Credit*, pp. 377–404; "Monetary Stabilization and Cyclical Policy," pp. 69–87; *Human Action*, pp. 538–86.

[41]Fritz Machlup, *The Stock Market, Credit and Capital Formation* [1931] (London: William Hodge & Co., revised ed., 1940), p. 224.

[42]Lionel Robbins, "Foreword" in F. A. Hayek, *Prices and Production* (New York: MacMillan, 1932).

[43]On the economic policies between the two World Wars, see my "Introduction" to Richard M. Ebeling, ed., *Selected Writings of Ludwig von Mises, Vol.*

III: The Political Economy of International Reform and Reconstruction (Indianapolis, IN: Liberty Fund, 2000), pp. xvii–xxii.

[44]Hayek, *Monetary Theory and the Trade Cycle*, pp. 113–14.

[45]Fritz Machlup, "The Rate of Interest as Cost Factor and as Capitalization Factor," *American Economic Review* (September 1935): 459–65.

[46]F. A. Hayek, "The Fate of the Gold Standard," [1932] in *Money, Capital and Fluctuations: Early Essays* (Chicago: University of Chicago Press, 1984), p. 129.

[47]Gottfried Haberler, "A New Index Number and Its Meaning," [1928] reprinted in Anthony Y. C. Koo, ed., *The Liberal Economic Order, Vol. II: Money, Cycles and Related Themes* (Brookfield, VT: Edward Elgar, 1993), pp. 107–8 & 113–14; the same criticism was made by Benjamin M. Anderson, "Commodity Price Stabilization a False Goal of Central Bank Policy," *The Chase Economic Bulletin* (May 8, 1929): 20. "The general price level is, after all, merely a statistician's tool of thought. Businessmen and bankers often look at index numbers as indicating price trends, but no businessman makes use of index numbers in his bookkeeping. His bookkeeping runs in terms of the particular prices and costs that his business is concerned with. . . . Satisfactory business conditions are dependent upon proper relations among groups of prices, not upon any average of prices."

[54]Christian Saint-Etienne, *The Great Depression, 1929–1938* (Stanford, CA: Hoover Institution Press, 1984), p. 3–33.

[49]Moritz J. Bonn, *The World Crisis and the Teaching of the Manchester School* (London: Cobden-Sanderson, 1931), pp. 13–14 & 26–27.

[50]Ludwig von Mises, "The Myth of the Failure of Capitalism," [1932] reprinted in Richard M. Ebeling, ed., *The Clash of Group Interests and Other Essays by Ludwig von Mises* (New York: Center for Libertarian Studies, 1978), p. 18.

[51]Richard Vedder and Lowell Gallaway, *Out of Work: Unemployment and Government in Twentieth Century America* (New York/London: Holmes & Meier, 1993), pp. 79–97.

[52]Rothbard, *America's Great Depression*, p. 209.

[53]Anderson, *Economics and the Public Welfare*, pp. 224–25.

[54]Saint-Etienne, *The Great Depression*, p. 29.

[55]Ludwig von Mises, "The Causes of the Economic Crisis: An Address," [1931] reprinted in Percy L. Greaves, ed., *Von Mises, On the Manipulation of Money and Credit* (Dobbs Ferry, NY: Free Market Books, 1978), pp. 173–203.

[56]Ibid., pp. 201–2.

[57]Edwin Cannan, "Not Enough Work for All," [1932] in the *Collected Works of Edwin Cannan, Vol. VII: Economic Scares* (London: Routledge/Thoemmes Press, 1997), p. 38.

[58]Mises, "The Current Status of Business Cycle Research and Its Prospects for the Immediate Future," [1933] reprinted in Percy L. Greaves, ed., *Von Mises, On the Manipulation of Money and Credit*, p. 211.

[59]Lionel Robbins, "The Ottawa Resolutions on Finance and the Future of Monetary Policy," *Lloyds Bank Limited Monthly Review* (October 1932): 432.
[60]Hayek, *Monetary Theory and the Trade Cycle*, pp. 21–22.
[61]Robbins, "The Ottawa Resolutions. . . ." pp. 435 & 437.
[62]John Maynard Keynes, "Am I a Liberal?" [1925] in *Essays in Persuasion* [1932] (New York: W. W. Norton, 1963), pp. 323–38.
[63]Keynes, "The End of Laissez-Faire," [1926] in *Essays in Persuasion*, pp. 312–22.
[64]Keynes, "A Short View of Russia," [1925] in *Essays in Persuasion*, pp. 297–311.
[65]John Maynard Keynes, *The Economic Consequences of the Peace* [1919] (New York: Harper & Row, 1971).
[66]John Maynard Keynes, *A Tract on Monetary Reform* (New York: Harcourt, Brace, 1924).
[67]Ibid., p. 177.
[68]Ibid., p. 187.
[69]F. A. Hayek, "Reflections on the Pure Theory of Money of Mr. J. M. Keynes," [1931–1932] in Bruce Caldwell, ed., *The Collected Works of F. A. Hayek, Vol. IX: Contra Keynes and Cambridge, Essays and Correspondence* (Chicago: University of Chicago Press, 1995), pp. 121–46 & 174–97.
[70]Ibid., p. 128.
[71]Hayek, "A Rejoinder to Mr. Keynes," ibid., p. 162.
[72]Donald Moggridge, ed., *The Collected Writings of John Maynard Keynes, Vol. XXI: Activities 1931-1939, World Crises and Policies in Britain and America* (New York: Cambridge University Press, 1982), pp. 289–339.
[73]Ibid., pp. 291–97.
[74]Paul A. Samuelson, "The General Theory," in Seymour E. Harris, ed., *The New Economics: Keynes' Influence on Theory and Public Policy* (New York: Alfred A. Knopf, 1947), pp. 146–47.
[75]Piero Sraffa, ed., *The Works and Correspondence of David Ricardo, Vol. I: On the Principles of Political Economy and Taxation* [1821] (New York: Cambridge University Press, 1951), p. 290.
[76]John Maynard Keynes, *The General Theory of Employment, Interest and Money* [1936] (New York: MacMillan, 1973), pp. 89–112.
[77]Ibid., p.105.
[78]Ibid., p. 161.
[79]John Maynard Keynes, "National Self-Sufficiency," *Yale Review* (June 1933): 758.
[80]Keynes, *The General Theory*, pp. 333–51.
[81]Keynes, "National Self-Sufficiency," pp. 761–62.
[82]Quoted in Roy F. Harrod, *The Life of John Maynard Keynes* (London: MacMillan, 1951), pp. 436–37.
[83]Ibid., pp. 192–93.

[84]Arthur Smithies, "Reflections on the Work and Influence of John Maynard Keynes," *Quarterly Journal of Economics* (November 1951): 493–94.
[85]Keynes, *The General Theory*, p. 129.
[86]Ibid., p. 164.
[87]Ibid., pp. 376–79.
[88]Ibid., p. 264.
[89]John Maynard Keynes, "Professor Tinbergen Method," *Economic Journal* (September1939): 558–68.
[90]Keynes, *The General Theory*, pp. 337–38.
[91]Ibid., p. xxiii.
[92]Jean Baptiste Say, "On the Demand or Market for Products," reprinted in Henry Hazlitt, ed., *The Critics of Keynesian Economics* (Princeton, NJ: D. Van Nostrand, 1960), pp. 12–22.
[93]John Stuart Mill, "Of the Influence of Consumption on Production," [1844] reprinted in Henry Hazlitt, ed., *The Critics of Keynesian Economics*, pp. 24–45.
[94]Ludwig von Mises, "Stones into Bread, the Keynesian Miracle," [1948] and "Lord Keynes and Say's Law," [1950] in *Planning for Freedom* (Grove City, PA: Libertarian Press, 4th ed., 1980), pp. 48–68; W. H. Hutt, *A Rehabilitation of Say's Law* (Athens, OH: Ohio University Press, 1974); and Steven Kates, *Say's Law and the Keynesian Revolution: How Macroeconomic Theory Lost Its Way* (Northhampton, MA: Edward Elgar, 1998).
[95]Keynes, *The General Theory*, p. xxxi.
[96]Ibid., pp.165–74 & 194–209.
[97]Ibid., pp. 147–64.
[98]L. Albert Hahn, "Is Saving a Virtue or a Sin?" in *The Economics of Illusion: A Critical Analysis of Contemporary Economic Theory and Policy* (New York: Squire Publishing, 1949), pp. 93–95.
[99]Mises, *Human Action*, pp. 257–326.
[100]Carl Landauer, "A Break in Keynes' Theory of Interest," *American Economic Review* (June 1937): 260ff.
[101]Dennis Robertson, "Mr. Keynes and the Rate of Interest," [1940] reprinted in William Fellner and Bernard F. Haley, eds., *Readings in the Theory of Income Distribution* (London: George Allen and Unwin, 1950) p. 440, suggested that Keynes seemed to have "a curious inhibition against visualizing more than two margins at once."
[102]Keynes, "Foreword to the German Edition," translated in James J. Martin, *Revisionist Viewpoints* (Colorado Springs CO: Ralph Myles Publisher, 1971), pp. 203–5; the translation of this foreword in the edition of *The General Theory*, pp. xxvi–xxvii, issued by the Royal Economic Society, is incomplete and inexact if compared to the original German, which is included in Martin's book.

[103]It is, however, the case that in May 1936 Keynes delivered a talk for BBC radio's "Books and Authors" series in which he reviewed Sidney and Beatrice Webb's pro-Stalinist book, *Soviet Civilization*, and praised the Soviet experiment. See, Donald Moggridge, ed., *The Collected Writings of John Maynard Keynes, Vol. XXVIII: Social, Political and Literary Writings* (New York: Cambridge University Press, 1982), pp. 333–34: "Until recently events in Russia were moving too fast and the gap between professions and actual achievements was too wide for a proper account to be possible. But the new system is now sufficiently crystallized to be reviewed. The result is impressive. The Russian innovators have passed, not only from the revolutionary stage, but also from the doctrinaire stage. There is little or nothing left which bears any special relation to Marx and Marxism as distinguished from other systems of socialism. They are engaged in the vast administrative task of making a completely new set of social and economic institutions work smoothly and successfully over a territory so extensive that it covers one sixth of the land surface of the world. The largest scale empiricism and experimentalism which has ever been attempted by disinterested administrators is in operation. Meanwhile the Webbs have enabled us to see the direction in which things appear to be moving and how far they have got. . . . It leaves me with a strong desire and hope that we in this country may discover how to combine an unlimited readiness to experiment with changes in political and economic methods and institutions, whilst preserving traditionalism and a sort of careful conservatism, thrifty of everything which has human experience behind it, in every branch of feeling and of action."

[104]John Maynard Keynes, *Two Memoirs: Dr. Melchior, A Defeated Enemy and My Early Beliefs* (London: Rupert Hart-Davis, 1949), pp. 82–83.

[105]Ibid., pp. 97–98.

[106]Ibid., pp. 98–99.

[107]Quoted in Donald E. Moggridge, *Maynard Keynes: An Economist's Biography* (London/New York: Routledge, 1992), p. 125.

[108]Adam Smith, *An Inquiry into the Nature and Causes of the Wealth of Nations* [1776] (New York: The Modern Library, 1937), p. 651.

[109]Frederic Bastiat, "What is Seen and What is Not Seen," [1850] in *Selected Essays on Political Economy* (Princeton, NJ: D. Van Nostrand Co., 1964), pp. 1–50.

[110]Hayek, *The Pure Theory of Capital*, pp. 409–10.

[111]Dudley Dillard, *The Economics of John Maynard Keynes: The Theory of a Monetary Economy* (Englewood Cliffs, NJ: Prentice-Hall, 1948), p. 1.

[112]Lawrence R. Klein, *The Keynesian Revolution* (New York: Macmillan, 1947).

[113]Ibid., p.179.

[114]Ibid., p. 180.

[115]Ibid., p. 177.

[116]Ibid., pp. 178–79.

[117]Mises, "Lord Keynes and Say's Law," p. 66; also, *Human Action*, p. 793.

[118]Mises, "Stones Into Bread, the Keynesian Miracle," pp. 53–55.

[119]Mises, "The Causes of the Economic Crisis," pp. 186–89; and "The Crisis and Capitalism," *Neue Freie Presse* No. 24099 (October 17, 1931).

[120]Mises, "The Current Status of Business Cycle Research. . . ," p. 211.

[121]Mises, *Human Action*, p. 777; also, "Wages, Unemployment, and Inflation," [1958] in *Planning for Freedom*, p. 149: "Inflation can cure unemployment only by curtailing the wage earner's real wages. But then the unions ask for a new increase in wages in order to keep pace with the rising cost of living and we are back where we were before, i.e., in a situation in which large scale unemployment can only be prevented by a further expansion of credit."

[122]Mises, "Capital Supply and American Prosperity," [1952] and "Wages, Unemployment and Inflation," [1958] in *Planning for Freedom*, pp. 188–205 & 146–47; "The Economic Role of Savings and Capital Goods," [1963] in Bettina Bien Greaves, ed., *Economic Freedom and Interventionism: An Anthology of Articles and Essays by Ludwig von Mises* (Irvington-on-Hudson, NY: Foundation for Economic Education, 1990), pp. 26–30.

[123]See Richard M. Ebeling, "A Rational Economist in an Irrational Age: Ludwig von Mises," in Richard M. Ebeling, ed., *The Age of Economists: From Adam Smith to Milton Friedman, Champions of Freedom*, Vol. 26 (Hillsdale, MI: Hillsdale College Press, 1999), pp. 69–120.

[124]Mises, *Human Action*, pp. 673–88; "Economics as a Bridge for Interhuman Understanding," [1945] in *Economic Freedom and Interventionism*, pp. 223–35; and "The Clash of Group Interests," [1945] in Richard M. Ebeling, ed., *Money, Method and the Market Process: Essays by Ludwig von Mises* (Norwell, MA: Kluwer Academic Press, 1990), pp. 202–14.

[125]Mises, "Planning for Freedom" [1945] in *Planning for Freedom*, pp. 5–6.

[126]Mises, "The Clash of Group Interests," pp. 209–10.

[127]Ludwig von Mises, *Omnipotent Government: The Rise of the Total State and Total War* (New Haven, CT: Yale University Press, 1944), p. 252.

Gene Epstein

Austrian Economics and the Popular Press

Ludwig von Mises, in my opinion, has made more long-lasting contributions to economic thought than any other economist of the twentieth century.

I personally owe a great deal to Austrian economics. After I had finished my M.A., I was working toward a Ph.D. in economics, as well as teaching economics in college, when suddenly the subject seemed empty to me. There just wasn't much intellectual meat in all those graphs and in all that math. Throughout my education I obviously had not had the good fortune to be exposed to Austrian economics. So I decided to quit and went to work on Wall Street as a commodities analyst.

I'm a browser—I will look at whatever books are in the stacks—and one day I came across Murray Rothbard's *Man, Economy and State.* It was a revelation to me. Those critical chapters about mainstream economics really hit home, and for the next few years I was a denizen of the Laissez Faire Book Shop, then on Mercer Street in Manhattan. I began to hang around Israel Kirzner's seminars. On occasion, I would hop a subway to the Polytechnic Institute where Murray Rothbard taught, and eventually I found my way back to economics. When I took a job as a senior economist at the New York Stock Exchange, my boss told me, "You know, you're the only guy I've ever met who reads economics for fun."

I heard a story, a joke, from the Chilean minister of finance that illustrates the impact of various interpretations of the news. Angry at the way crony capitalism had made a mess of things in

Asia, God decides to end the world in three days. He invites Clinton, Yeltsin, and Kim Dae Jung of Korea to his office in the sky and tells them of his plans. Clinton returns to the Oval Office, calls in Vice President Gore, and says, "I've got some good news and some bad news. The good news is that God exists. The bad news is that He is going to end the world in three days. Let's party!" Yeltsin appears before the Duma, the Russian Parliament, and tells them, "I have some bad news and some bad news. The first bad news is that contrary to what we believed, God does exist. The other bad news is that the tyrant will end the world in three days." Kim Dae Jung appears on national TV in Korea and says, "People of Korea! I have good news and I have good news. The first good news is that God called me up to the sky along with Clinton and Yeltsin to share His thoughts with us. The other good news is that in three days the Asian crisis will be over!"

Market, Process, and Productivity

> What one witnesses in a market economy at any point in time is nothing but an attempt by market participants to take advantage of newly discovered or created possibilities. In the course of seeking to implement these plans, market participants notice, again, further market possibilities that had hitherto escaped attention. . . . This process is kept continuously boiling by the incessant injection of unexpected changes and surprises. The process of creative discovery is never completed, nor is it ever arrested.[1]

Israel Kirzner, in his various books on entrepreneurship and the market process, tries to explain how the standard microtheory of economics really does not describe the basis of reality. The basis of market reality is process and change—what Joseph Shumpeter, the neo-Austrian, the quasi-Austrian, has called creative destruction.

But the way market reality is reported by the media is often unreal. When these misperceptions are taken as truth, as they frequently are, we end up in a tangled web. To explain this point, I offer the following examples.

The *New York Times* ran a story called "America's Treadmill Economy." It began with this sentence: "While productivity may be a national goal, conflicting pressures are getting in the way, pushing companies to add thousands of hours of labor as they fight to hang onto increasingly demanding and flighty customers."[2] That sounds like bad news to me. We have met the enemy, and it is the American consumer. This desperation to hang onto "increasingly demanding and flighty customers" is bad for productivity. A sidebar to this story carried a formula that defines productivity. (Apparently the writer had studied too much mainstream economics.) The formula was: Productivity equals output per worker hour. In order words, it is ratio, a fraction. The total output of the economy is the numerator; the total worker hours of the economy are the denominator.

Now in defense of this little formula, I would say that up to a point it does make sense. Bear in mind that those who defend it are quite sophisticated. They would, of course, agree that the division of labor, increased capital accumulation, better technology, and education increase output per worker hour. And this makes it possible for the numerator of that fraction—the total output of the economy—to go up faster than the denominator—the worker hours. In certain industries, introducing labor-saving devices will move labor out of the industry, so that worker hours decline as output goes up.

So if the formula does make some sense, what does it mean? It means that if you hold total output even, but you increase the number of hours worked to hold onto your "flighty customers," this leads to lower productivity.

In the first sentence, the writer is talking about a new era thesis, which is that productivity is actually soaring. (That this has been mismeasured is another issue.) "Critics of the new era thesis note that a corporation can raise profitability, at least for a while, without improving productivity. It can invest more in marketing and innovation, for example, to make a product or service seem different, and better, than a competitor's. The issue, they say, isn't that the growing service sector is less efficient than manufacturing or harder to measure. . . . Rather the critics say, the drag on productivity comes from the great quantities of labor that are expended, in both manufacturing and the service sector, to hold on to customers or to lure them away from other companies."[3] Profitability and productivity are somehow no longer in sync. The key sentence reads, "Rather the critics say, the drag on productivity comes from the great quantities of labor that are expended in both manufacturing and the service sector to hold onto customers or to lure them away from other companies." You are employing more labor in your particular industry in order to develop a new product, in order to change the nature of your product, and when you do that, the writer argues, productivity goes down. This is because, according to the formula, your output is staying the same but—in order to hold your customers—you are increasing the number of worker hours in order to develop or market a new product.

The *Times* article provided three examples. The first example was Gillette, a company near and dear to my heart. What does Gillette do that is bad for productivity? Well, Gillette spends tens of millions of dollars in the redesign and testing of innovations, such as the Mach III razor. This may seem like a good thing to do, but according to the formula, it is not. The new or retooled machinery and the advertising and promotional outlays related to the redesign and testing of such innovations show up in the national productivity data as thousands of hours of labor input.

The *Times* writer somewhat contemptuously quotes a Gillette spokesman: "'What we have managed to do is add to the value of the shaving experience,' said John F. Bush, a vice president of Gillette, 'and we get a higher price and a greater profit margin when we do this.'" The writer then goes in for the kill in a summary of the situation: "Yet Gillette, a much admired manufacturer, may not be doing much more than a struggling service company like AT&T to build the nation's income through greater productivity."[4]

Maybe the problem with this analysis is obvious to you. Standard productivity measures do try to take into account a better product. Something that economists agree with, but that the reporter missed, is that some accommodation has to be made for quality and for the way in which the market system brings about greater quality. So if we examine this formula, yes, the number of worker hours that go into producing this product have increased, but the product is better. And maybe that makes a difference to the customer. I, for one, agree with the Gillette vice president that the Mach III has "added to the value" of the shaving experience, and I don't mind paying a little extra for it. So maybe productivity hasn't declined. Maybe the formula doesn't work in this situation. Maybe there is something wrong with this story.

The writer also examined the information specialist position at AT&T. The company hired workers, mainly women, to respond to calls to a special information number. The work was very labor-intensive because these information specialists offer real hands-on, personal treatment to the customer who is requesting information. The writer interviewed one of these information specialists, a Mrs. Singh. "Mrs. Singh and her colleagues . . . are asked to be pleasant and patient. Ask one to list the names and phone numbers of all the delicatessens on Sixth Avenue in Manhattan, and she . . . will go patiently through 30 delis that come up on the screen before the caller has had enough. . . . 'You get a warm feeling from these conversations,' Mrs. Singh said. 'You don't come away from the job feeling brain dead.'" The reporter, however, comes down hard on Mrs. Singh: "But Mrs. Singh's role represents a considerable deterioration in productivity."[5] Arrest this woman.

What is Mrs. Singh doing? She is improving the value of AT&T service. She and her colleagues put in many worker hours giving people the kind of help that you otherwise really can't get anymore. The service is popular, people are calling for information, and Mrs. Singh is earning her keep. However, according to the formula, Mrs. Singh is bad for productivity, bad for productivity in this collectivist sense. But what AT&T is really doing, as an entrepreneurial firm, is discovering its true product: It is discovering different ways to please its customers.

Market Process and Pricing

There was an article about pork in the *New York Times,* which began in its typically colorful style: "While much of the nation is splurging on pork chops, ham, and bacon, allegations of price-gouging are being leveled against the meatpackers that turn hogs into pork products and, to a lesser extent, against the giant supermarket chains that sell them."[6]

The price of pork plummeted and the reason for this is explained in the *Times'* clever headline to its article: "Too Many Piggies Went to Market."[7] Hog farmers had become very optimistic about selling pork to the former Soviet Union, as well as to Japan. When the Japanese started to buy cheaper cuts of pork, rather than the more expensive ones, and the Russian market fell apart, the farmers had to sell their hogs on the domestic market. But because the farmers had raised a lot of hogs in anticipation of increasing foreign markets, there was an oversupply, and the price fell.

So what the story is saying is that although the country is enjoying itself, gorging on pork chops, something terrible is happening. And while the writer is complaining about this something terrible the meatpackers and grocery stores are doing, he is not discussing market reality. The meatpackers' price is not nearly as volatile on the upside or on the downside as is the farm price, and that goes with the territory. It is the nature of the commodities markets. The figures reported in the story show that the meatpackers' price went down as well, reflecting the fallen farm price. Why is that a problem?

What is so confusing about this story is that the retail prices, the prices at the grocery, did not come down at all, yet the grocery story is viewed as the lesser evil. Why isn't this a problem?

Let's examine what occurred at the retail level. I researched some figures from the U.S. Department of Agriculture. In 1995, 12.9 pounds of pork were consumed per person. By 1998, when supplies got tighter and the retail price increased, a record amount of pork was sold in the retail sector. How could that be? The price of pork is relatively elastic: You have to cut the price in order to move the product.

What has happened is that pricing on the retail level has been affected by new technology. Cash registers have been replaced by scanners. You swipe the goods across the scanner, and the price and sale are recorded. This enables the retailer to vary prices much more often, much more efficiently, than previously (and empirical data show this to be true). The price is not stamped on the good, a labor-intensive task, but somewhere near the good. There is no need for the cashier to remember prices, because the prices are "in the computer."

But this is only part of it. The stores also exercise entrepreneurship in pricing. Stores no longer lower prices: They discount prices. If a pork roast usually sells for $4 a pound, and your local grocery features it for a three-day-only sale at $2 a pound, you will rush to the store to grab up this bargain (and probably pick up a few nonbargains while you are there). The $4 per-pound price remains posted to remind you of the deal you are getting and to reference this setpoint price.

Then the government inspectors come in, average the sale and nonsale prices, and report that pork is selling for $3 per pound. This is duly reported in the *New York Times* and henceforth taken as gospel. However, that is not the real price per pound. For every pound sold at $4 that week, assume five pounds are sold at the $2 price. The real weighted average price is then $2.33 per pound, so, in fact, the real price has plummeted at the retail level as well. But because the government inspectors are unaware of it, because they don't look at quantities—they weren't taught to do so, and they don't have the time. And because the *New York Times* trusts the government's reports, and people trust the *New York Times*, a myth is perpetuated.

Another example of massive misinterpretation has to do with job creation and destruction. A newspaper article reported in December 1997, "The American economy showed surprising strength last month by creating 404,000 new jobs." Was that true?

Every month the government reports nonfarm payrolls based on a nationwide survey of 390,000 business establishments. The survey simply requests the number of employees on the payroll. In October 1997, it was reported that there were 124,561,000 jobs in the U.S. In November 1997, that figure had grown to 124,965,000. Payrolls had grown by 404,000 new employees. But in reporting that 404,000 new jobs had been created, no attention was paid to the number of jobs that had been eliminated. We know that some one million jobs are eliminated every month. We know that 100,000 businesses fail each year. Businesses are cutting back and eliminating jobs every month. To report that 404,000 new jobs were created in November 1997 is telling only half the story. It doesn't relate the net figure. I would rewrite that first sentence to read: "The American economy showed surprising strength last month by creating about 1,404,000 new jobs, but since about one million jobs were eliminated, the net gain was 404,000."

Another example is shown in two quotations: one from the *New York Times*, the other from the *Wall Street Journal*. The *Times* wrote: "The number of planned job cuts by United States business rose in November from a year earlier, putting the annual total on track for the largest number of cuts in five years, according to the monthly survey conducted by Challenger, Gray & Christmas, an unemployment firm."[8] A similar story ran in the *Wall Street Journal*: "Layoffs are as brisk as ever: More than half a million job cuts have been announced in the U.S. so far this year, according to a tally of published reports by Chicago outplacement firm Challenger, Gray & Christmas."[9] Now Challenger, Gray & Christmas is an entrepreneurial firm, but they are entrepreneurial in an unfortunate way. They have gained a lot of attention because they are supposedly keeping track of job cuts, which they do by reading the newspapers and following press releases. Now if the Mom-and-Pop shop down the street is going to have a layoff, or if 100,000 companies are going to go under, that will not enter into their calculations. So, obviously, these reports do not tell the story of what is actually going on in the marketplace.

I looked to unemployment insurance claims, which would seem to be a real reflection of workplace activity. In 1991, during the recession, there were some 450,000 unemployment insurance claims per week. By 1998, in the sixth year of economic expansion, unemployment insurance claims were running over 300,000 per week. There were over 15 million people in 1998 filing for unemployment insurance at a time when the labor markets were extremely tight, when the unemployment rate was 4.4 percent, the lowest rate in about thirty years. Nonetheless, there is still this incredible parade of one-third of a million people a week leaving jobs and getting jobs.

To return to the Challenger, Gray & Christmas estimates, they reported that 56,000 jobs had been eliminated in a month. Over the course of a year, that's some 600,000 job cuts. Compared to the unemployment claims figures, it appears that the Challenger, Gray & Christmas annual figure is equal to two weeks' worth of the unemployment insurance office tally. Again, the newspapers take their numbers from a Challenger, Gray & Christmas-type firm, and the incorrect figures are given absolute-fact status.

It appears from these examples—which, unfortunately, are not isolated cases—that reporters suffer a sort of myopia about the market process. A sure cure would be that business writers be required to study the Austrian economists. But that is not likely to happen. What can be done, and what needs to be done, is that young people trained in free market economics take on a career in journalism and make it their mission to report the truth.

Notes

[1]Israel M. Kirzer, *Discovery and the Capitalist Process* (Chicago: University of Chicago Press, 1985).
[2]"America's Treadmill Economy," *New York Times*, March 3, 1998, p. 2.
[3]Ibid.
[4]Ibid.
[5]Ibid.
[6]*New York Times*, January 6, 1999, p. A2.
[7]Ibid.
[8]"Many Brake Lights on the Economic Road," *New York Times*, December 13, 1998.
[9]*Wall Street Journal*, December 28, 1998.

Gleaves Whitney

Ludwig von Mises: The Man Behind the Book

Introduction

Imagine that you are the audience in the studio of the game show *Jeopardy!* The category is "Great Economists." Alex Trebek reads the following to the contestants:

> The last name of this famous economist begins with "M." He was born into a Jewish family in the nineteenth century, raised in a German-speaking country, and lived the last thirty-three years of his life in the English-speaking world. At the time of his death, this economist had a loyal, brave band of disciples willing to fight against the intellectual fashions of the day.[1]

Most *Jeopardy!* contestants would not need much time to come up with, "Who is Karl Marx?" And they would be correct. Everything fits the description of Marx, down to the last thirty-three years of his life in the English-speaking world. But those with an even higher economic IQ would know that the other correct response is, "Who is Ludwig von Mises?" This is one of those remarkable coincidences in our intellectual history.

We can add up the number of books and articles Mises wrote, the number of teaching posts he held, the number of students he taught. But how do we calculate the sum total of the man? How do we measure the depth of his understanding? The degree of his intellectual courage? His impact on the history of ideas? That is the challenge we face when speaking of Ludwig von Mises.

Mises was a titan who left a deep imprint on the long road to freedom. Just as all philosophy is a footnote to Plato, so it is increasingly apparent that free market economics is an extension of Mises. He ranged beyond his two great Austrian predecessors, Carl Menger and Eugen von Böhm-Bawerk. The evidence of his impact is abundant, from college faculties to think tanks.[2]

Thus it can be fairly said: In Ludwig von Mises, we encounter a significant man who was educated in a significant tradition that equipped him to enter a significant debate, out of which he wrote a significant book that has had a significant impact.

While speaking of significant things, we should add that Mises had a significant wife. Margit von Mises was a force in her own right, helping lead the renaissance of Austrian economics in the mid-1970s, and living to almost 103 years of age to champion the cause of her husband. Hayek thought Ludwig's marriage to Margit softened his edges considerably.

Mises was agnostic; he was not an observant Jew. He respected people who had a faith, but did not count himself as one of them. Nevertheless, a theme to which I will recur is that he was the modern-day version of an ancient Hebrew prophet, a prophet in the sense of the Hebrew *nabî*—a messenger of timeless truths, an interpreter of eternal laws, a judge rendering a judgment of the nations.[3] In the modern age, Mises was a voice in the wilderness—a true prophet in a world teeming with false ones.

A Significant Man

Let us look more closely at this assertion that Mises was a significant man. It has been said that providence brings forth men to match the times. Mises certainly appeared at the right time and the right place to test this proposition. Permit me to lay out his life in brief and, just as important, his response to life; you can then decide if he was significant.

Ludwig von Mises was born in 1881. The Austro-Hungarian empire of his youth was a remnant of the *ancien régime*, one of the last great Old World monarchies. It was often remarked that he retained the manners of the Old World throughout his 92 years on this earth: a true gentleman-scholar.

Mises had the good fortune to grow up in one of the intellectual capitals of the world, Vienna, where he received virtually all his schooling. After he earned his doctorate at the University of Vienna, the First World War broke out and he served in the Austro-Hungarian army as a captain in the artillery. He spent much of the war on the Russian front, the mere mention of which should make us realize how fortunate the world is not to have lost him at that point.

In 1920, two years shy of his fortieth birthday, Mises secured international recognition for an article he had written about socialism. It was a timely piece. Recall that the Bolsheviks had come to power in the new Soviet Union only three years before, in 1917. In his article, Mises set out to prove that economic calculation in a socialist regime is a house of cards. In the absence of a free market, prices cannot do what they do best, which is convey information about what goods and services are genuinely valued. No economic calculation, no economy. Ergo: In a socialist state there is really no economy.[4]

This was just the first famous article in a series of works that Mises would produce in response to the crises of his day. And crises there were aplenty. In addition to the First World War and Bolshevik Revolution, there was the dissolution of the Austro-Hungarian empire. These events, however, were mere dress rehearsals for what was to come: The hyperinflation of the 1920s, the Great Depression of the 1930s, the rise of Nazism, the *Anschluß* by the Third Reich, the outbreak of the Second World War, then the Cold War and the ever-looming threat of nuclear holocaust. Without exaggeration, it can be said that Mises' professional life coincided with one of the most horrific periods in the history of the West. In the midnight-dark year of 1940, Mises opined—and here the Hebrew prophet in him is evident, the *nabî*—"Occasionally I entertained the hope that my writings would bear practical fruit and show the way for policy, and to that end I have constantly searched for evidence of an ideological change. But I have never allowed myself to be deceived. I recognized that my theories merely explain the decline of a great civilization; they do not prevent it. I set out to be a reformer, but only became the historian of decline."[5]

Mises wrote those words at the low ebb of his intellectual life, in 1940. Yet at the high tide of his influence, many years later, he was appreciated for being much more than a historian of decline. Henry Hazlitt described his friend and mentor as "the greatest economist of his generation, one of the great social thinkers of our age, a powerful and original mind [that] saw economics not as some narrow specialty, but as a study of nothing less than the whole realm of human action, human decision."[6]

Another friend, Hans Sennholz, observed that Mises was "the most important economist of the century. But he was more than a great economist with a keen analytical mind. He was the most undaunted and uncompromising champion of economic and political liberty. For more than half a century he was a rallying-point for the forces of freedom, never wavering or compromising, imperturbable and unyielding, unaffected by the scorn and ridicule of his adversaries, or by the temptations of the world. By his writings, Ludwig von Mises has sown the seeds of a regeneration that are bearing fruit the world over."[7]

This high praise inspires deeper inquiry into what it was in the inner man that made Mises significant. Anyone who becomes acquainted with this remarkable man will be struck by one virtue in particular: his courage. Imagine you are an Austrian during the very worst time to be an Austrian. It is the twilight of the Empire, stirred up in places that are still making headlines—Kosovo, Sarajevo, Bosnia. Then, as now, it was a boiling cauldron of ethnic unrest. At the beginning of your career, World War I erupts because of your country's inability to deal with the unrest. You are part of that tragic "generation of 1914," and you lose many friends in battle. After four horrible years, it turns out that your country fought for nothing. Worse, it ends up on the wrong side of the Armistice. An unsettling peace is imposed. Civil unrest is a daily reality. The economy goes south. That was Austria in the first third of the twentieth century. Could it get worse?

Yes, it could—and it did. In these desperate conditions, an apparent savior appears out of the North. His mesmerizing speeches promise to restore order and pride. The only problem is that the savior is the leader of a fanatical band of thugs who happen to hate Jews. You are Jewish. To your chagrin, your gentile neighbors pour out into the streets to welcome Hitler and his legions of goose-stepping troops. You know that you are a marked man, and doubly so: Not only are you Jewish, but the new regime is hostile to your ideas. Your writings and teachings put you at grave risk. As an intellectual enemy of the Reich, the Nazis are determined not only to destroy your body, but your work.

You flee the country with little more than what you can carry on your back. Your house is ransacked by the Nazis. All your personal papers—the fruits of almost three decades of work—are stolen, shipped to Berlin, and then to Moscow, and kept under lock and key for decades.

You seek refuge in Switzerland, an island of liberty in a sea of tyranny. A safe harbor, right? Wrong. The Swiss government pressures you to leave because it considers your presence "a political liability and a danger to its security."[8]

This is dreadful news. You are not a young man anymore. You are almost sixty years of age; you are newly married. Under ordinary circumstances, most contemporaries your age would be thinking about retirement. Not you. Thoroughly uprooted, you have no home, no job, no prospects.

The one stroke of good luck is that you are able to make it to the United States. In America, life is not bad. You get invited to some parties at first, but then people discover that you are extreme and unyielding in your views. It is not that you are impolite, not at all. But word has gotten out that when you and your wife are at a dinner party and you learn that there are Marxists present, you firmly tell her to get her coat and gloves. You are leaving!

From your keen mind comes a steady stream of books and papers—in your new language, no less. The reception, however, is not what you had hoped for. Your American colleagues have fallen under the spell of Keynes; they are thoroughgoing interventionists. They write you off as quaint, out of the mainstream. Despite your accomplishments, there is never an offer from an Ivy League university. The most you will be able to secure is a visiting professorship at New York University, where you will be consigned to teach in a basement classroom. Any professional advancement will be blocked. And you are "punished" for being outspoken, unyielding, and principled to a fault. Your wife observes that the more you write, the harder you fight for your ideas, the more enemies you make.[9]

That's the scenario. That was Mises' life in the first half of the twentieth century. Now, the $64,000 question: In light of everything just described, you are asked what your one regret in life is. Your answer: That you have not been even *more* unyielding, *more* uncompromising, and *more* principled!

That was Ludwig von Mises, a man who demonstrated rare courage throughout his life. And I submit that this was a quality that he shared with the Hebrew prophets.

A Significant Tradition

What about the significant tradition I mentioned, the tradition into which Mises was educated? It is the Enlightenment, sometimes known as the Age of Reason. The spirit of the Enlightenment was famously characterized by the German philosopher Immanuel Kant, who proclaimed that the Enlightenment meant nothing less than humankind's emergence from intellectual immaturity. This immaturity was not due to "lack of intelligence, but lack of determination and courage to use that intelligence without another's guidance. *Sapere aude!* as Kant exhorted his fellow *philosophes.* "Dare to know! Have the courage to use your own intelligence!"[10]

The English historian Paul Johnson distills the significance of the Enlightenment with characteristic insight: "For the first time in human history, and with growing confidence and audacity, men arose to assert that they could diagnose the ills of society and cure them with their own unaided intellects." They didn't need God's revelation to do it.[11]

That was the tradition into which Mises was educated. He believed that one of the noblest endeavors a person could undertake was to discover the timeless, immutable laws that govern our world and shape human behavior. Mises believed that just as there are immutable laws governing nature, so there are universal laws of human nature, especially human nature in action. Again, his mission relates Mises back to the prophets of old, who also communicated timeless truths to anyone with ears to hear.

Enlightenment thinkers believed that we humans have a faculty that enables us to comprehend the universal laws of nature and human nature—and that is reason. Reason is the foundation of all Mises' thinking and work. In his memoir of the founders of the Austrian School, what did he praise? Reason.[12] In his eulogy of Wilhelm von Röpke, his contemporary and also a great economist, what did he praise? Reason.[13] In his magnum opus, *Human Action,* what did he praise again and again and again? Reason. Reason is the constant in his work, like a metronome that keeps musicians on beat.

From this it follows that one violates the dictates of right reason at one's peril. Yet it happens all the time. Mises knew, better than most who call themselves economists, that "[i]t is possible for a government to damage an economy greatly by ignoring or defying [the laws of economics], and many governments have done so in the twentieth century."[14] He knew well what his friend Henry Hazlitt immortalized in *Economics in One Lesson:* ignoring long-term consequences and secondary effects is the most common source of error in economics.[15] "Man has only one tool with which to fight error," he said, and that is "reason."[16]

I know that at one level this sounds ho-hum. Who could be against reason? But put Mises' defense of reason in its cultural context:

- The irrational was being explored in turn-of-the-century Vienna by Freud, who had just completed *The Interpretation of Dreams.*
- The irrational was being privileged in philosophical discourse, in the work of Bergson and Nietzsche.
- The irrational and the violent were being raised to first principles of political thought in theorists like Sorel *(Reflections on Violence),* and in the new totalitarian "isms"—Leninism, Fascism, Nazism.
- The irrational was being celebrated in modern art—look at Dada and Surrealism—and in modern music like the *Symphony Fantastique* by Berlioz.
- Even advances in physics were undermining rationality: witness Einstein's relativity theory and Heißenberg's "uncertainty principle."

Now Mises' philosophy doesn't sound so ho-hum. Indeed, a vigorous defense of reason during the first decades of the twentieth century was nothing short of revolutionary. (An interesting word, "revolution." The old meaning of the word is best explained by picturing a wheel that turns, turns, turns back to its starting point. A true revolution returns to something fundamental. That's precisely what Mises is about in an age of war, genocide, and disorder. Like a Hebrew prophet, he was challenging his civilization to return to the timeless truths revealed by right reason. It was he who was revolutionary.)

A Significant Debate

Now, what about the significant debate I mentioned? Every man has a passion. For Mises, that passion was freedom. He was an intellectual freedom fighter his entire adult life. The battle he joined was over the contested ground of freedom in the modern world. Take all the major debates he engaged in, and they were many, and they all swirl around this one great idea: human freedom.

Mises did not carry on his battle in isolation. He, like every thinker, had an intellectual genealogy. In the family tree of liberty, the giant among giants is John Stuart Mill. His work *On Liberty* is the catechism of freedom-lovers throughout the world. In fact, Mises, like Hayek, claimed Mill as one of his own—"Austrian" even![17]

Mill, you will recall, famously laid down the criterion by which interference with the individual is justified:

> The sole end for which mankind are warranted, individually or collectively, in interfering with the liberty of action of any of their number, is self-protection. . . . The only part of the conduct of anyone, for which he is amenable to society, is that which concerns others. In the part which merely concerns himself, his independence is, of right, absolute. Over himself, over his own body and mind, the individual is sovereign.[18]

Proceeding from this principle, Mises debated Marxists, Keynesians, and interventionists of all stripes. Raising a prophetic voice, Mises said that man had to choose between freedom and slavery. Either he could be free in a market economy, or he could be a slave in a socialist regime. Ultimately, there was no mythical Third Way.

As a champion of classical liberalism, Mises knew that freedom means nothing if not possessed by the individual; that the individual is the absolute owner of his life, to use and dispose of as he sees fit; that all a man's social actions should be voluntary; that respect for every other person's life, liberty, and property is the ethical basis of an open and humane society.

Such a social framework calls for limited government. Indeed, the legitimate function of government is pretty much restricted to assisting an individual in his self-defense against violence, theft, fraud, and broken contracts.[19]

But note this well. Mises is not libertarian to the point of advocating anarchy or condoning antisocial behavior. Listen to how he frames human freedom: "A man's freedom is most rigidly restricted by the laws of nature. . . . If he chooses to indulge in gratifications that produce definite effects upon the functions of his body or his mind, he must put up with these consequences."

Furthermore,

> Man cannot have both the advantages derived from peaceful cooperation . . . within society and the license of embarking upon conduct that is bound to disintegrate society. He must choose between the observance of certain rules that make life within society possible and the poverty and insecurity of the "dangerous life" in a state of perpetual warfare among independent individuals.

He gives an example:

> A man who absorbs poison harms himself alone. But a man who chooses to resort to robbery upsets the whole social order. While he alone enjoys the short-term gains from his action, the disastrous long-term effects harm all the people. His deed is a crime because it has detrimental effects on his fellow men. If society were not to prevent such conduct, it would soon become general and put an end to social cooperation and all the boons the latter confers upon everybody.

Reaping the consequences of antisocial behavior, Mises concludes, "is no less rigid a law . . . of all human action than are the laws of physics."[20] Again, we hear in the Austrian a prophetic voice, conveying timeless truths and interpreting eternal laws for a people who wish to be free.

A Significant Book

I just mentioned the phrase "human action," which brings us to the commemoration of the fiftieth anniversary of the book by the same title. In its thousand pages, Mises makes one of the most sustained defenses of freedom and individualism ever penned. He shows how social cooperation results when you give free play to human knowledge, choice, and action. He argues that economics is the study not of some amorphous social mass, but of how you and I as individuals express our values in the marketplace.

There are a number of neologisms in the book, like "praxeology" and "catallactics," words that may put some neophytes off. Serious readers will also need several foreign language dictionaries to plow through the work. But Mises' argument, at base, is not difficult to understand. In fact, it is really quite intuitive. Simply put: The value of goods is not inherent in the goods themselves, or the labor put into them, but in the minds of acting men and women. Because economic value, like beauty, is in the eye of the beholder, it will vary from person to person, and even within the same individual over time.

Murray Rothbard humorously explained it this way: "I could spend thirty years of labor time and other resources working on the perfection of a giant steam-powered tricycle. If, however, on offering this product no consumers can be found to purchase this tricycle, it is economically valueless." No amount of labor or material can change that brute fact.[21]

This is the essence of "subjectivist economics," a great leap forward from the classical theory of value held by Adam Smith, David Ricardo, and their followers. And if the subjective theory of value sounds rather commonsensical nowadays, then it is a tribute to Mises and his teachers, Carl Menger and Böhm-Bawerk. It also shows the standing *Human Action* has acquired, as a kind of summa of Austrian economics. Indeed, it has been called "The Capitalist Manifesto."

"Every once in a while," wrote Rothbard, "the human race pauses in the job of botching its affairs and redeems itself by producing a noble work of the intellect. . . . To state that *Human Action* is a 'must' book is a greater understatement. This is the economic Bible of the civilized man."[22]

In the course of his argument, Mises slays a host of dragons known variously as socialism, Marxism, statism, collectivism, interventionism—all arrayed against the free market. One of the chief villains of the book is Lenin, who sought to empower an elite that would wield absolute control over an economy's "commanding heights." The Bolsheviks' agenda was "to organize the *whole* national economy like the postal system," to make the whole of society "one office and one factory," and to transform *all* citizens "into hired employees of the state."[23]

In one of the most powerful passages ever to come from the hand of Mises, he observed:

> The champions of socialism call themselves progressives, but they recommend a system which is characterized by rigid observance of routine and by a resistance to every kind of improvement. They call themselves liberals, but they are intent upon abolishing liberty. They call themselves democrats, but they yearn for dictatorship. They call themselves revolutionaries, but they want to make the government omnipotent. They promise the blessings of the Garden of Eden, but they plan to transform the world into a gigantic post office.

Yes. "The post office is the model for the construction of the New Jerusalem. The post-office clerk is the prototype of future man. Streams of blood have been shed for the realization of this ideal."[24]

The significance of *Human Action* is immense, but what I am concerned with here is what *Human Action* reveals about the mind of Ludwig von Mises. *Human Action* is the work of

- a courageous man with a strong character and steadfast determination to refute the follies of his age;
- a rational man, educated in the Enlightenment ideal and demonstrating a mastery of history and logic as his arguments unfold;

- a passionate man whose love of freedom was second to none;
- a philosophical man who understood that true freedom is inseparable from right reason;
- a systematic man who formulated the correct methodology for economic science;
- a persistent man who, after formulating the correct methodology for economic science, took the next difficult steps and constructed the entire body of economic analysis on that method;
- a polemical man who knew that capitalism had so enriched the common man that he would be the envy of the princes of bygone ages;
- a prophetic man, whose jeremiad amounts to a warning to America, to the West, to the world, a warning not to let government overstep its bounds.[25]

Human Action is all of these things and more. In the interest of time, permit me to broach just two of the book's themes that are more implicit than explicit, and that may go unnoticed in one's initial encounter with it. These two subtexts also tell us much about the author.

One of the book's implicit themes is America. *Human Action* is the work of a man who loved America and who wanted our nation to recover the promise of freedom that inspired our founding. Remember the context. When Mises was writing the 1940 book on which *Human Action* would be based,[26] Europe was bristling with arms; its civilizational legacy was being destroyed by two viciously totalitarian regimes—Nazi Germany and the Soviet Union. Where did Mises seek sanctuary but in the great outpost of freedom, the United States. To be sure, he knew our nation's weaknesses, especially after the Keynesian 1930s. Yet he greatly admired the Founders and their gift of freedom to the world. He believed that America alone was still free to choose between individualism and democracy on one hand, and compulsion and totalitarianism on the other. And he believed that the decision of the American people would determine the outcome for the whole of humankind.[27]

Another implicit theme in the book is humanism. I mean the term in its old, venerable sense: humanism as an interest in the full intellectual, moral, cultural development of the human person. By this definition, *Human Action* is the work of a Renaissance man who wanted to carry forward one of the great conversations in Western civilization, and that is how to ennoble man to reach his full potential. I have not seen this link developed in the literature about Mises. But as I was rereading the book, I was struck by the humanistic impulse throughout. Mises plumbs such humanistic themes as:

- human dignity, as seen in his defense of free will;
- human choice based on that free will;
- a constitutionally ordered polity that allows for the expression of choice and self-determination;
- an unfettered marketplace in which men and women can act on their freely chosen values; and,
- a critique of socialist ignorance of the true nature of man.

What motivated Mises' deep dislike of Marxism, I believe, was not just that it obliterated economic calculation, but that it obliterated man. It was antihumanistic. That is the greater indictment. Mises wrote, "German Marxists coined the dictum: If socialism is against human nature, then human nature must be changed. They did not realize that if man's nature is changed, he ceases to be a man."[28] Again and again, we see Mises fighting to uphold human dignity and freedom against the Marxists and interventionists who would straitjacket man into an ideology that serves their own self-serving ends. That is why *Human Action* is a preeminently humanistic work.

To conclude, I need to mention one thing *Human Action* and its author are not. This is necessary because more people talk about the book than read it.

Mises was not antigovernment, and nowhere did Mises call government per se evil. What may be more surprising to you still: Nowhere did Mises call bureaucracy per se evil. The police department, for example, is properly run as a bureaucracy. What Mises was against was the bureaucratization of society. He was against the concentration of coercive power and the arbitrary use of power against law-abiding citizens.

Mises was a keen student of history and knew that limited government is one of the greatest accomplishments of humankind. It has been imperfectly enjoyed by only a portion of the human race, and, where enjoyed, its hold is precarious. The experience of the twentieth century offered this Austrian abundant evidence of how tenuous constitutional government is. One needs courage to achieve it, and vigilance to maintain it.

He admired the American system of government because it was established to provide government, to be sure, but government that was delegated, enumerated, and limited. Our Founders drew from their knowledge of thousands of years of human history during which many peoples struggled for liberty and limited government. There were many defeats, and some victories, along the way. Studying and meditating on these lessons of history, our Founders distilled their wisdom into the documents that serve as the foundation of our experiment in limited government: the Declaration of Independence, Articles of Confederation, state constitutions, Constitution of the United States, and Federalist papers.[29]

We continue to amass evidence that Mises was not antigovernment. In 1997, Bettina Greaves, perhaps the oldest living student of Mises, discovered a "lost" manuscript among the Austrian's papers. Written in 1943, it is called "Mexico's Economic Problems." And guess what Mises wrote? "The economic backwardness of a part of Mexico's agricultural population justifies intervention on the part of the government. It is all right for the government to advise the peons how to establish and to run cooperatives. Even small subsidies for newly formed cooperatives may be advocated. But it would be a mistake to subsidize them permanently or to grant them tax privileges."[30]

Hardly the words of an anarchist.

A Significant Impact

To assess the significance of the man and the book, again, we must put Mises into context. He was part of the great migration of intellectuals, many of them Jewish, from central Europe to the United States in the 1930s and 1940s, a migration that produced a sea-change in twentieth-century American intellectual life.[31] Both the left and the right benefited from this pooling of talent. Henry Hazlitt remarked how ironic it was that the two "most eminent . . . defenders of English liberty, and of the system of free enterprise which reached its highest development in America should now be two Austrian exiles." He was of course referring to Mises and Hayek.[32]

George Nash, in his seminal book, *The Conservative Intellectual Movement in America,* lays out Mises' influence in the very first chapter. He was a cornerstone of the libertarian wing of postwar conservatism, a counterrevolutionary in a world of "overweening statism, entrenched bureaucracy, and seemingly triumphant philosophies of the Left." He played a pivotal role in "the intellectual rehabilitation of individualism in America at the close of World War II."[33]

Indeed, a list of the individuals whom Mises influenced reads like a Who's Who. In the economic sphere, his students included Friedrich von Hayek, who won the Nobel Prize, and Gottfried Haberler and Fritz Machlup, both of whom served as president of the American Economic Association. Also among his disciples were the powerful polemicists Henry Hazlitt and Murray Rothbard.[34]

In the political sphere, Mises had an indirect influence on leaders like Ronald Reagan and Michigan's own John Engler.

Even in the sphere of popular culture, Mises has made his impact felt. About a year ago, he was the subject of a Batman comic strip![35]

Why this continuing impact? I have argued that Mises was like the Hebrew prophets of old, a messenger of timeless truths, an interpreter of eternal laws—in this case, the laws of human action in the marketplace. He devoted his life to defending reason in an irrational age. Moreover there was the powerful testimony of his conduct of life, his courage to go against the tide no matter what the personal cost. Then there was his hope. Not blind optimism, but the virtue of hope, which is quite a different thing. This quality of hope was expressed in his first essay for *The Freeman* (its first volume). Mises argued that there is no historical determinism that precludes a return to classical liberalism. Humans are not passive but active; we can will what we want. This is an encouraging message for those who are feeling jaded, which I think includes many conservatives these days.[36]

Assessment

No doubt about it: *Human Action* is a significant work, and it is right that we celebrate its fiftieth anniversary. Nevertheless, the book has not been uniformly embraced on the Right. Cultural or traditionalist conservatives argue that Misesian analysis does not go far enough. In its preoccupation with observable human action, it overlooks how important are the worldviews, ethical systems, and religious faiths that motivate that action. It is as though conservatives are yelling from the rooftops, "It's *not* the economy, stupid—it's the culture!"

Cultural conservatives argue that there is a lot more to *homo economicus* than economics. There is our soul, our love, our moral sense that enables us to choose right or wrong. These constitute the ultimate ground of economics—the choices that we have already made in our hearts before we ever choose in the marketplace. That is why economics points beyond itself, to "meta-economic" concerns, to those things which are above and beyond the mere material aspects of our existence.

Meta-economic factors are especially important in a capitalist system because it is the most powerful economic system ever devised. It is the most efficient way to express human values. It will deliver what people want in superabundance. So: If a society values child pornography, capitalism will deliver, better than any other system. If the masses want psychic hotlines, capitalism will deliver, better than any other system. If the majority want human clones to serve as cheap labor, capitalism will deliver, better than any other system.[37]

This last example sounds outrageous, I know. But remember, it wasn't too long ago that there were gulags and concentration camps on European soil, and slaves on our own. That is why moral reins will forever be needed to keep the massive economic horsepower unleashed by capitalism from running wild. Runaway capitalism stirs up antisocial forces that bring about a society's destruction.

To be fair, Mises and the libertarians would remind conservatives that they are hardly advocating an amoral society, much less an immoral one. For the free market to work, people need, at the very least, to refrain from violence, theft, fraud, perjury, and unilaterally breaking contracts. Whether these basic values come from the Ten Commandments or the Golden Rule or a democratically held social gospel really does not matter to libertarians. The source in a pluralistic society is not so important as the fact that people act on these values.

Yet many conservatives would challenge this easy latitudinarianism. The source of social values is important. It is not enough for us all to be, say, Utilitarians. A transcendent system of sanctions—such as found in Judaism and Christianity—is superior to Utilitarianism because a transcendent system won't drift with the winds of convenience, sophistry, and pleasure. Judaism and Christianity hold fast to certain fundamental laws, the violation of which is a violation of God's will. Judeo-Christian anthropology asserts that the human person is more than *homo economicus*, more than an accidental collocation of atoms, more than a bundle of nerve endings seeking pleasure and avoiding pain. Indeed, the human person is created in the image and likeness of God. What a powerful affirmation of the dignity of the human person, a dignity that no economic actor, or system, should violate.

Pope John Paul II challenged Americans with precisely this message during his recent trip to North America. He criticized the pervasive "neo-liberalism" of our day. We tend to be dominated by an economic system that is "based on a purely economic conception of man," one that regards "profit and the law of the market as its only parameters, to the detriment of the dignity of and the respect due to individuals and peoples." The trouble with neo-liberalism, as with Marxism, is that it sees people only as economic actors. It sees only bodies, not souls. Yet any good social order will not neglect the salvation and care of souls.

The Pope and his conservative allies are not saying that everybody in America has to be a believing Jew or Christian. But among our citizenry, there must be a critical mass of theists who adhere to an absolute system of transcendent values that are not prone to utilitarian drift. Their right to express their values must be rigorously protected. For in a pluralistic society, these believers are the anchors that keep society from crashing against the rocks of rampant egotism and hedonism. They make sustainable prosperity possible.

The conservative critique of Mises is not to diminish his great achievement in *Human Action*—only to put it in perspective. His paean to freedom was, to be sure, a much-needed antidote to the poisonous totalitarianisms of the modern age. Yet the conservative critique challenges us to accept that man is more than what he does in the marketplace; and that the wealth of this world is as nothing compared to the treasures of the next.

Notes

[1]For the uncanny parallels between Marx and Mises, I am grateful to David Ramsay Steele, *From Marx to Mises: Post-Capitalist Society and the Challenge of Economic Calculation* (La Salle, IL: Open Court, 1992), p. xv.

[2]The president of the Mackinac Center, Lawrence Reed, hung a portrait of Mises in the Center's library, beneath which reads the plaque:

Ludwig von Mises
(1881–1973)

Preeminent scholar of the "Austrian School" and the Greatest Economist of the 20th Century. "Without economic calculation there can be no economy. Hence, in a socialist state wherein the pursuit of economic calculation is impossible, there can be—in our sense of the term—no economy whatsoever."

[3]Bruce Vawter, "Introduction to Prophetic Literature," in *The New Jerome Biblical Commentary,* ed. Raymond E. Brown, Joseph A. Fitzmyer, and Roland E. Murphy (Englewood Cliffs, NJ: Prentice Hall, 1990), pp. 186–87.

[4]Ludwig von Mises, "Economic Calculation in the Socialist Commonwealth," translated by S. Adler, in *Economic Planning: Critical Studies of the Possibilities of Socialism,* edited by Friedrich Hayek (London: Routledge & Sons, 1935); originally published in German as "Die Wirtschaftsrechnung im sozialistischen Gemeinwesen," *Archiv für Sozialwissenschaft und Sozialpolitik,* 47 (1920–21): 86–121.

[5]Ludwig von Mises, *Erinnerungen von Ludwig von Mises,* Foreword by Margit von Mises (Stuttgart and New York: Gustav Fischer Verlag, 1978), p. 76: *"Wenn die Rückkehr zum Kapitalismus wirklich ausgeschlossen ist, wie man allgemein behauptet, dann ist der Schicksal unserer Kulture besiegel ... [A]ber... der [K]apitalismus hebt sich nicht selbst auf. Die Menschen wollen ihn abschaffen, weil sie im Sozialismus oder im Interventionismus das Heil erblicken.*

"Ich habe machmal die Hoffnung gehegt, daß meine Schriften eine praktische Wirkung erreichen und der Politik den Weg weisen würden. Ich have immer nach den Anzeichen eines ideologischen Wandels Umschau gehalten. Doch ich habe mich eigentlich nie darüber getäuscht, daß meine Theorien den Niedergang der großen Kultur erklären, ihn aber nicht aufhalten. Ich wollte Reformer werden, doch ich bin nur der Geschichtsschreiber des Niedergangs geworden."

[6]Henry Hazlitt, eulogy of Ludwig von Mises, October 16, 1973, quoted by Margit von Mises, in Greaves and McGee, *Mises: An Annotated Bibliography*

(Irvington-on-Hudson, NY: Foundation for Economic Education, 1993), p. vii.

[7]Sennholz, "Postscript," to Ludwig von Mises, *Notes and Recollections* (South Holland, IL: Libertarian Press, 1978), p. 147.

[8]Mises, *Notes,* p. 138.

[9]Greaves and McGee, *Mises,* p. 365.

[10]Immanuel Kant (1784), quoted in Peter Gay, *Age of Enlightenment* (New York: Time, 1966), p. 11.

[11]Paul Johnson, *Intellectuals* (New York: Harper & Row, 1988), pp. 1–2.

[12]Ludwig von Mises, *The Historical Setting of the Austrian School of Economics* (New Rochelle, NY: Arlington House, 1969).

[13]Ludwig von Mises, "Wilhelm Röpke, RIP," *National Review,* March 8, 1966, p. 200. Mises wrote, "In the midst of moral and intellectual decay, he was an inflexible harbinger of the return to reason. . . ."

[14]Russell Kirk, *Economics: Work and Prosperity* (Pensacola, FL: Beka Books, 1989), p. 92.

[15]Henry Hazlitt, *Economics in One Lesson,* any edition.

[16]Ludwig von Mises, *Liberalism: In the Classical Tradition,* translated by Ralph Raico, foreword by Louis M. Spadaro, preface by Bettina Bien Greaves (Irvington-on-Hudson, NY. and San Francisco: Foundation for Economic Education and Cobden Press, 1985); original German edition, *Liberalismus* (Jena: Gustav Fischer, 1927).

[17]Mises, *Human Action,* p. 496n.

[18]John Stuart Mill, *On Liberty* (Amherst, NY: Prometheus Books, 1986), p. 25.

[19]Paraphrase of Karl Hess, quoted in Jerome Tuccille, *Radical Libertarianism* (New York: Bobbs-Merrill, 1970); quoted in Brad Miner, *The Concise Conservative Encyclopedia* (New York: The Free Press, 1996), p. 137.

[20]Mises, *Human Action,* p. 280.

[21]Murray N. Rothbard, "The Essential Von Mises," in *Planning for Freedom, and Sixteen Other Essays and Addresses,* by Ludwig von Mises, 4th ed. (Spring Mills, PA: Libertarian Press, 1980), pp. 235–39.

[22]"Human Action," advertisement for *Human Action: The Scholar's Edition,* Ludwig von Mises Institute web site <www.mises.org>.

[23]Cf. Ludwig von Mises, *Bureaucracy* (Cedar Falls, IA: Center for Futures Education, 1983), p. vi.

[24]Mises, *Bureaucracy,* pp. 124, 125.

[25]Mises, *Human Action,* pp. 859–60.

[26]Ludwig von Mises, *Nationalökonomie: Theorie des Handelns und Wirtschaftens* (Genf: Editions Union, 1940).

[27]Mises, *Bureaucracy,* p. vii.

[28]Mises, *Bureaucracy,* p. 103.

[29]Cf. Tom G. Palmer, "The Great Bequest," *Freeman,* March 1999, p. 29.

[30]Editor's endnote number 3, from Eduardo Turrent, "Mises on Mexico," *Freeman,* March 1999, p. 22.

[31]H. Stuart Hughes, *The Sea Change,* any edition.

[32]Henry Hazlitt, *New York Times Book Review,* October 1, 1944, p. 5.

[33]George H. Nash, *The Conservative Intellectual Movement in America: Since 1945* (Wilmington, DE: Intercollegiate Studies Institute, 1996), p. 2, 7–10.

[34]For praise of Murray Rothbard's understanding of praxeology, especially as demonstrated in his book *Man, Economy, and State,* cf. review by Ludwig von Mises, "New Treatise on Economics," *New Individualist Review,* 2 (Autumn 1962): 39–42.

[35]Paul Pope, *The Batman Chronicles,* 11 (Winter 1998): 2–19.

[36]Ludwig von Mises, "Trends Can Change," *Freeman* (January 8, 1951): 300–301; reprinted in Mises, *Planning for Freedom and Twelve Other Essays and Addresses* (South Holland, IL: Libertarian Press, 1952, 1962, 1974).

[37]For this insight, I am indebted to Dr. Gary Wolfram, economics professor, Hillsdale College.

George Roche

The Revolt Against Reason

Ludwig von Mises was born in Austria in 1881. He wrote his first book while he was still a university student. He served as an artillery officer on the eastern front in the "Great War," as World War I was known. Afterward, he became the chief economist for the Chamber of Commerce in Vienna. Although he was a retiring, almost reclusive, scholar, he gradually gained an international reputation, based on a series of important articles, books, and lectures that championed nineteenth-century classical liberalism. (By this, of course, I do not mean modern liberalism. In the twentieth century, the liberals hijacked the name, but not the meaning.)

In 1938, it became clear that the Nazis were about to arrest Mises as an "enemy of the state." He had offended them not only because of his public criticisms of National Socialism, but also because he was of Jewish ancestry. He fled to Switzerland and eventually moved to the United States, where he assumed a teaching position at New York University.

He died in 1973 at the age of ninety-two after a long and distinguished career. His students, protégés, and devoted fans included economists, small business owners, corporate executives, politicians, scholars, teachers, and high school and college students. Most of his books remain in print and are just as relevant today as when they were first written.

Mises left his personal library to Hillsdale College. He explained his decision by writing, "Hillsdale, more than any other educational institution, most strongly represents the free market ideas to which I have given my life." That is a remarkable testimony—and a remarkable legacy. For twenty-six years, Hillsdale has hosted the Ludwig von Mises Lectures and published the Champions of Freedom series in Mises' honor. We have sought in our own way to keep his memory and his work alive.

Mises and the Fall of the Berlin Wall

When the history of the twentieth century is written, Ludwig von Mises may well be remembered as the foremost economist of our age. Certainly, the history of one period during this century ought to include his name writ large: the one that will forever be remembered as the time when the Berlin Wall came crashing down. The man who took out the first brick was Ludwig von Mises. He did it with such brilliant books as *Socialism* and *Human Action.*

Today's college students were in elementary school when the Berlin Wall fell in 1989. It probably doesn't mean all that much to them. But I can assure them that it was a world-shaking event. At the end of World War II, the victorious Allied Powers—that is, the United States, Britain, France, and Russia—divided Germany into four sectors. In the late 1940s, the American, British, and French sectors combined to form a free and democratic nation known as West Germany. The Russian sector, under orders from Moscow, became a communist state called East Germany.

In August 1961, the East German government began to erect a concrete brick barrier along the border between East Germany and West Germany.[1] Officials claimed that the "Wall" was necessary to keep Westerners out. But it was, of course, really meant to keep East Germans in. They had been fleeing their supposed "socialist paradise" in droves. For example, 160,000 fled in the eight months prior to the erection of the Wall. In August 1962—almost one year to the day after the Wall went up—an eighteen-year-old boy was shot trying to climb over. He would be the first of one hundred reported fatalities over the next three decades. Still, escape attempts continued. East German citizens—like their counterparts behind the "Iron Curtain" in Hungary, Czechoslovakia, Bulgaria, Rumania, Poland, and Russia—desperately wanted their freedom, and they were willing to risk their lives for it.

You and I take freedom for granted. We live in a nation that has, from the very beginning, allowed more religious, political, and economic liberty than any nation in recorded history. But freedom has not been the norm. Indeed, for most of this century, most of the countries of the world have not been free. And millions of people living under totalitarian domination have died.

Socialism (1922)

It is only in this grim historical context that Ludwig von Mises' life and work can be fully understood and appreciated. Mises began writing seminal articles and books on the free market at a time when virtually all of his peers, with a few notable exceptions, were being seduced, and traduced, by the utopian dreams of socialism.

In 1922, Mises broke ranks within his profession and published a very courageous and very prophetic book—*Socialism: An Economic and Sociological Analysis.* This book had a profound impact on the intellectual community in Europe and the United States. It did not, of course, convert ardent socialists into free marketers, but it did lead many students and scholars who had flirted with socialism to change their minds. F. A. Hayek, who would later become one of Mises' protégés and who would win the Nobel Prize in Economics, confessed, "*Socialism* shocked our generation, and only slowly and painfully did we become persuaded of its central thesis."

What is that thesis? It is that socialism, despite all its lofty aims, cannot work. Why?

- Because it cannot predict which industries will be winners or losers in the marketplace.
- Because it cannot provide an adequate substitute for prices, which are the only reliable signals that can tell producers what to produce.
- Because it cannot force consumers to buy what they do not want to buy.
- Because it cannot create more wealth by penalizing productivity, confiscating private property, or redistributing income.
- And, most important, because it cannot change human nature or the way that individuals make decisions.

Human Action (1949)

That last point became the main point of *Human Action,* Mises' monumental treatise on economics, which appeared in 1949. This book argues that all theories of economics must properly be based on the supremacy of the individual. Why? Because the rational, purposeful, day-to-day decisions of ordinary men and women are what constitute the market and are thus the basis of all human endeavor.

Please understand that Mises was writing about economics in a way that was fundamentally different from the way nearly everyone else in his profession was writing at the time. Most economists didn't care about the individual—they cared only about large groups and socioeconomic classes, about statistics and mathematical formulas, about abstract theories and models of equilibrium. Furthermore, they assumed that government was the primary actor in the economy and that government could, and should, intervene to produce desirable economic and social outcomes.

Mises, on the other hand, observed that the market is not made up of groups or of impersonal forces but of flesh-and-blood men and women who make their own decisions and their own choices. He went on to prove that the market is unpredictable, because of constantly changing conditions and because of the limits of knowledge. Therefore, he concluded, it is not government edicts but the millions of individuals—acting alone in their own limited spheres of influence with their own limited knowledge—that really drive the economy, create wealth, and spread the benefits of prosperity.

Socialism versus Reason

In *Human Action,* Mises went on to warn that the greatest danger to Western society would come with the increasing concentration of political and economic power in the hands of the state. He used the example of communism in the Soviet Union and Eastern Europe to point out that the peril was real indeed.

One of my favorite chapters is "The Revolt Against Reason." I believe that it may be one of the most forceful and eloquent repudiations of the modern liberal mentality that I have ever read. It opens with the observation:

> It is true that some philosophers were ready to overrate the power of human reason. They believed that man can discover by ratiocination [reasoning] the final causes of cosmic events, the inherent ends the prime mover aims at in creating the universe and determining the course of its evolution. They expiated on the "Absolute" as if it were their pocket watch. They . . . drafted schemes for an earthly paradise in which pure reason alone should rule. They failed to realize that what they called absolute reason and manifest truth was the fancy of their own minds. They blithely arrogated to themselves infallibility and often advocated intolerance, the violent oppression of all dissenters and heretics. They aimed at a dictatorship either for themselves or for men who would accurately put their plans into execution. There was, in their opinion, no other salvation for suffering mankind.[2]

There is no doubt that Mises understands the ways in which reason can be perverted and exalted to undeserved status. But he adds that this is "no argument again reason," when reason is understood as man's capacity for rational thought. He acknowledges the fact that "reason is man's most particular and most characteristic feature." But in the last one hundred years, there has been a widespread intellectual "revolt against reason," led mainly by socialist politicians, journalists, and scholars. They have targeted economics for special criticism because economics is the Achilles' heel of all socialist theories. By the end of the nineteenth century, classical liberals had thoroughly discredited socialism. And as Mises writes,

> The communist ideas were done for. The socialists were absolutely unable to raise any objection to the devastating criticism of their schemes and to advance any argument in their favor. It seemed as if socialism was dead forever.
>
> Only one way could lead the socialists out of this impasse. They could attack logic and reason and substitute mystical intuition. . . .[3]

Karl Marx, the co-author of *The Communist Manifesto* and the father of Soviet communism, was the socialists' "johnny-on-the-spot" with the handy solution:

> Human reason, he [Marx] asserted, is constitutionally unfitted to find the truth. The logical structure of the mind is different with various social classes. There is no such thing as a universally valid logic. What mind produces can never be anything but "ideology," that is, in the Marxian terminology, a set of ideas disguising the selfish interests of the thinker's own social class. Hence, the "bourgeois" mind of the economists is utterly incapable of producing more than an apology for capitalism.[4]

Does this sound familiar? It certainly should. Modern liberals with anticapitalist bias basically parrot Marx when they argue that the free market system allows the "rich to get rich at the expense of the poor," that "self-interest and the profit motive lead to exploitation," and that "government must regulate the economy to prevent 'unfair competition' and 'economic injustice.'" And it doesn't stop with economics. The revolt against reason, which Mises saw concentrated in economics, has spread to modern education. And it now has a name: Political correctness. Political correctness has three main doctrines. The first is that there are certain ideas, issues, and actions that are simply unacceptable within the academic community and that it is the main mission of education to eradicate them. That is why hundreds of schools have attempted to enforce speech codes and "sensitivity training" and to punish students who don't buy into the establishment's liberal biases.

The second doctrine of political correctness is that all differences in ideas, values, and lifestyles are equally valid, and any attempt to prefer one over the other—or to devote more attention to one than to the other—is an act of prejudice. Moreover, the differences between people—blacks and whites, men and women, rich and poor, Westerners and non-Westerners—are more important than any qualities they share in common. For this reason, political correctness holds that questions of race, gender, class, and power are the real issues that govern the economy and every other area of life.

The third doctrine of political correctness is that Truth with a capital "T" does not exist and that it cannot be taught. What has been passed off as truth is merely the collective prejudice of the dominant ruling class and culture. Students must be shown how to deconstruct what they think is true. If you ask, "How, if truth does not exist, can anyone believe in political correctness?" you have caught onto the contradiction in this doctrine. But, as Mises often pointed out, some academics thrive on contradiction.

Mises would have been disappointed, but not disheartened, by this new "front" in the war against reason. In his lifetime, he witnessed the Great Depression and two world wars. He was forced to give up his home, his possessions, and his country to escape execution at the hands of the Nazis. Even in those dark times, he found cause for optimism and hope.

I knew him when we were both involved with the Foundation for Economic Education in New York. Imagine a short-statured, distinguished, very proper old gentleman. Lew was a very formal man with Old World manners who immediately put you in mind of turn-of-the-century Vienna. But he had a sense of humor, too. He liked to use the occasional joke or humorous aside to pierce common socialist presumptions. He knew that if economics was about human action, it had to be taught with humanity.

Ludwig von Mises never gave up on the battle for freedom. He never stopped believing that reason and truth would ultimately triumph. Let us share his faith; let us perpetuate it.

Notes

[1]The border necessitated a system of staggered natural and manmade barriers, including barbed wire, trenches, and the Berlin Wall.

[2]Ludwig von Mises, *Human Action: An Economic Treatise* [1949] (Irvington-on-Hudson, NY: Foundation for Economic Education, 4th rev. ed., 1996), p. 72.

[3]Ibid., pp. 73–74.

[4]Ibid., p. 74

Richard M. Ebeling

Two Variations on the Austrian Monetary Theme: Ludwig von Mises and Joseph A. Schumpeter on the Business Cycle

Mises and Schumpeter at the University of Vienna, and After

Ludwig von Mises entered the University of Vienna as a student in 1900. A year later, Joseph Schumpeter began his matriculation there as well. Both received their doctoral degrees in Roman and Canon Law in 1906.

These were exciting years to be a student at the University of Vienna for anyone interested in economics, especially Austrian economics. Following is a very abridged selection illustrating the faculty and course offerings in economics during this time:[1]

Eugen von Böhm-Bawerk (returned to teaching summer semester 1905, after serving as Finance Minister of Austria-Hungary)
  Introduction to Economics
  Investigations into Political Economy
  Topics on Themes in Economic Theory (for advanced students only; began summer semester 1906)
Karl Grünberg
  Introduction to Economics
  History of Economics
  Economic History of Recent Time
  On Socialism
Johann von Komorzynski
  Fundamental Principles of Economics
  The Theory of Prices

Credit and Banking
Direct Personal Income Tax in Austria
Victor Mataja
Investigations into Social Policy
Carl Menger (retired summer semester 1903)
Introduction to Economics
Public Finance with Special Consideration to Austrian Tax Law
Robert Meyer
Investigations into Public Finance
Eugen von Philippovich
Introduction to Economics
Economic Policy
Public Finance with Special Consideration to Austrian Tax Law
Richard Schüller *(Privatdozent)*
International Trade Policy
Friedrich von Wieser (replaced Menger winter semester 1903)
Introduction to Economics
Economic Policy
Public Finance with Special Consideration to Austrian Tax Law
Theory of Money

In 1906, both Mises and Schumpeter participated in Böhm-Bawerk's advanced seminar, along with Otto Bauer (a leading Austrian socialist of the postwar period), Rudolf Hilferding (a leading Marxist), Emil Lederer (a socialist and later co-founder of the Graduate Faculty at the New School for Social Research in New York), and Felix Somary (later a prominent banker and diplomat).

Mises, in his *Notes and Recollections*, described the seminar:

> When Böhm-Bawerk opened his seminar it was a great day in the history of the University and the development of economics. As the subject matter of the first seminar, Böhm-Bawerk chose the fundamentals of the theory of value. From his Marxian position, Otto Bauer sought to dissect the subjectivism of the Austrian value theory. With the other members of the seminar in the background, the discussion between Bauer and Böhm-Bawerk filled the whole semester. Bauer's brilliant intellect was very impressive; he was a worthy opponent of the great master whose critique had mortally wounded Marxian economics. I believe that in the end Bauer had to admit to himself also that the Marxian labor theory of value was untenable.[2]

Mises does not tell of his own contributions to that seminar, but in his memorial essay on Schumpeter's life and work, Gottfried Haberler reported, "A member of that seminar told the author of the present essay that in the heated debates between Böhm-Bawerk and the Marxists, Schumpeter attracted general attention through his cool, scientific detachment. The seemingly playful manner in which he took part in the discussion . . . was evidently mistaken by many for a lack of seriousness or an artificial mannerism."[3]

In 1909, Schumpeter was given the status of *Privatdozent* at the University of Vienna. In the summer semester 1909, he taught an "Introduction to the Study of Political Economy for Beginners," and in the winter semester 1910, he offered "The Entrepreneur and the Capitalist (An Analysis of the Modern Economy, with Special Consideration to the Capitalistic Tendency Towards Concentration and Its Relation to the Money Market)." In 1909, he was appointed professor of political economy at the University of Czernowitz in the eastern part of the Austro-Hungarian Empire. And in 1911, he accepted a position on the faculty at the University of Graz, 150 miles south of Vienna, which he held until 1921. In late 1918–early 1919, he served on a commission for the socialization of industry in Berlin. From March to October 1919, Schumpeter was Finance Minister of Austria. In 1921 he became president of the Biedermann Bank in Vienna, which went bankrupt in 1924. In 1925, he accepted a chair at the University of Bonn, Germany. During 1927–28 and 1930, he was a visiting professor at Harvard University. He accepted a permanent position at Harvard in 1932 and remained there until his death in 1950.[4]

Mises received his status as *Privatdozent* at the University of Vienna in 1913. For the winter semester 1913–1914, he taught a course called "Money and Banking." For the summer semester 1914, he taught "Bank Credit." Then in the late summer of 1914, his army reserve unit was called up for active duty, and Mises spent the next three and half years as an artillery officer, most of the time on the eastern front. In late spring 1918, he was called back to Vienna to serve as an economic analyst for the Austrian General Staff, after having been the officer in charge of Military Currency Control in Austrian-occupied Ukraine following the Treaty of Brest-Litovsk in March 1918. In 1919, he resumed his teaching as a *Privatdozent* at the University of Vienna and continued to do so every semester until he moved to Geneva in October 1934 as Professor of International Economic Relations at the Graduate Institute of International Studies. He had been employed, beginning in 1909, at the Austrian Chamber of Commerce as an economic advisor and analyst, a position he formally held until 1938. In 1920, he organized his famous *Privatseminar*, which continued until the late spring of 1934. He left Geneva in July 1940 and moved to the United States, where he lived until his death in 1973. From 1945 to 1969, he was a visiting professor in the Graduate School of Business Administration at New York University.

(An interesting commonality between Mises and Schumpeter is that both were offered visiting professorships in Japan in the mid-1920s, and both turned the offer down.)

Was Schumpeter an Austrian?

To suggest that both Mises and Schumpeter offered variations on the "Austrian" monetary theme in some of their writings implies that both were in some since members or adherents or users of the methods of the Austrian School of Economics. There would be little dispute about Ludwig von Mises' credentials in this context, but Schumpeter is a different matter. Mises stated in no uncertain terms, "Because Austrian economics is a theory of human action, Schumpeter does not belong to the Austrian School. . . . Economics, to him, is a theory of 'economic quantities,' and not of human action. Schumpeter's *Theory of Economic Development* is a typical product of the equilibrium theory."[5] Friedrich A. Hayek, too, argued that while having been trained at the University of Vienna under Wieser and Böhm-Bawerk, "In the course of time he moved further away from the characteristic tenets of the Austrian School so that it became increasingly doubtful later whether he could still be counted as a member of that group."[6]

One has only to refer to Schumpeter's own words on this matter. In his first book, *The Nature and Essence of Theoretical Economics*, published in 1908, Schumpeter declared, "From a methodological and epistemological viewpoint, pure economics is a 'natural science' and its theorems are 'laws of nature.'"[7] In the same year that his first book appeared, he wrote a letter to Leon Walras in which he said, "I shall always try to work on the foundations that you have laid and to continue your efforts."[8] And there are, of course, the famous passages from his *History of Economic Analysis*, in which he said that "as far as a pure theory is concerned, Walras is in my opinion the greatest of all economists. His system of economic equilibrium, uniting, as it does, the quality of 'revolutionary' creativeness with the quality of classic synthesis, is the only work by an economist that will stand comparison with the achievements of theoretical physics."[9] While the Austrians had found the right starting point in the concept of marginal utility, they could not climb all the way up the analytical ladder that led to Walrasian general equilibrium because of their "defective technique" that prevented them from understanding "the meaning of a set of simultaneous equations."[10]

The Austrians' defective technique, in Schumpeter's view, was their insistence on a "causal–genetic" theory.[11] Indeed, Böhm-Bawerk had taken Schumpeter to task for rejecting the causal–genetic approach, saying, "Under the admitted influence of a certain epistemological school of the natural sciences, Schumpeter, for instance, wants to avoid the concepts of cause and effect and substitute for them the 'more perfect' mathematical concept of 'function'. . . . The *cirulus vitiosus* and the *petitio principii* lose their logical fear if we no longer distinguish between cause and effect, between which causality proceeds in a certain direction, but if we merely recognize mutual interdependency."[12]

On the other side, Israel Kirzner, in his own expositions on the Austrian theory of entrepreneurship, has pointed out many similarities between his own conception of the entrepreneur and that of Schumpeter's, while still making it clear that the emphases in the two conceptions of the role of the entrepreneur in the market process are not the same.[13] And Erich Streissler, in an essay on "Schumpeter and Hayek: On Some Similarities in Their Thought," argued that in the early part of the twentieth century, Schumpeter "took up so many of the ideas then current only in the Austrian economic tradition that any hypothetical historian of economic thought, not knowing Schumpeter to be an Austrian, could immediately trace him to this school. . . . [T]he innovative 'Schumpeterian' entrepreneur, the glorified figure of the capitalist process, is actually one of Wieser's ideas, which Schumpeter merely amplified and embellished."[14] And on the topic of credit expansion and the business cycle, Streissler even went so far as to say that he considered Schumpeter's version to be more "Austrian" in some ways than the formulations developed by either Mises or Hayek![15]

The books by Mises and Schumpeter most relevant for such a comparison are, of course, Mises' *Theory of Money and Credit* and Schumpeter's *Theory of Economic Development.* Schumpeter's book first appeared in 1911. Mises' was published the next year. Both issued revised editions at about the same time, with the second edition of Mises' *Theory of Money and Credit* appearing in 1924, and Schumpeter's second edition of *The Theory of Economic Development* in 1926. The English translations of *The Theory of Money and Credit*[16] and *The Theory of Economic Development*[17] appeared in 1934.

Schumpeter presented briefer, English-language expositions, first in "The Explanation of the Business Cycle," published in *Economica* (December 1927)[18] and then again in "The Instability of Capitalism," which appeared in the *Economic Journal* (September, 1928).[19] Mises published a restatement of his theory of the business cycle in the monograph *Monetary Stabilization and Cyclical Policy* in 1928.[20] (An English translation of Mises' monograph had been sent to T. E. Gregory of the London School of Economics in 1930 for assistance in finding a British publisher; unfortunately, no publisher could be found and this earlier translated manuscript is now lost.)

It is in the context of these writings (and a few others) that we will discuss their theories of credit expansion and the business cycle. What are the common elements that can be seen in their expositions? I would suggest they are: (a) the non-neutrality of money; (b) that credit expansion has the ability to create a discrepancy between savings and investment; (c) that such a credit expansion can bring about a redirection of investment activities through a process of "forced savings"; and, (d) the "boom" phase of the business cycle eventually results in a depression, and this depression phase is a "normal" and "healthy" process that brings the market economy back to equilibrium. But the "stories" they tell in using these ideas are quite different.

Schumpeter's Theory of Economic Development and the Business Cycle

In the famous essay "Money and the Social Product," published in 1917/1918, Schumpeter attempted to formulate a theory of the value of money using a variation of the equation of exchange.[21] He points out that his analytical framework is built on the earlier writings of such economists as Menger, Wieser, Knut Wicksell, Walras, Alfred Marshall, Irving Fisher, and Edwin Kemmer. But he adds in a footnote, "A book whose power and originality the critics have overlooked because of some minor points, is that of von Mises," referring to *The Theory of Money and Credit.*[22] In *The Theory of Economic Development,* Schumpeter accepted the Austrian causal–genetic theory of the origin of money and its value and referred to Mises' *Theory of Money and Credit* for a demonstration that the theory did not suffer from circular reasoning in explaining the value of money.[23] And he credited Mises with having coined the "extremely happy expression 'forced saving,'" though Mises later denied that he had either invented or even used the term, but he did say, "To be sure, I described the phenomena" in *The Theory of Money and Credit.*[24] Our interest is not with the particular theoretical construction Schumpeter developed for his theory of the value of money (other than to point out parenthetically that he did not develop his framework in a way that would be totally consistent with his own vehement defense of methodological individualism).[25]

In the latter part of the essay he turns to a discussion of the "dynamic" aspects that result from changes in the quantity of money. Though at several points in the analysis he emphasizes that in the long run the general effect of an increase in the supply of money is a rise in prices, with no necessary change in the total quantity or composition of goods and services produced, he then discusses the non-neutral manner in which changes in the quantity of money can in fact influence "real relationships" in the market.

> To begin with, increases in the quantity of money never occur uniformly for all people. Further, people are never completely aware of the nature of the process, so that, at least for some time, they act as if they received higher incomes, when the

> sum of incomes remains constant. For both reasons, prices never rise uniformly—neither the prices for consumer goods relative to each other nor the prices of consumer goods relative to those of the means of production. Thereby the price rise ceases to be merely nominal. It means a real shift of wealth on the market for consumer goods and a real shift of power on the market for the means of production, and it affects the quantities of commodities and the whole productive process. No doubt, not all these effects are permanent. . . . But very frequently such re-establishment of the status quo is impossible. Newly-won positions may be permanently held and old ones permanently lost, and much in the life of the economy may thereby change—forms of business organization, direction and methods of production, etc.[26]

Schumpeter analyzes the pattern of events that are likely to arise from increases in the quantity of money when its origin is (a) an increase in the quantity of gold-money entering the economy, either as additional consumer demand for final output or an increase in specie reserves in the banking system as some of that deposited gold becomes a basis for new loan-making; (b) an increase in fiat money for financing government spending, such as in wartime; (c) the creation of additional bank credit without additional gold reserves as backing, and the accompanying lowering of the interest rate to induce additional borrowing for investment purposes; (d) an increased demand for investment borrowing by entrepreneurs, which is satisfied through an expansion of bank credit without a prior lowering of the interest rate.

The initial impact occurs when the money has entered the economy and first affects the markets, depending on how that additional money is used to increase money demand. The effect then sequentially spreads through the rest of the economy, influencing the pattern of relative demands, the allocations of real resources among sectors of the economy, and the relative income positions of various groups in the society. The specific consequences will depend precisely on the paths by which the money spreads itself through the economy.[27]

The importance of the non-neutrality of money was clearly an aspect of monetary analysis that Schumpeter never abandoned.

In his *History of Economic Analysis,* which was his last major enterprise, he pointed out that "the Austrian way of emphasizing the behavior or decisions of individuals and of defining exchange value of money with respect to individual commodities rather than in respect to a price level of one kind or another has its merits, particularly in the analysis of an inflationary process; it tends to replace a simple but inadequate picture by one which is less clear-cut but more realistic and richer in results."[28]

But it is in *The Theory of Economic Development* that Schumpeter constructed his conception of the role of credit expansion, forced savings, and the business cycle. The starting point of his analysis is an explanation of the circular flowing economy in which the patterns of consumer demand, the methods of production, and the quantities and distribution of the means of production are assumed to be unchanging. Thus the processes of production and the streams of expenditures as payment for factor services repeat themselves in the same relative patterns period after period. Likewise, the finished goods created by the processes of production meet the same relative structure of demand for that output, with the same stream of receipts from sales of final output. In the circular flow, the prices of the factors of production fully reflect their imputed value from the value of consumer goods. As a result, cost prices equal sale prices for an equilibrium throughout the entire economy.[29]

Since production is perfectly synchronized with consumption and is repeated period after period, Schumpeter reaches his peculiar conclusion that in the stationary economy labor and land absorb all income, with no implicit interest income earned by savers (or capitalists), because savings is not required in the equilibrium of the circular flow.[30] Each period the owners of the firms that produce goods earn receipts equal to the sums they need to purchase the same relative quantities of factors of production to repeat the production processes in the next period. Hence, "waiting" appears not to be required; and if waiting is not required, then what "premium" is needed since no time-sacrifice is incurred?

Of course, it is the very focus on the repetition of the production processes in an equilibrium that led Schumpeter to the false notion that in the circular flow an implicit interest return for forgoing present consumption seems unnecessary. Even in the stationary economy, the owners of the firms who direct the means of production in their repeated productions have the choice to continue their production processes or withhold a portion (or even all) of the receipts from rehiring and repurchasing the factors of production they employed last period, and utilize those receipts for other purposes. Schumpeter said that the owners of the firms receive a "wage" for managing the production processes, and therefore their wages are part of the full imputation of the value of final output to labor and land. But hidden in these managerial wages must, therefore, be a premium for not consuming any portion of the receipts needed to continue the production processes in the same way each period. The owner-managers are, in fact, acting as their own capitalists in providing the factors of production with income until the next period's production processes are completed.[31]

Schumpeter does not argue that no change occurs in his conception of the circular flow. There can be changes in population and resulting modifications in the structure of relative demands and the availability of capital and labor, for example, that require adjustments in the types of goods produced and even in the combinations of labor and capital with which they are manufactured. But what is crucial for him in this process of adjustment and change within the circular flow is that they do not involve "revolutionary" changes in the methods of production. They are merely adaptations of the given resources and technological knowledge to moderate or incremental shifts in the relative demands for goods and combinations of the factors of production. They require nothing more from the managers of the production processes than marginal adjustments within the existing order of things in the market economy. As such, they introduce no inherent instabilities or difficulties of productive transformation within the economic system.[32]

Development, as understood by Schumpeter, involves something quiet different: "Development in our sense is a distinct phenomenon, entirely foreign to what can be observed in the circular flow or in the tendency towards equilibrium. It is a spontaneous and discontinuous change in the channels of the flow, disturbance of equilibrium, which forever alters and displaces the equilibrium state previously existing."[33]

What types of changes, then, represent "development"? They are: (a) a new good or a significant change in the quality of the good marketed; (b) new methods of production with which goods are produced; (c) the opening up of new markets, that dramatically transforms economic activities; (d) the discovery and utilization of new resources; and (e) radical changes in the organizational structures of industry.[34]

For these developmental changes the means of production must be combined in new, revolutionary ways. It involves withdrawing the means of production from their routine and repeated processes of production in the circular flow and redirecting them into new channels not known or utilized before. Eventually these radically new ways of doing productive activities will be absorbed and routinized and be made part of a new pattern of a circular flow. But in the period between their initiation and their integration, the market economy is thrown into a setting in which the preceding production and equilibrium conditions no longer serve as a benchmark from which to evaluate the economic relationships of the market.

"Enterprise" is the name Schumpeter assigns to this process. And "entrepreneurs" are those who bring about these transformations. In Schumpeter's circular flow, however, neither enterprise nor entrepreneurship exist. In the circular flow there are neither profits nor losses and no new methods of production. The businessman is merely the overseer of standardized processes. "[E]veryone is an entrepreneur only when he actually 'carries out new combinations,' and loses that character as soon as he has built up his business," Schumpeter argued, "when he settles down to running it as other people run their businesses."[35]

For Schumpeter, the circular flow, the stationary state, market equilibrium are not merely analytical tools of thought, conceptual points of reference, with which to theoretically understand and logically explain the workings of the market order: They are actual conditions the market not only hits upon but operates within for observable periods of time.[36] There are times when neither entrepreneurship nor development may be occurring within a market to any significant degree, and the economy can be referenced as being so much more or less from the actual equilibrium state conforming to the established routinized processes of production.[37]

Now logically if the market economy is in a state of equilibrium and the conditions that have generated that equilibrium continue and are expected by the market participants to continue, then there is no place for the entrepreneur as the adjuster of production to new circumstances, because there are no new circumstances. But since Schumpeter admits that even in the circular flow of the stationary state, changes can and do occur in the form of changes in population and changes in the patterns of consumer demand, it logically follows that those who direct the processes of production must attempt to redirect the factors of production under their control to reflect these potential changes. They must attempt to anticipate when these changes will occur, to what degree, and what adjustments are needed in the uses and combinations of the factors of production (even in a setting in which the technological knowledge about how resources might be combined does not change to any significant degree). If those who control the means of production fail to do so, profit opportunities will be missed and losses will be incurred that, in principle, might have been avoided. Thus, though Schumpeter tries to deny the title of "entrepreneur" to those who "merely" adjust the given production techniques to changing circumstances in the circular flow, their task is no less entrepreneurial. They, too, bring about "new combinations" to meet new market situations, and in the process, they inevitably think of and imagine new and different ways of bringing about a "harmony" between the wants of the consuming public and the application of the means of production to satisfy those wants.[38]

The entrepreneur is the leader who breaks out of the routine, who has the will, authority, and "weight" to bend the routinized processes of production out of the inertia and rationality of the existing knowledge and ways of doing things. His is not the image of the "heroic" leadership of military combat or political struggle. "He 'leads' the means of production into new channels. But this he does, not by convincing people of the desirability of carrying out his plan or by creating confidence in his leading in the manner of a political leader . . . but by buying [the means of production] or their services, and using them as he sees fit."[39]

How precisely does the entrepreneur lead the means of production into new avenues in Schumpeter's analysis? This brings us to his theory of the process by which credit expansion can create a discrepancy between the equality of savings and investment in the circular flow and the phenomenon of "forced saving."

The difficulty for the entrepreneur in the circular flow is that all the receipts earned from the sale of finished consumer goods are "spoken for" in the sense that each unit of money is earmarked for particular production factors in the repetition of existing production processes. There are no financial means available to the entrepreneur for bidding away factors of production in revolutionizing "new combinations."[40]

Schumpeter gives negligible attention to the possibility that those entrepreneurs who conceive of new, more profitable ways to apply the means of production could enter the financial markets and bid the required monetary resources away from those who, until now, have been receiving loans to continue their routinized processes of production. In his schema of the circular flow, banking as normally thought of hardly exists. The manufacturers of goods receive the required means for continuing production in the next period from the sale of finished goods in the previous period. In this sense, Schumpeterian entrepreneurs have no one to bid against, since existing producers of goods have no intention of parting with the financial resources needed to maintain their own enterprises. Banking, the use of credit, and credit creation come into existence and take on a real role in the market process only in the context of the entrepreneurs' demand for access to the means of production.

Hence, entrepreneurs have only one source for the funding required for their revolutionizing enterprises: the additional credit created for them by the banks to which they apply for loans. Schumpeter distinguishes between "normal" and "abnormal" credit:

> Normal credit creates claims to the social dividend, which represent and may be thought of as certifying services rendered and previous delivery of existing goods. That kind of credit, which is designated by traditional opinion as abnormal, also creates claims to the social product, which, however, in the absence of past productive services could only be described as certificates of future services or of goods yet to be produced. . . . Both serve the same purpose as means of payment and

> are externally indistinguishable. But the one embraces means of payment to which there is a corresponding contribution to the social product, and the other means of payment to which so far nothing corresponds—at least no contribution to the social product.[41]

In other words, normal credit represents savings out of past production, and thus reflects monetary claims against quantities of goods or of factors of production that are not being utilized for present consumption or current uses, but which are instead being made available for the production of future goods. Abnormal credit, on the other hand, represents monetary claims that do not flow from any past production and current savings of goods or factors of production; instead, these additional money claims are introduced into the market economy, and then can compete for the use of those same goods against those whose existing money holdings reflect contributions to previous production.

> The essential function of credit in our sense consists in enabling the entrepreneur to withdraw the producers' goods which he needs from their previous employments, by exercising a demand for them, thereby to force the economic system into new channels. . . . [I]n so far as credit cannot be given out of the results of past enterprise or in general out of reservoirs of purchasing power created by past development, it can only consist of credit means of payment created *ad hoc,* which can be backed neither by [specie] money in the strict sense nor by products already in existence. It . . . consists in creating a new demand for, without simultaneously creating a new supply of, goods.[42]

Thus, "abnormal" credit creation has as its purpose precisely to bring about a redirection of the means of production out of those channels representing an equilibrium nexus of consumption choices and production decisions. The entrepreneur enters the market for factors of production and bids them away from those who have been using them for those routinized processes of production, and "he takes his place beside the previous producers and his purchasing power beside the total previously existing."[43]

This generates a rise in prices, first for the factors of production, for it is through the entrepreneurs' act of bidding up factor prices that those factors are induced to leave their present employments. But this is followed by a rise in consumer goods prices, as those factors of production attracted to these new entrepreneurial enterprises spend their higher money incomes on various finished goods and services. But the essential element in this process, Schumpeter argues, is the phenomenon of "forced savings."

> The price-raising effect of bank money gives rise to the phenomenon of "forced savings." Without wishing to save, people are forced to do so by the reduction in real income through the rise in prices. This releases means of production and the stock of goods at the disposal of the economy for productive purposes is increased, its fund for immediate consumption is diminished. . . . "[B]anking operations" can make possible an enrichment of the productive apparatus of the economy. They cause a shift in purchasing power among individuals and, if this shift favors the expansion of production, a transfer of means of production to those individuals to whom credits are granted by means of newly created credit. . . . New men and new plans come to the forefront that otherwise would have always remained in the background. . . . The banking world constitutes a central authority of the economy whose directives put the necessary means of production at the disposal of innovators in the productive organism. . . . The essence of modern credit lies in the creation of such money. It is the specifically capitalistic method of effecting economic progress.[44]

What sets the limit on the amount of "abnormal" credit the banking system can create to feed the demands of entrepreneurs for the factors of production? Originally writing in the period before the demise of the gold standard, Schumpeter argued that the more new credit created and the higher prices rise, the greater the pressures brought about for potential domestic withdrawals of specie reserves and the greater the likelihood of gold redemption and export of gold for importation of less expensive foreign goods.

Thus the limits of credit expansion are set by the resulting inflation being only temporary and moderate.[45]

How long does the upswing of the inflationary boom last? In Schumpeter's scheme of things, the natural end to the inflationary stage of the business cycle comes when those entrepreneurial innovations and transformations of the means of production are completed, with new supplies of goods coming onto the market, bringing with them a deflationary reversal of the rise in prices.[46] Now the "self-deflationary" process sets in, that is, a fall in prices inevitably follows. From the revolutionized methods of production come increased quantities of goods and services, manufactured in new ways that enable their sale at lower prices because of the introduction of improved cost-efficient techniques of production. But reinforcing the decline in prices due to the increase in goods offered on the market, the entrepreneurs who previously borrowed those quantities of "abnormal" credit for their enterprises now repay their loans; thus, the total quantity of circulating media returns to what it had been before the entrepreneurs received the new credits.[47]

Furthermore, during the upswing the rising costs induced by the competitive bids of entrepreneurs pushes many businesses into economically untenable positions, with a widening circle of business failures or at least narrowed profits. Now when these greater quantities of more and improved goods arrive on the market and sell at lower prices, more established firms find themselves unable to withstand the new market pressures. They are driven to losses and even bankruptcy.

Then, the depression phase of the business cycle sets in. But for Schumpeter the resulting depression is to be neither bemoaned nor interfered with. The depression, he stated, "we may call the 'normal' process of resorption and liquidation."[48] It is the process through which the market economy searches for a new equilibrium, given the dramatic changes in the directions and methods of production introduced permanently into the market as a positive result of the innovations financed during the boom phase. Not only must entrepreneurs find their proper relationships within the new situation their activities have brought into existence, the "mere businessman" of the circular flow must adapt to the changed circumstances.

At the same time, the very disruption of the previous equilibrium, since it has overthrown many routinized relationships of the earlier circular flow, creates uncertainties, hesitations, and rigidities of various sorts to adjusting to the new circumstances. These hesitations and rigidities can only delay recovery and intensify the duration and depth of the depression period.[49]

Any attempts to mitigate the depressionary phase of the business cycle will only prolong the period of normal liquidation and adjustment. The essence of the depression is the need for adjustment in the "real factors," for example, modifications in the allocation of resources among sectors of the economy, the adaptation of new methods of production, and changes in the structure of relative prices among finished consumer goods and among the factors of production. Interventions would only retard the finding of a new set of equilibrium relationships. Monetary expansion to bolster older industries and artificially maintain cost-price relationships that are no longer relevant would only delay the final outcome. Schumpeter argued:

> [O]ur analysis led us to believe that recovery is sound only if it does come of itself. For any revival which is merely due to artificial stimulus leaves part of the work of the depressions undone and adds, to an undigested remnant of maladjustment, new maladjustment of its own which has to be liquidated in turn, thus threatening business with another crisis ahead. Particularly, our story provides a *presumption* against remedial measures which work with money and credit. For the trouble is fundamentally *not* with money and credit, and policies of this class are particularly apt to keep up and add to, maladjustment, and to produce additional trouble in the future.[50]

Though he classes the credit expansion that finances his entrepreneurial process "abnormal," Schumpeter considered it the foundation for economic progress. It is an alien element introduced into the market order that breaks the economic system of the constraint of "given" structures of production. It is a revolt against the wishes of consumers as expressed in their decision to consume so much of their income and not less in the form of additional savings to voluntarily fund the innovations of routine-breaking would-be entrepreneurs.

Instead, they are "forced" to save a greater portion of their income through restricting their consumption due to the higher prices brought about by the entrepreneurs who have bid away resources and labor for their "revolutionizing" projects. A greater scarcity of final goods and services is created due to the inability of the established firms to continue to employ the same requisite quantities of factors of production to maintain their respective levels of final output. The consumers are finally "rewarded" for their imposed frugality when the new methods of production undertaken by the entrepreneurs bring forth an enlarged horn of plenty.

Before the full benefits of that forced savings can be enjoyed by consumers, the market order must pass through a wrenching adjustment to the new possibilities in the form of a depression. The maladjustments must be cleared away for the economy to return to a state of balanced relationships between expenditures and receipts, consumption and production, consumer prices and the cost-prices of the factors of production. What are the "maladjustments" that the market must "liquidate" to return to the equilibrium of the circular flow? The maladjustments are the remaining older modes and methods of production, the preceding distributions and combinations of the factors of production, the past relative amounts of various consumer goods and services produced by existing firms that are now inconsistent with the new conditions that the entrepreneurial changes have created and imposed upon the market order that was and are incompatible with the market order that now will be and must be.

Crucial to Schumpeter's "story" is the confidence that nothing will interfere with the entrepreneurs' ability to bring new methods of production to completion and begin to produce the larger quantities of better quality and less costly goods and services that are their goal. The "abnormal" credit expansion that sets the entrepreneurial processes in motion operates by providing those entrepreneurs with the financial means to bid factors of production away from their prior employments. As a consequence, factor incomes rise for those employed in the new ways; those factors of production utilize their enhanced money incomes to increase their demands for various consumer goods and services; the prices of those final goods are pushed up as well, which increases the receipts of the manufacturers of those finished goods.

But the implicit assumption is that the old-method producers of consumer goods are not able to match and outcompete the new entrepreneurs, even if money receipts have increased and therefore improved their capacity to bid anew to retain or draw back into their sectors of the economy the resources required to continue their levels of production. The entrepreneurs must be "fed" with ever greater quantities of "abnormal" credit so that their monetary positions are always sufficient to maintain their demands for the factors of production to complete their projects. The "periods of production" necessary to bring these new projects to completion must be shorter than the period of time over which prices will have been pushed up sufficiently from these counterbids for the employment of the factors of production, and before the banks would be threatened with sufficiently large losses of reserves that they would have to bring the "abnormal" credit expansion to a halt. If that point is reached before the new entrepreneurial "combinations" are completed, they will be "starved" for cash and left in various incomplete states. The "malinvestments" would then be the entrepreneurial projects for which the necessary credit was unavailable.[51]

Schumpeter in designing this particular "story" of the business cycle seems to have followed too closely Wicksell's analysis of the results from a credit expansion.[52] In *Interest and Prices,* Wicksell constructs a model in which a lowering of the "money rate" of interest below the "natural rate" induces a shift in investment plans from a one-year period of production to a two-year period of production. At the end of the first year, consumers find that the quantities of consumer goods are less than expected, and they are "forced" to save more than they had planned; but they are rewarded with a greater quantity of goods at the end of the two years. As Wicksell explained:

> The real savings which is necessary for the period of investment to be increased [to two years] is in fact *enforced*—at exactly the right moment—on consumers as a whole; for a smaller quantity

> than usual of consumption goods are available for the consumption of the second year. At the end of the [second] year . . . when the two years period of production comes to an end and the available quantity of consumption goods has increased correspondingly, the consumers will receive some reward for their abstinence.[53]

Mises, like Schumpeter, was greatly influenced by Wicksell's analysis. But Mises reached very different conclusions about the nature and the phases of the business cycle.

Mises' Monetary and Malinvestment Theory of the Business Cycle

While Schumpeter attempted to construct a theory of economic development, in the context of which he presented a theory of the business cycle as part of the development process, Mises' purpose was different. In *Notes and Recollections,* Mises explained that Karl Helfferich's claim, made in his 1903 book, *Money,*[54] that the theory of marginal utility was unable to serve as a successful framework for analyzing the value of money was the stimulus for his own investigation into the problems of money and banking.[55] The culmination of that study was *The Theory of Money and Credit.*

In his reminiscences, Mises described the tasks he had set for himself in that work. First, he wished to show the applicability of marginal utility theory for explaining the value of money, starting with Carl Menger's theory of cash balance holdings by individuals.[56] Rather than operating purely within an equilibrium framework, Mises developed a dynamic sequence analysis (which he called "the step-by-step method") for demonstrating the following processes: (a) the emergence of money from the arena of directly exchanged commodities; (b) the "regression theorem," by which he applied marginal utility analysis to the value of money, by showing the temporal sequence through which the purchasing power of money yesterday, today, and tomorrow are interconnected; (c) how changes are brought about in the general value, or purchasing power, of money through increases or decreases in the demand for or supply of money; and (d) the determination of the exchange ratios between different kinds of money (his formulation of the purchasing power parity theory).

Second, he wished to demonstrate, by using the same sequence analysis, the influence of credit expansion in generating the business cycle, or more precisely: (a) the development of two different types of credit in banking: commodity credit (based on fully backed reserves) and circulation credit (fiduciary media, not fully backed by reserves); (b) how the existence of circulation credit influences the purchasing power of money on the market; (c) the relationships between money, credit, and market rates of interest; and (d) the effect of increases in circulation credit in bringing about a temporary lowering of the market rate of interest below a Wicksellian "natural rate" that induces unsustainable, more "roundabout" processes of production that culminate in crisis and depression.[57]

Our concern, as with Schumpeter, is in focusing on those aspects of Mises' analysis that will enable us to understand his theory of credit expansion and the business cycle.

Taking his lead from Menger's work on the origin of money,[58] Mises applied the Austrian "causal–genetic" process analysis to explain the emergence of money from the field of directly exchanged commodities and its value in the arena of exchange. The difficulties that often block successful barter lead individuals to search for other, indirect avenues to consummating desired transactions. The differing qualities and degrees of marketability among goods result in individuals adapting to particular commodities as the money goods that combine the features most useful to facilitate indirect exchange.[59]

The distinct "value of money" originates at that point in time when a particular commodity is no longer valued purely for its usefulness as either a consumer or producer good, but as a medium of exchange as well. From that point on, that good's exchange value is made up of two components: its subjective value for use as an ordinary good and its subjective value for use as a medium of exchange. Over time, as that good's role as money increases through a widening circle of transactions, its market value as a medium of exchange may supersede or even totally supplant its importance as an ordinary commodity.

Since the subjective value of the medium of exchange to any potential holder or user of the money-good is dependent upon its estimated real purchasing power over other goods in the market, Mises demonstrates that the present valuation of money is derived from a "historical component": its objective exchange-value in the preceding period. This preexisting purchasing power of money serves as the starting-point in the present period for the (marginal) evaluation of money's usefulness to market participants. In turn, the resulting interactions of demanders and suppliers of money generate a new array of price ratios between money and the goods against which it exchanges. The new objective exchange value of money then serves as the starting point for the subjective (marginal) valuations of money's utility to individuals in the next period. This does not result in "circular reasoning," as some critics charged, because Mises showed that money's value in the market can always be "regressed" to the point at which its value as a money began (that is, that point in the past at which the good was first used and valued not only as an ordinary commodity, but as a medium of exchange as well).[60]

Every change in either the demand for or supply of money brings about a modification in the value of the medium of exchange. But true to Mises' insistence upon a rigorous adherence to methodological individualism, he argues that any theoretical understanding of how such changes in the purchasing power of money are brought about must start with the specific individuals whose particular new demand for or supply of money sets in motion the process leading to a changed value of money on the market.[61] From this point in the market order the effects of the change in the demand for or supply of money work their way through the entire economic system in a temporal–sequential process, culminating in a decrease or increase in the general purchasing power of the monetary unit.

The shift from one value of money on the market to another, however, will not be neutral in its effects: That is, it will bring about a change in the relative income and wealth positions of various individuals and it will modify the structure of relative prices and the allocation of resources among competing sectors of the economy.[62] Mises' exposition of the non-neutrality of money was clear and concise:

Changes in money prices never reach all commodities at the same time, and they do not affect the prices of the various goods to the same extent. Shifts in the relationships between the demand for, and the quantity of, money for cash holdings generated by changes in the value of money from the money side do not appear simultaneously and uniformly throughout the entire economy. They must necessarily appear on the market at some definite point, affecting only one group in the economy first, influencing only *their* judgments of value in the beginning and, as a result, only the prices of commodities these particular persons are demanding. Only gradually does the change in the purchasing power of the monetary unit make its way throughout the entire economy.

For example, if the quantity of money increases, the additional new quantity of money must necessarily flow first of all into the hands of certain definite individuals—gold producers, for example, or, in the case of paper money inflation, the coffers of the government. It changes only *their* incomes and fortunes at first and, consequently, only *their* value judgments. Not all goods go up in price in the beginning, but only those goods demanded by these first beneficiaries of the inflation. Only later are prices of the remaining goods raised, as the increased quantity of money progresses step by step throughout the land and eventually reaches every participant in the economy. But even then, when finally the upheaval of prices due to the new quantity of money has ended, the prices of all goods and services will not have increased to the same extent. Precisely because the price increases have not affected all commodities at one time, shifts in the relationships in wealth and income are effected which affect the supply and demand of individual goods and services differently. Thus, these shifts must lead to a new orientation of the market and of market prices. . . .

It is only because changes in the purchasing power of money never affect all commodities everywhere simultaneously that they bring with them . . . still other shifts in wealth and income. The groups which produce and sell commodities that go up in price first are benefited by the inflation, for they realize

> higher profits in the beginning and yet they can still buy the commodities they need at lower prices, reflecting the previous stock of money. . . . At the same time, those whose incomes remained nominally the same suffered from the inflation, as they were forced to compete in making purchases with those receiving . . . inflated incomes. . . . For some time they had to pay prices already affected by the increase in the quantity of money, with money incomes related to previous conditions.[63]

Mises' theory of the business cycle begins with his distinction between money proper and money-substitutes. Transactions may be facilitated in one of two ways: through the buying and selling of goods for quantities of the actual money good or the buying and selling of goods for quantities of perfectly secure claims to an equivalent sum of the actual money good. The latter are treated in market transactions as being, say, as "good as gold," if market participants are confident that the substitutes are redeemable "on demand" at full face value. They are viewed in market transactions as being perfectly interchangeable with the sum of the commodity-money they represent since they are supposed to be receipt-claims for the actual specie. A unique quality to money-substitutes, unlike other claims to various commodities, is that they may in principle circulate indefinitely, passing from hand-to-hand, never being redeemed for the commodity money they represent. They may be as widely used and generally accepted as a medium of exchange as the actual commodity money. Indeed, if they carry sufficient confidence, money-substitutes can, in principle, completely replace the actual commodity money in most market transactions.[64]

Mises argued that such money-substitutes could be of two types: "We may use the term Money-Certificates for those money-substitutes that are completely covered by the reservation of corresponding sums of [commodity] money, and the term Fiduciary Media for those which are not covered in this way."[65] Both are accepted in market transactions and are indistinguishable from each other. Within an economic community, changes in the quantity of money-certificates need not have any impact on the purchasing power of money from "the money side" of the economy. An increase in the number of money-certificates is matched by an equivalent decrease in the quantity of commodity money held as cash balances and utilized in facilitating transactions; a decrease in the number of money-certificates is matched by an increase in the quantity of commodity money held as a cash balance and utilized in facilitating transactions. (This assumes no net increases in the supply of commodity money within the economic system.)

In the case of fiduciary media, on the other hand, the result is potentially different. Banks of deposit and money-substitute issuance can increase the quantity of less than fully covered money-substitutes with no corresponding decrease in the quantity of commodity money in circulation. They can do so by extending loans to potential borrowers in the form of money-substitutes (notes, check-money, etc.) without a matching increase in commodity money deposits with their institutions.

To explain the nature of this process, Mises distinguished between what he called "commodity credit" and "circulation credit." But for purposes of clarity, we will use the terminology offered by Fritz Machlup for the same categories, and which Mises endorsed: "transfer credit" and "created credit."[66]

In the case of transfer credit, one of the two parties to a transaction makes a "sacrifice" in the present. Specifically, he defers his access to a portion of his income or real resources for a period of time. His sacrifice is matched by the opportunity the other party now has to use that income or those resources until such a time as he is expected to return what he has borrowed, plus any interest agreed upon as the price for having had use of those "present goods." In the case of "transfer credit," the act of "savings" must precede or be simultaneous with the act of "investment."

In the case of "created credit," the borrower is given a sum of money-substitutes representing a degree of purchasing power over a quantity of goods in the market, with no corresponding "sacrifice" on the part of another member of the economic community.[67] The bank's ability to issue money-substitutes that are as readily accepted and are viewed as interchangeable with either commodity money or money-certificates enables the recipient to have access in the market to goods that no one has voluntarily chosen to set aside for use by the borrower. An act of new "investment" can occur independent of any increased "savings."

This possibility developed, Mises argued, because of the blending of two separate functions within the banking industry:

the depository function and the lending function. An individual who deposits a sum of commodity money in a bank in exchange for money-substitutes redeemable on demand (notes or checks that may be written against his account) has made no decision to defer consumption and save. The money-substitutes are merely a more convenient form in which to hold ready cash in anticipation of possible acts of exchange. "The claim that he has acquired by his deposit is also a present good for him. The depositing of the money in no way means that he has renounced immediate disposal over the utility that it commands. . . . [T]his is not a credit transaction, because the essential element, the exchange of present goods for future goods, is absent."[68]

But banks began to act as if these deposits were in fact savings against which they could extend loans in the form of money-substitutes. Real savings would have involved individuals depositing sums of money with a bank for a stipulated period of time during which depositors could not withdraw those sums "on demand." On the basis of the purchasing power represented by those deposits, loans could be made for periods of time synchronized with the period of time the "savings" are to remain in the bank.

Instead, banks began to pyramid issuance of money substitutes in the form of loans on top of the already outstanding money-substitutes that represented claims on demand by depositors of commodity money. This necessarily meant that some portion of the banks' outstanding money-substitutes could not be fully covered by existing reserves if a sufficient number of holders of those money-substitutes were to demand payment within the same narrow timeframe. "Consequently the chief rule to be observed in the business of credit-issuing banks is quite clear: it must never issue more fiduciary media than will meet the requirements of its customers for their business with each other." It therefore falls upon the banks to maintain a ratio of reserves relative to outstanding claims of money-substitutes that assures their everyday ability to meet potential withdrawals on demand.[69]

This sets an upper limit on the ability of any one bank to issue fiduciary media. Issuing money-substitutes in excess of the economic community's willingness to hold them will result in a drain on reserves though direct withdrawals or by claims from other banks through the clearing-house mechanism. This is no less true for a bank that has centralized reserves within the banking system; it, too, would be threatened with the loss of commodity money to those demanding redemption of their money-substitutes.[70] Only a central bank that renounced redemption of money-substitutes would be free from that threat. But then the collapse of the monetary order could threaten if continual issuance of greater and greater amounts of money-substitutes generated an increasing rate of inflation, which would finally result in money-substitute holders escaping into a "flight for real goods."[71]

In Mises' framework, therefore, credit creation by the banking system had evolved in a manner that exceeded the bounds in which investment would be limited to actual savings. And it had introduced an element in the market order that had the potential to influence the purchasing power of money beyond the limits that would have been set by the demand for commodity money and money-certificates, on the one hand, and the supply of commodity money and money-certificates on the other. Fluctuations in the purchasing power of money, from the "money-side," now could be influenced by an additional factor other than the profitability of the production of the commodity money relative to the demand for it.

Furthermore, the introduction of "created credit" into the market order, Mises argued, set the stage for the business cycle—with few of the positive effects that Schumpeter considered so praiseworthy in the process.

Banks have the capacity to expand the quantity of fiduciary media in the market, but only by making it profitable for potential borrowers to take a greater number of loans. If uninfluenced by "created credit," the rate of interest that tends to prevail is Wicksell's "natural rate." This would be the rate of interest at which savings and investment would be equal if not for the intervention of disruptive monetary factors. Investments undertaken would only be those whose anticipated rate of return was greater than the rate of interest at which the borrowed funds may be obtained. And the "roundaboutness," or time structure, of the investments undertaken would be confined to the savings available to sustain the projects to completion and maintain the factors of production during the "period of production." Additional investment would be dependent on an increase in savings, which would provide the income and resources to initiate more "roundabout" production projects and sustain the factors of production during a longer production period. The shift in time-valuations toward greater savings would decrease the "natural rate" of interest, and the resulting lower interest rate for loans would make profitable potential investment projects not economically justifiable at the previous higher "natural rate."[72]

However, banks can set the money rate of interest at which they actually extend loans to a level below the Wicksellian natural rate:

> [T]he number and extent of these [loan] requests are not independent of the credit policy of the banks; by reducing the rate of interest charged on loans, it is possible for the banks indefinitely to increase the public demand for credit. . . . If it is possible for the credit-issuing banks to reduce the rate of interest on loans below the rate determined at the time by the whole economic situation (Wicksell's *naturlicher Kapitalzins* or natural rate of interest), then the question arises of the particular consequences of a situation of this kind. Does the matter rest there, or is some force automatically set in motion which eliminates this divergence between the two rates of interest? . . . Our task now is merely to discover the general economic consequences of any conceivable divergence between the natural and money rates of interest, given uniform procedure on the part of the credit-issuing banks.[73]

With the new "created credit," investment borrowers bid resources and labor away from the manufacture of consumer goods and from production processes with short time horizons (a lesser degree of "roundaboutness") to undertake investment projects with lengthier periods of production. To attract resources and labor into more time-consuming investment activities, the borrowers of "created credit" have to bid up the price of the required factors of production to draw them from their alternative uses in the economy.

The new "created credit" now passes to those factors of production as higher money incomes. They become the "second-round" recipients of the credit expansion. Unless those factors of production were to undergo a change in time-valuations, and therefore in their willingness to save, their real demand for consumer goods will be the same as it was before the increase in the supply of money-substitutes. Therefore when they increase their money demand for finished goods and services, it is more or less in the same proportion of income as before.

As a result, consumer good prices start to rise as well. But because of the reallocation of resources away from consumer good production, the quantities of such goods available are smaller than they had been, which intensifies their price rise. As the factors of production expend their higher money incomes on desired consumer goods, the sellers and producers of those goods became the "third-round" recipients of the new "created credit." Producers of consumer goods now increase their demand for the same scarce factors of production to draw them back into the consumer goods sectors of the economy and into investment projects with shorter time horizons. The factors of production drawn back into the final consumer stages of the production processes become the "fourth-round" recipients of the new "created credit."

Those who initially had taken the "created credit" off the loan market now find it increasingly difficult to complete some longer-term investment projects in the face of the rising costs created when factors of production move back to the consumer good sector of the economy. A "crisis" begins to emerge as the numbers of such affected longer-term investment projects grow. The demand to banks for additional "created credit" to continue these longer-term projects pushes market interest rates up, creating an even greater crisis in the investment sectors of the economy. The expansionary or "boom" phase of the business cycle now turns into the "depression" phase, as more long-term investment projects collapse, are left unfinished, or are restructured to operate on a smaller scale with less profits than anticipated. The result is malinvestments of capital in economically unsustainable processes of production.

The only way some of these investment activities could be temporarily saved would be for the banks to increase the quantity of "created credit" again. But this would merely set the same process in motion again, with the same inevitable result. If the banks were to try to prevent this inevitable result through ever greater increases in "created credit," the outcome would be higher prices in general, with a threatened collapse of the society's monetary system.[74]

What is the role of "forced savings" in this process? During the early phase of the business cycle, the prices of consumer goods rise as labor and resources are drawn from consumer goods production into longer-term, more roundabout investment projects. Some members of society are "forced" by these higher priced finished goods to provide the means of production required to begin the new investment activities through an imposed reduction in their level of consumption. But the imposed frugality does not last until the more roundabout processes of production are completed. The very rise in consumer goods prices that restrains the buying habits of those whose money incomes have not yet increased in line with the prices of the goods they normally purchase also brings about a countershift toward increased profitability for the processes of production closer to the consumer goods sectors of the economy. Resources are drawn back to consumer goods production, increasing their supplies to some extent and, thus, reducing the intensity of the enforced saving.

But this very reversal toward "less roundabout" processes of production and periods of investment undermines the ability and opportunity to complete the very longer-term investment projects "created credit" initially fostered. The crisis phase of the business cycle shows that many processes of production were misdirections of society's scarce resources, rather than stepping-stones to economic progress and development. Entrepreneurs have not led the market order to a higher plan of technical and productive capability; they have been misled by the distortion of a central market signal—the rate of interest—into beginning projects that cannot be completed or maintained in operation, or which fail to earn anticipated returns.

> Sooner or later, the crisis must inevitably break out as the result of a change in the conduct of the banks. The later the crack-up comes, the longer the period in which the calculations of

> the entrepreneurs is misguided by the issue of additional fiduciary media. The greater this additional quantity of fiduciary money, the more factors of production have been firmly committed in the form of investments which appeared profitable only because of the artificially reduced interest rate and which prove to be unprofitable now that the interest rate has again been raised. Great losses are sustained as a result of misdirected capital investment. Many new structures remain unfinished. Many of those already completed, close down operations. Still others carry on because, after writing off losses that represent a waste of capital, operation of the existing structure pays at least something.[75]

Mises also argued that there may be some permanent improvements in the process of capital formation and the creation of more productive roundabout methods of production. But rather than an inherent and inevitable positive result of the business cycle, any permanent benefits brought forth by the forced savings of the "boom" would be side effects, results of the redistribution of wealth caused by the non-neutral manner in which individuals, industries, and income groups had been affected during the credit expansion. If income is permanently redistributed toward individuals inclined to save, then the "natural rate of interest" will be lowered; some troubled projects may find the savings required to sustain them. But to the extent that this were to happen, Mises argued, there was no way to anticipate it or estimate its magnitude, since it would be totally dependent on the particulars of historical circumstance. Just as conceivably, there could be a change in the opposite direction—that is, a decline in the amount of savings—intensifying the degree to which investment projects are categorized as malinvestments (i.e., misallocations of scarce resources and capital).[76]

Like Schumpeter, Mises considered the depression a healthy phase of liquidation and adjustment, an elimination of maladjustments left over from the boom period of the business cycle. But Mises' interpretations of "maladjustments" and needed "adjustments" were not the same as Schumpeter's. What the depression reveals, in Mises' analysis, is the misdirection and overextension of investment projects begun under the stimulus of "created credit" expansion and artificially lowered interest rates. The misallocations of resources created during the "boom" must now be rearranged for consistency with the underlying "real" relationships of available savings, consumer demand, and the limited availability of scarce factors of production for use among competing present and future-oriented processes of production.

> Credit expansion . . . diverts capital investment away from the course prescribed by the state of economic wealth and market conditions. It causes production to pursue paths which it would not follow unless the economy were to acquire an increase in material goods. As a result, the upswing lacks a solid base. It is not *real* prosperity. It is *illusionary* prosperity. . . . Sooner or later it must become apparent that this economic situation is built on sand.[77]

But Mises' view of the need for market-directed readjustment of production, employment, wages and prices was similar to Schumpeter's. In 1931, as the Great Depression was becoming worse, Mises argued:

> If everything possible is done to prevent the market from fulfilling its function of bringing supply and demand into balance, it should come as no surprise that a serious disproportionality between supply and demand persists, that commodities remain unsold, factories stand idle, many millions are unemployed, destitution and misery are growing and finally, in the wake of these, destructive radicalism is rampant in politics. . . . With the economic crisis, the breakdown of interventionist policy . . . becomes apparent. Hampering the functions of the market and the formation of prices does not create order. Instead it leads to chaos, economic crisis.[78]

The Conclusions of Mises and Schumpeter on the Business Cycle

Credit creation through the banking system was the essence of the phenomenon of the business cycle for both Joseph Schumpeter and Ludwig von Mises. It was the motor that set the engine in motion. "Normal credit" for Schumpeter and "transfer credit" for Mises represent resources set aside from past production to support demands for investment in market equilibrium. "Abnormal credit" for Schumpeter and "created credit" for Mises represent media supplied by the banks that enabled the undertaking of investments in excess of the existing savings in the market.

Both "abnormal credit" and "created credit" provided the monetary means through which entrepreneurs were able to enter the market and bid away resources and labor from existing employments for their new enterprises and new investment projects. This reallocation of factors of production toward these new projects was possible because the credit expansion initially increased the buying power of the entrepreneurs relative to the other members of the society who had not received the additions to the supply of money substitutes. Precisely because money was non-neutral in its effects in both Schumpeter's and Mises' analyses, those involved in the undertaking of existing processes of production would be unable to compete successfully with those whose monetary positions has been enhanced through the increase in bank credit. The new investments in excess of "real savings" were partly financed through a rise in prices that imposed reduced purchases for goods and services on others in the society. The resources and labor required for these entrepreneurs were squeezed out of the market through "forced savings." And both Schumpeter and Mises concluded that the boom phase of the business cycle must end in a depression and a period of adjustment and liquidation.

But here the similarities ended. The initiator of the boom phase in Schumpeter's conception is the innovative entrepreneur; he is the one who possesses the vision of transforming the fields of production. The banks are essential but merely accommodative responders to the financial needs of the entrepreneur. The initiators of the boom in Mises' conception are the banks, who are guided either by the motive of financial gain from extending loans or by the influence of ideological forces,[79] to lower interest rates and stimulate borrowers' demand for investment funds in excess of real savings. The entrepreneurs are induced by the banks to start new investment projects they would not have undertaken if the higher "natural rate" of interest had continued to prevail on the market.

In Schumpeter's scheme of things, the boom comes to an end when the new investment projects and processes financed by "abnormal credit" have been completed; greater quantities of goods now appear on the market, prices fall, and entrepreneurial loans are repaid (resulting in a contraction of the then-existing quantity of credit on the market). In Mises' scheme of things, the boom comes to an end when consumer goods prices rise due to the greater scarcity of finished goods and the higher money incomes earned by factors of production in the investment goods sectors of the economy, as well as interest rates that begin to rise back toward the "natural rate"; many of the new, more roundabout investment projects are now found to be unsustainable and cannot be completed, and financial losses are suffered.

In Schumpeter's view, the depression is a period of adjustment and liquidation. The existing market order and processes of production must conform to the new methods and techniques of production introduced by the entrepreneurial innovators. In Mises' view, the depression is also a period of adjustment and liquidation; the resources, labor, and capital goods drawn into the new investment projects, now seen as unprofitable and misdirected, must be revalued and reallocated for application in alternative uses consistent with the underlying "real" conditions in the market.

In spite of these differences, however, there is one final thing that Schumpeter and Mises share: The mainstream economics profession has chosen to ignore their theories of the business cycle. But what both attempted to do, each in his own way, was to formulate a dynamic microeconomic temporal–sequence analysis in which the monetary elements were interconnected with the allocation and investment of the "real" factors of production. Macroeconomic phenomena were grounded in microeconomic foundations. In this, both Mises and Schumpeter remain ahead of our time.

Notes

[1]I have listed only those professors to whom Ludwig von Mises referred as significant economists at the University of Vienna during this period in Ludwig von Mises, "The Historical Setting of the Austrian School of Eco-

nomics," [1969] reprinted in Bettina Bien Greaves, ed., *Austrian Economics: An Anthology* (Irvington-on-Hudson, NY: The Foundation for Economic Education, 1996), p. 74, or in Ludwig von Mises, *Notes and Recollections* [1940] (South Holland: IL: Libertarian Press, 1978).

[2]Mises, *Notes and Recollections,* pp. 39–40.

[3]Gottfried Haberler, "Joseph Alois Schumpeter, 1883–1950," *Quarterly Journal of Economics* (August 1950): 338.

[4]Haberler, "Joseph Alois Schumpeter," pp. 338–39.

[5]Mises, *Notes and Recollections,* pp. 36–37.

[6]F. A. Hayek, "Joseph Schumpeter (1883–1950)" in *The Collected Works of F. A. Hayek, Vol. 4: The Fortunes of Liberalism* (Chicago: University of Chicago Press, 1992), p. 160.

[7]Quoted in Richard Swedberg, *Schumpeter: A Biography* (Princeton, NJ: Princeton University Press, 1991), p. 28.

[8]Ibid., p. 31.

[9]Joseph A. Schumpeter, *History of Economic Analysis* (Oxford: Oxford University Press, 1954), p. 827.

[10]Ibid., p. 918.

[11]Ibid., p. 908.

[12]Eugen von Böhm-Bawerk, *Capital and Interest,* Vol. 3 (South Holland, IL: Libertarian Press, 1959), pp. 228–29; on the Austrian causal–genetic theory of price formation, see Hans Mayer, "The Cognitive Value of Functional Theories of Price," [1932] in Israel M. Kirzner, *Classics in Austrian Economics: A Sampling in the History of a Tradition, Vol. 2: The Interwar Period* (London: William Pickering, 1994), pp. 55–168.

[13]Israel M. Kirzner, *Competition and Entrepreneurship* (Chicago: University of Chicago Press, 1973), pp. 72–73, 79–81 & 125–31; *Perception, Opportunity and Profit: Studies in the Theory of Entrepreneurship* (Chicago: University of Chicago Press, 1979), pp. 111–12 & 115–19.

[14]Erich Streissler, "Schumpeter and Hayek: On Some Similarities in Their Thought," in Fritz Machlup, Gerhard Fels, and Hubertus Müller-Groeling, eds., *Reflections on a Troubled World Economy: Essays in Honor of Herbert Giersch* (New York: St. Martin's Press, 1983), p. 358; see also Erich Streissler, "The Influence of German and Austrian Economics on Joseph A. Schumpeter," in Yuichi Shionoya and Mark Perlman, eds., *Schumpeter in the History of Ideas* (Ann Arbor, MI: The University of Michigan Press, 1994), pp. 13–38.

[15]Ibid., pp. 360–61.

[16]Ludwig von Mises, *The Theory of Money and Credit* [1912; 2nd revised ed., 1924] (Indianapolis: Liberty Classics, [3rd revised ed., 1953] 1981).

[17]Joseph A. Schumpeter, *The Theory of Economic Development* [1911; 2nd revised ed., 1926] (Cambridge, MA: Harvard University Press, 1934).

[18]Joseph A. Schumpeter, "The Explanation of the Business Cycle," [1927] in Richard V. Clemence, ed., *Essays on Entrepreneurs, Innovations, Business*

Cycles, and the Evolution of Capitalism by Joseph A. Schumpeter [1951] (New Brunswick, NJ: Transaction Publishers, 1991), pp. 21–46.

[19]Schumpeter, "The Instability of Capitalism," [1928] in ibid., 47–72.

[20]Ludwig von Mises, "Monetary Stabilization and Cyclical Policy," [1928] in Percy L. Greaves, ed., *Von Mises, On the Manipulation of Money and Credit* (Dobbs Ferry, NY: Free Market Books, 1978), pp. 57–171; reprinted in Israel M. Kirzner, ed., *Classics in Austrian Economics: A Sampling in the History of a Tradition, Vol. 3: The Age of Mises and of Hayek* (London: William Pickering, 1994), pp. 33–111.

[21]Joseph A. Schumpeter, "Money and the Social Product," [1917/1918], *International Economic Papers*, No. 6 (1956), pp. 148–211; for a critique of Schumpeter's framework by another Austrian economist, see Gottfried Haberler, "Critical Notes on Schumpeter's Theory of Money—The Doctrine of the 'Objective' Exchange Value of Money," [1925] in Anthony Y. C. Koo, ed., *Selected Essays by Gottfried Haberler* (Cambridge, MA: The MIT Press, 1985), pp. 531–52.

[22]Schumpeter, "Money and the Social Product," p. 149.

[23]Schumpeter, *The Theory of Economic Development*, p. 48; though he added that in contrast to when he wrote the first edition of the book, "he would not now consider this way of introducing the element of money to be satisfactory."

[24]Ibid., p. 109; Mises, "Monetary Stabilization and Cyclical Policy," p. 121; see also, the interesting survey article by Fritz Machlup, "Forced or Induced Saving: An Exploration Into Its Synonyms and Homonyms," [1943] in *Essays in Economic Semantics* (New York: New York University Press, 1975), pp. 213–40.

[25]See Joseph A. Schumpeter, "On the Concept of Social Value," [1909] in *Essays*, pp. 2–6 & 19.

[26]Schumpeter, "Money and the Social Product," p. 191.

[27]Ibid., pp. 192–98.

[28]Schumpeter, *History of Economic Analysis*, p. 1090.

[29]Schumpeter, *The Theory of Economic Development*, pp. 3–56.

[30]Ibid., p. 46.

[31]See Eduard März, *Joseph Schumpeter: Scholar, Teacher & Politician* (New Haven, CT: Yale University Press, 1991), Chapter 8, "Schumpeter and the Austrian School of Economics," pp. 131–43, for a discussion of Böhm-Bawerk's criticisms of Schumpeter's theory of interest. On the general topic of the illusion of synchronized production eliminating the idea of a "period of production," see Fritz Machlup, "Professor Knight and the 'Period of Production,'" [1935] in Kirzner, *Classics in Austrian Economics*, Vol. II, pp. 275–315; F. A. Hayek, "The Mythology of Capital," [1936] in William Fellner and Bernard F. Haley, eds., *Readings in the Theory of Income Distribution* (London: George Allen and Unwin, Ltd., 1950), pp. 355–83; and Murray N. Rothbard, *Man, Economy and State*, Vol. I (Los Angeles: Nash Publishing Co., [1962] 1970), pp. 385–86.

[32]Schumpeter, "The Instability of Capitalism," pp. 47–60; "The Explanation of the Business Cycle," p. 25.
[33]Schumpeter, *The Theory of Economic Development*, p. 64.
[34]Ibid., p. 66.
[35]Ibid., p. 78.
[36]See, e.g., his discussion of the idea and uses of the "equilibrium" concept in Joseph A. Schumpeter, *Business Cycles: A Theoretical, Historical, and Statistical Analysis of the Capitalist Process*, Vol. I (New York: McGraw-Hill Book Co. Inc., 1939), pp. 31–71.
[37]Ibid., p. 69.
[38]Rothbard, *Man, Economy and State*, Vol. II, pp. 493–94; on Böhm-Bawerk's criticisms of Schumpeter's distinction between the innovator and the imitator (or adapter) in the processes of production, see Eduard März, *Joseph Schumpeter*, pp. 140–41. A primary distinction that Kirzner tries to draw between his notion of the entrepreneur and that of Schumpeter is that in the latter's conception entrepreneurship involves disrupting the prior equilibrium state, while in Kirzner's view, the task of the entrepreneur is to discover disequilibrium discrepancies that have arisen independent of any innovation. In Schumpeter's framework, the Kirznerian "entrepreneur" would be those directors of the means of production in the circular flow who adjust productive activities to marginal changes in market circumstances within the given market organizational structures and techniques of production. Of course, in actuality, entrepreneurs do both.
[39]Schumpeter, *The Theory of Economic Development*, p. 89.
[40]Ibid., p. 108.
[41]Ibid., pp. 101–2.
[42]Ibid., p. 106.
[43]Ibid., p. 108.
[44]Schumpeter, "Money and the Social Product," pp. 205–6; "The Explanation of the Business Cycle," p. 40; "The Instability of Capitalism," pp. 67–68.
[45]Schumpeter, *The Theory of Economic Development*, p. 113; "The Explanation of the Business Cycle," pp. 36–37.
[46]Schumpeter, *The Theory of Economic Development*, p. 233: "The average time which must elapse before the new products appear—though of course actually dependent upon many other elements—fundamentally explains the length of the boom. . . . This time is determined first technically, then by the tempo in which the multitude follow the leaders. . . . This appearance of the new products causes the fall in prices, which on its part terminates the boom, may lead to a crisis, must lead to a depression, and starts all the rest."
[47]Schumpeter, *The Theory of Economic Development*, pp. 232–33; "The Explanation of the Business Cycle," p. 38.

[48]Schumpeter, *The Theory of Economic Development,* p. 236.

[49]Ibid., pp. 238–39; "The Explanation of the Business Cycle," pp. 34–35.

[50]Schumpeter, "Depressions: Can We Learn from Past Experiences?" [1934] in *Essays,* p. 117.

[51]For a general critique of Schumpeter's theory of the business cycle by a prominent Austrian, see Murray N. Rothbard, *Man, Economy and State,* Vol. II, pp. 747–51; and, Rothbard, *America's Great Depression* [1963] (Los Angeles: Nash Publishing Co., 1972), pp. 69–71.

[52]In saying this, there is no direct textual evidence that Schumpeter was guided by Wicksell in constructing his theory of the business cycle. Yet the similarity is close enough to suggest the conclusion that, perhaps, a Wicksellian influence was at work on him, since Schumpeter was well versed in Wicksell's writings.

[53]Knut Wicksell, *Interest and Prices* [1898] (New York: Augustus M. Kelley, 1965), pp. 155–56, emphasis in the original; see also Richard M. Ebeling, "Money, Economic Fluctuations, Expectations and Period Analysis: The Austrian and Swedish Economists in the Interwar Period," in Willem Keizer and Bert Tieben, eds., *Austrians In Debate* (New York: Routledge, 1997), pp. 42–74, especially pp. 43–51.

[54]Karl Helfferich, *Money* [1927] (New York: Augustus M. Kelley, Publishers, 1969), pp. 525–34.

[55]Mises, *Notes and Recollections,* p. 43.

[56]Carl Menger, *Grundsätze der Volkswirtschaftslehre,* 2nd ed. (Vienna: Hölder-Pichler-Tempsky A.G., 1923), pp. 241–331.

[57]Mises, *Notes and Recollections,* pp. 57–62 & 107–10.

[58]Carl Menger, "On the Origin of Money," [1892] reprinted in Richard M. Ebeling, ed., *Austrian Economics: A Reader* (Hillsdale, MI: Hillsdale College Press, 1991), pp. 483–504, and in Israel M. Kirzner, ed., *Classics in Austrian Economics,* Vol. I, pp. 91–106.

[59]Mises, *The Theory of Money and Credit,* pp. 42–46.

[60]Ibid., pp. 117–46; see also Ludwig von Mises, *Human Action, A Treatise on Economics* (Irvington-on-Hudson, NY: The Foundation for Economic Education, 1996), pp. 408–11; Rothbard, *Man, Economy and State,* Vol. I, pp. 160–65 & 231–37; and Murray N. Rothbard, "The Austrian Theory of Money," in Edwin G. Dolan, ed., *The Foundations of Modern Austrian Economics* (Kansas City: Sheed & Ward, Inc., 1976), pp. 160–71.

[61]Mises, *The Theory of Money and Credit,* pp. 153–60.

[62]Ibid., pp. 160–68, 237–43; and Mises, "The Suitability of Methods of Ascertaining Changes in the Purchasing Power of Money for the Guidance of International Currency and Banking Policy," [1930] in Richard M. Ebeling, ed., *Money, Method and the Market Process: Essays by Ludwig von Mises* (Norwell, MA: Kluwer Academic Press, 1990), pp. 79–81; *Human Action,* 412–13 & 416–22.

[63]Mises, "Monetary Stabilization and Cyclical Policy" [1928], pp. 95–96; also *Ludwig von Mises, Nation, State and Economy* [1919] (New York: New York University Press, 1983), pp. 156–58; and Ludwig von Mises, "The Non-Neutrality of Money," [1940] in Ebeling, ed., *Money, Method and the Market Process*, pp. 69–77.

[64]Mises, *The Theory of Money and Credit*, pp. 67–73; Mises, "The Position of Money Among Economic Goods," [1932] in Ebeling, ed., *Money, Method and the Market Process*, pp. 63–64; *Human Action*, pp. 432–34; Murray N. Rothbard, *What has Government Done to Our Money?* (Auburn, AL: The Ludwig von Mises Institute, 1990), pp. 43–45.

[65]Mises, *The Theory of Money and Credit*, p. 133; *Human Action*, p. 433.

[66]Fritz Machlup, *The Stock Market, Credit and Capital Formation* [1931] (London: William Hodge and Co., Ltd., 1940), p. 224; and Fritz Machlup, *Führer durch die Krisenpolitik* (Vienna: Julius Springer, Publisher, 1934), p. 137; see Mises, *Notes and Recollections*, p. 60: "Fritz Machlup very capably translated the two distinct concepts with the terms, 'transfer credit' and 'created credit.' Only by the making of this distinction . . . can the way be paved for understanding how the creation of fiduciary credit explains the business cycle phenomena."

[67]Mises, *The Theory of Money and Credit*, pp. 296–97.

[68]Ibid., p. 301.

[69]Ibid., p. 362.

[70]Ibid., pp. 363–64.

[71]Mises, "Monetary Stabilization and Cyclical Policy," p. 129; Mises, however, admits the possibility that the purchasing power of the monetary unit could continue to decrease even at an increasing rate, without an abandonment of that type of money in the society, *The Theory of Money and Credit*, pp. 256–57.

[72]Mises, *The Theory of Money and Credit*, pp. 393–94 & 399; "Monetary Stabilization and Cyclical Policy," pp. 122–23.

[73]Mises, *The Theory of Money and Credit*, pp. 398–99.

[74]Ibid., pp. 401–3; "Monetary Stabilization and Cyclical Policy," pp. 118–30.

[75]Mises, "Monetary Stabilization and Cyclical Policy," pp. 129–30.

[76]Mises, *The Theory of Money and Credit*, pp. 385–87; "Monetary Stabilization and Cyclical Policy," pp. 121–22 & 126–27.

[77]Ludwig von Mises, "The Causes of the Economic Crisis," [1931] in Greaves, ed., *von Mises, On the Manipulation of Money and Credit*, p. 183.

[78]Ibid., pp. 201–2.

[79]Mises, "Monetary Stabilization and Cyclical Policy," pp. 136–38.

CHARLES MURRAY

Mises and the Philosophy of Freedom

In thinking about Mises and the philosophy of liberty, I had to come to grips with a tension that exists between what Mises has said about certain things and what I say about certain things. I will give just one example. Here is a quotation not from *Human Action* itself, but from *Liberalism and the Classical Tradition*:

> We liberals do not assert that God or nature meant all men to be free because we are not instructed in the designs of God and of nature and we avoid on principle drawing God and nature into a dispute over mundane questions. What we maintain is only that a system based on freedom for all workers warrants the greatest productivity of human labor and is therefore in the interests of all the inhabitants of the earth.[1]

And then I turn to a much less distinguished book—of interest only because I wrote it—in which I said:

> I have been discussing the virtues of economic freedom without mentioning the point that is now most broadly accepted, the freer a market is the more abundantly it produces wealth. I have not dwelled on it because to me, as to many libertarians, it is a secondary issue. The free market's efficiency is a plenty pleasant bonus. It would be morally superior to socialism even if it were less efficient in producing wealth.

A bit earlier in the same book, I begin a discussion by saying, "Freedom is first of all our birthright." In both, I am expressing a somewhat different tradition than Mises does.

My purpose here is not to set myself up against Mises by any means, but to use him as a point of departure. And in so doing, I am reminded of a quotation from the *Constitution of Liberty* by Friedrich Hayek, which says, in effect, that the case for freedom must be stated anew for each generation.[2] I agree that emphases need to be changed for this generation and this era—not because what Mises said is less true now than it used to be, but because, as Hayek said, "As times change you need to restate the case in ways which make sense and are also true for that generation." In that regard I have in mind two conditions that I think change what needs to be emphasized about freedom. The first condition is simply the huge wealth that now exists throughout the United States. The second condition has been prompted by the bizarre morality play that recently took place in Washington, D.C. and the ways in which concepts of virtue and of character have been subjected to a variety of considerations, most of them ill-advised and philosophically very flabby.

With regard to that, I have two assertions to make. Recalling the quotation from Mises about economic productivity being that which distinguishes the liberal, note that I am going to use the word "liberal" as it should be used. The important aspect of the liberal tradition is that it liberates human productivity and increases wealth for everyone. That Mises made a number of statements of this sort indicates that economic productivity was dominant in his thinking. My first assertion is that economics isn't good enough anymore. The second has to do with the issue of rationality. Consider the following quotation from Mises:

> The organization of human society according to the pattern most suitable for the attainment of the ends in view, is a quite prosaic and matter-of-fact question, not unlike the construction of a railroad or the production of cloth or furniture. However lofty the sphere in which political and social questions are placed, they still refer to matters that are subject to human control and they must consequently be judged according to the canons of human reason. In such matters no less than in all other mundane affairs, mysticism is only an evil. Problems of social policy are problems of social technology and their solu-

> tions must be sought in the same ways and by the same means at our disposal in the solution of other tech-nical problems by rational reflection and examination of the existing conditions.[3]

This is another statement that is true, but which I don't think is enough anymore.

Regarding my first assertion that economics isn't good enough anymore: Liberals today, unlike those of even a half-century ago, live in a society where many of the practical arguments for a pure liberal state no longer carry their old force. It remains true that the welfare state acts as a drag on economic growth, but the problem is that liberalism is such a powerful system that even a moderate amount of freedom suffices to generate huge amounts of wealth. It would have been impossible for the United States of 1900 to install a welfare state without going bankrupt; it is not impossible in 1999 for the United States to have a welfare state and not go bankrupt. We have proved for some decades now that Adam Smith's remark that there is a great deal of ruin in a nation applies to modern economies as well. We can have a great deal of contamination of a free market system and still do very well economically. Furthermore, the drag is getting less obtrusive all the time.

A few years ago, I made a calculation in which I was trying to estimate whether we could satisfy the left's fondest desire for equalitarianism. The left oftentimes says that if you have a really just, socially just, system you will have one in which the minimum income is equal to half the median income: not just a poverty line, not just providing enough for the basics of life, but half the median income is the least that anyone can make. In the late 1980s it looked to me as though we could do that in the United States if we replaced every form of social welfare transfer that we have with a simple cash transfer. It was an iffy calculation then. I don't think it is anymore. I think we could probably take what we are spending now and without question provide half the median income in cash for everybody. And to that extent, a lot of the reasons we wanted economic freedom in the past became a lot less urgent; the case for radical reform is also made more difficult by increasing income inequality. I am convinced that it is correct to say that a great deal of what has happened in terms of income in the last twenty years has been that things have gotten a lot fatter at the rich end of the tail. Whereas the median income for the entire population has gone up modestly, for many years at a time it has not gone up at all. Why is this important? It is hard to say we have to have a freer economy, which, by the way, will enable people at the upper end to make even more than they do now, when we have a situation where they are doing quite well as things stand.

The case for radical reform can be made, but I don't think you do it by appealing primarily to economics as of 1999. I think we have to go back to basics, and those basics have to do with how human beings live satisfying lives. Here are two examples of what I mean. The first example is something we are told that we must worry about by the pop psychology books—self-fulfillment. In terms of self-fulfillment in our personal lives, in terms of our own talents, an old principle stated by Aristotle is extremely apt: People enjoy the exercise of their realized capacities; the more complex and demanding the capacity—and the more it is exercised—the greater the enjoyment. Look to your own lives and see if this doesn't make sense. If you think of something that you really enjoy, whether it is your profession or your hobby, it is very likely that it is something you do very well. And the more you are challenged, the more you enjoy it. If you are a really good chess player and you are put up against a really poor chess player, you won't enjoy the game as much. There has to be the right balance between abilities and challenges.

Other ways in which people lead satisfying lives have to do with some very fundamental roles: those of parent, of spouse, and of neighbor. Why is being a parent satisfying? It has to do with what you accomplish with your child, the relationship you have with that child. If you changed the diapers, dried the tears, helped with the homework, and lived through all of the things that a child lives through, you can take a great deal of satisfaction in being a parent. If you send your child off to boarding school at age seven, after years of being in a nanny's care, it is probably true that you don't have as much satisfaction in being a parent. The same is true of being a spouse and of being a neighbor.

Whether it is the principle of achieving self-fulfillment by the use of our talents, or whether it is having fulfilling roles in our personal lives and social lives, there are a few requirements involved. First, we have to have responsibility for the outcomes. If we don't have responsibility for the outcome, there is no way we can say to ourselves, "I did well." It is not necessary to have total responsibility; it can be shared responsibility, but there has to be the opportunity to be able to say, "This happened because of something I did." Second, there has to be effort involved. It is a very common human understanding that satisfaction is intimately related to how hard we work for something.

What does all this have to do with freedom? It has to do with the fact that those rich roles that we play depend on the individual responsibility for our lives that can only come with freedom. We need to look at what has happened to social policy over the last fifty years in this country not by how much money we have spent, and not by whether we have let people get on welfare and live lives of ease at the expense of the taxpayers. The right way to look at what has happened to social welfare over the last fifty years is that it has diluted our lives; it has lessened the content. It has stripped the role of neighbor and moved the functions of neighborhood to the government offices downtown. For some parts of the population, it has certainly diminished the role of spouse. If you want to know why men are not involved with their babies, why they don't feel compelled to marry, and why women don't feel compelled to make them marry, it can be traced to the ways in which being a father, especially if you are a low-income person in this country, has been diluted.

We like to think that people who have some special skill can be successful, if only given the right opportunities. It isn't necessarily true. Consider, for example, somebody who is below average in everything: below average in intelligence, below average in looks, below average in personality, below average in industriousness. Average means that half of the population is above and half below. (By the way, I have been hissed on college campuses for this observation. They probably wanted me to say, "below the median in intelligence," and were unhappy with my lack of precision.) This means that there are a lot of people who are below average. Take a fellow who is working on a loading dock, and who is not making an impressive amount of money. We can look at his situation in two ways. One is that by working on the loading dock and taking home a paycheck, he can say to himself with perfect legitimacy, "By doing this I am making a life for my wife and my children." He has an authentic reason to be proud of himself. Or suppose this same fellow knows that if he leaves tomorrow, if he does not bring home another dollar, his family will be just as well off as they are now. At this point he is a chump for working at that job. This diminishing of the roles that make life satisfying is a real consequence of social welfare policy.

The second assertion is that rationality is not good enough anymore. I believe that our capacity for reason is that which sets us apart from all other animals. It is our genius, our excellence. And there is nothing in what I am about to say that will diminish that in any way, shape, or form. What I mean, and why I am taking issue with the quotation I selected from Mises, is that many liberals have the sense that if only we get the rules right, everything else will follow. I do not think that this is appropriate. My proposition is that over the last two centuries liberals have steadily retreated from a rich consideration of the moral prerequisites for a liberal state. The twentieth century had many thinkers arguing that voluntary exchange is morally preferable. But we have not had much talk about what kind of culture is required for a liberal state to work. We can contrast that with Adam Smith, probably the most brilliant person who dealt with this issue. In his *Theory of Moral Sentiments,* which in many ways is even better than *Wealth of Nations,* we have a fully articulated discussion of human nature, the nature of social relations, and how these dynamics interact with economic freedom to produce a society that is both cooperative and benevolent. Let me stress that part about human nature. Smith, along with other moral philosophers of his time, accepted that one could not draw large conclusions about political and economic relationships independent of one's analysis of human nature. That seems to me to be exactly right. Before you can decide whether a given way of governing is good for human beings, you have to decide what human beings are like. Are human beings essentially good but capable of being corrupted by bad institutions? Are human beings essentially evil, and so have to be restrained by good institutions? Does man have a moral sense? We don't usually think of these things as having political implications, but they do.

If you think that a certain program will work, that is because you believe human beings act in a certain way. Smith had a brilliant way of stating this. He said, in effect, that he was a psychologist before there was a thing called psychology. He said that human beings are not necessarily good, but they do have a few traits we can depend on. One is self-love. Why does the "invisible hand" work? The invisible hand works because people are pursuing their own interests, but Smith spun this in a way that is fully understandable. He said that there is another mainspring of human action that is very important, and that is that human beings have an innate desire for the approbation of other human beings. Now this could go bad, if you are running with the Hell's Angels, for example. But if you are dealing with other kinds of populations, by and large, human beings give you approbation if you are socially cooperative, socially useful. You can achieve great things, Smith argued, if you rely on these aspects of human nature. He then linked those aspects to the ways in which a free society and economy encourage them. He also understood that human beings have to bring something to the polity before it can work. In this he was right in line with the Founders. Madison, for example, said that to suppose any form of government will secure liberty and happiness without virtue in the people is a chimerical idea. And I could give you quotes that say virtually the same thing from Washington and Adams. The Founders were not Pollyannas in this regard. Read the *Federalist Papers* if you want some very profound statements about human frailty, but virtue was a necessary aspect of a free society. The best statement, the best single paragraph, comes not from a liberal founding father, however, but from a conservative hero—Edmund Burke.

> Men are qualified for civil liberty in exact proportion to their disposition to put moral chains upon their own appetites.... Society cannot exist unless a controlling power upon will and appetite be placed somewhere; and the less of it there is within, the more there must be without. It is ordained in the eternal constitution of things, that men of intemperate minds cannot be free. Their passions forge their fetters.[4]

We don't write like that anymore. It is a brilliant statement, entirely persuasive of the relationship between virtue and a free society. Not only do we not write like that anymore in terms of the elegance of the prose, we don't write about those issues anymore. By "we," I mean liberals. Starting in the nineteenth century we shifted our focus; the economists had a very good idea and a very powerful construct, and that very powerful construct was self-interest. So whether it was Ricardo or Malthus or Carlyle or Mill or Spencer, they could take that construct of self-interest and make it explain a lot. They did the right thing in the sense that it is truly a powerful construct. But they neglected the other half of the equation, and that also extends, I think, into the twentieth century.

Some time ago when I was going through *Human Action* for another project, I tried to find statements about social welfare and how to deal with people who fall between the cracks in a free market. What Mises said was, "It is a sad fact that physical disability prevents many people from playing an active role in social cooperation. It is the operation of the laws of nature that makes these people outcasts. They are stepchildren of God or nature. We may fully endorse the religious and ethical precepts that declare it man's duty to assist his unlucky brethren who nature has doomed."[5] But the recognition of this duty does not answer the question concerning by what methods man should assist the less fortunate. I have no quarrel with anything in that passage as to its truth, but it is a pretty icy, detached statement. What a remarkable contrast it offers to someone like Smith, who wrote in *Theory of Moral Sentiments*: "He is certainly not a good citizen who does not wish to promote by every means in his power, the welfare of the whole society of his fellow citizens."[6] Now I am treading on dangerous ground: I know this because I am myself ambivalent about what I am saying.

A couple of years ago, my wife and I would attend Quaker meetings, where you sit quietly until moved to say something; then you stand up and say it. One time the oldest member of the meeting, a wonderful man of about 90 years old, stood up and read from a passage about Cain and Abel, the famous passage in which Cain, when asked where his brother is, replies, "Am I my brother's keeper?" The old gentleman concluded by saying, "Are we our brother's keeper? Of course we are." In many ways I was a good libertarian because my reaction to that statement was, "The hell I am!" And that is the expected response if you have been told for years that admitting to being your brother's keeper also means you ought to be in favor of an expansion of Medicaid. The fact is that while I sat there, like Quakers are supposed to do, and reflected upon his words, I finally was brought kicking and screaming to the realization that, yes, I do think that we are our brother's keeper in a moral sense: There is a moral obligation upon us to help those in need. But that does not mean that it is therefore appropriate for the government to do so. That kind of recognition is something we need more of.

However, rationality is not enough. This has to do with the notion that people don't have to have virtue to make a free society work. Suppose that tomorrow Russia miraculously got a leader with total power who was an absolutely scrupulous devotee of classical liberalism, and who proceeded to install the perfect classical liberal system in Russia. Every law, every rule about the money supply, about property rights, about everything is exactly right: How long do you think that would last in Russia today? Maybe hours, maybe longer, but Russia has no cultural capital that is appropriate for the requirements of a free society. You have to bring to the table all sorts of trust, good faith, and an understanding that when somebody makes a profit, that is not necessarily stealing. It is not enough to have the right institutions.

I never considered myself to be naive until recently. I had always been under the impression that if I am called as a witness and I raise my right hand and say, "I swear to tell the whole truth and nothing but the truth," it meant something morally and legally. But lawyers have known for many years what we have only just discovered—that those words are empty. They don't mean a thing. What you are required to do is tread a very narrow line whereby you give some alternative explanation, however implausible, for your words and actions, deflecting the situation so that they can't quite pin anything on you. This is a real problem because our legal system depends on people taking the requirement to tell the truth very seriously. We are playing with fire when we say that we can have a distinction between the culture of this country with regard to things like character and the operation of a free society. I do not think those things should be divorced as they have been.

Let me make a simple comparison: George Washington and Bill Clinton. In 1789 the most brilliant political document in the history of mankind was written: the Constitution of the United States. In terms of the framework that was given to us, we started out as best as you can. The story of Washington's eight years as president, when everything he did was a precedent, is phenomenal. Every other leader in our history has been deconstructed to a "fare-thee-well," but we cannot deconstruct George Washington. He remains a tower of integrity, a tower of character and of judgment, who made this political institution work.

In the case of Bill Clinton, forget what he says, because what is worrisome is what everyone else is saying. A lot of libertarians make the argument that this personal stuff is personal, that it is nobody's business. I say that it is precisely those of us who are liberals/libertarians, who believe in limited government, who must understand that in a limited government it is even more important that our leaders be rich in character. That is because the way to lead in a free society is by moral example and by exhortations backed by moral authority.

We need to think about what we mean when we say that we believe in freedom. Sometimes we try to duck the responsibilities freedom commands. Sometimes we lose sight of the basics, caught up in anger over the latest Supreme Court decision, or in our desire to defeat a certain congressional nominee, or in our disappointment over a particularly objectionable law. What I hope we can do is step outside politics from time to time and remember the intensely idealistic vision behind the specifics. Libertarianism, liberalism, limited government—all these words refer to a vision about how people should be able to live. It is a vision about how people may endow their lives with meaning, about living their lives according to their deepest beliefs and taking responsibility for the consequences of their actions. So when we form our coalitions to reach some political end, we need to be careful. Freedom cannot be viewed as something expedient. We need to revere the truth that only freedom enables people to live fully human lives.

Notes

[1]Ludwig von Mises, *Liberalism: The Classical Tradition* (Irvington-on-Hudson, NY: Foundation for Economic Education, 1996), p. 22.

[2]F. A. Hayek, *The Constitution of Liberty* (Chicago: University of Chicago Press, 1960), p. 1.

[3]Ludwig von Mises, *Liberalism: The Classical Tradition* (Irvington-on-Hudson, NY: Foundation for Economic Education, 1996), p. 6–7.

[4]*The Portable Conservative Reader,* edited, with an introduction and notes, by Russell Kirk (New York: Viking Penguin, Inc., 1982), p. 48.

[5]Ludwig von Mises, *Human Action: A Treatise on Economics* (Irvington-on-Hudson, NY: Foundation for Economic Education, 1996), p. 839.

[6]Adam Smith, *The Theory of Moral Sentiments* (New Rochelle, NY: Arlington House, 1969), pp. 445–46.

Hans Sennholz

Ludwig von Mises: Valiant Defender of Capitalism

Soon after my immigration to the United States in December 1949, it became clear to me that I needed some American education in order to compete and succeed in the American labor market. As a young German doctor of political science, a graduate of the University of Cologne, I surely could have found a position as a college instructor of the German language. But such a career, merely utilizing my native tongue, presented no challenge and offered no opportunities for career advancement and financial success. I concluded, therefore, that I needed American knowledge in order to find my way in the New World and that I had to earn an American degree, which, it was hoped, would open all doors.

During the summer of 1950 I visited several universities in the New York area, such as Columbia University, Fordham University, the New School of Social Research, Pace University, and New York University. When I discovered in a catalogue that Professor Ludwig von Mises was teaching at New York University, my choice was clear. I had read his book *The Theory of Money and Credit* during my Master's studies at the University of Marburg and since then had admired him as the most rational and logical monetary theorist. I was then unaware of his many other writings.

When I first approached the professor, stating my hope to study with him and write a doctor's thesis under his tutelage, he was rather discouraging. "Everyone wants to write a dissertation with me. Everyone thinks he can do it," he remarked haughtily. I was hurt, but not discouraged; after all, I had overcome many obstacles in my education in Germany. When I repeated my request six weeks later, he was a different professor—friendly, cooperative, and most helpful in suggesting and discussing a topic for my thesis. He never revealed to me why he changed his mind and consented to work with me. Five years later, in 1955, I was to become his first Ph.D. student at New York University, one of four who passed the school's rigorous requirements.

Soon after my graduation, in gratitude for his sponsorship, fatherly counsel, guidance, and instruction, my wife and I created a *Festschrift* in his honor, titled *On Freedom and Free Enterprise,* which she edited with contributions from nineteen of his eminent friends, colleagues, and former students. My wife presented the *Festschrift* to him at a banquet at the University Club in March 1956. Professors Hayek and Machlup and Leonard Read of the Foundation for Economic Education were our jubilee speakers. A year later, as professor of economics at Grove City College, I persuaded my employer to grant Professor Mises an honorary doctor of law degree (LL.D.) at its seventy-seventh commencement, on June 8, 1957. It was to be Professor Mises' first academic honor.

Throughout his life Professor Mises did not receive the recognition he deserved. To swim against the mainstream of academic fashion is to invite disapproval, animosity, and even hatred; to be a nonconformist is to be an extremist, a revolutionary, or even a traitor. In the eyes of many academics, Professor Mises was an insurgent who meant to restore a thoroughly discredited system: laissez–faire capitalism. They were right in one respect: He meant to defend it against the onslaught of socialism, which, in his judgment, was devoid of truth and contrary to human nature. He unmasked it and fought it with all his mental, moral, physical, and spiritual powers. Yet, he was ever fearful that socialism would triumph over reason and freedom, and that Western civilization, which builds on them, would perish in the end. Although he never revealed it in his writings, he was deeply pessimistic about the future of mankind.

Ludwig von Mises did not live to see the disintegration of the Soviet empire and the worldwide efforts to discard socialism. But just fifteen years after his passing his many students could witness the dissolution of that empire for the very reasons he had described so well in his writings. They could observe how the communist world, which was forever stuck in the mire of poverty, misery, and chaos, finally disintegrated. In 1989, the communist regimes of Eastern Europe collapsed or were overthrown, and a great surge of economic reform spread to those countries. The prosperity of the capitalistic world offered a material example to the East European countries which they hoped to emulate. While many thousands of students and workers were demonstrating and agitating for a "democratic revolution," the intellectuals of the communist world remained silent, having lost their faith in Marxism–Leninism. Their gradual disillusionment with the official ideology quietly contributed to the erosion of communism as a system of political and economic organization.

Professor Mises' incisive critique of socialism and brilliant defense of capitalism greatly contributed to the disillusionment of the intellectuals. When he appeared on the ideological scene shortly after World War I, socialism was enjoying a virtual intellectual monopoly. Karl Marx had pointed the way, and the Soviet revolution in Russia had created a force that meant to sweep the world. Famous visitors to Russia would report that "they had seen the future and that it works." They were convinced that they were living in an age in which "all roads lead to communism."

Indeed, nearly all roads had been leading to communism since Karl Marx had penned his *Communist Manifesto* in 1848 and the first book of *Das Kapital* in 1867. There had been little intellectual opposition because the classical economists from Adam Smith to his immediate successors, Thomas Robert Malthus, David Ricardo, James Mill, J. R. McCulloch, and Nassau William Senior, had propagated a labor theory of value that had opened the gates for socialism. Karl Marx skillfully took advantage of the open gates by advancing his theory of the inevitability of the coming of socialism. It is bound to come "with the inexorability of a law of nature"; it is the final goal of mankind's history when all human wishes and desires are fulfilled. He then fortified his inevitability theory with a doctrine of polylogism that would reject all criticism of socialism as an ugly symptom of selfish capitalistic class interest. He and his followers never tired of charging the critics of socialism with capitalistic ill-will, hostile disposition, and naked selfishness. Anyone who dared to raise his voice against the doctrines of socialism was proscribed and outlawed.

The foundation of Marx's economic teaching is his "iron law of wages," which had been fully developed by his intellectual predecessors—Claude Henri de Rouvroy, St. Simon, Charles Fourier, Robert Owen, William Thompson, Louis Blanc, and Pierre-Joseph Proudhon. The law contends that wage earners cannot earn more than is needed for them to produce enough children to operate the mines and factories. If wages rise above this natural level, the wage earners will produce more children than are needed, which will reduce wage rates again to the natural level. No labor market reforms, no minimum wage law, no labor union can lift the laborers above the level of bare subsistence. They are doomed to be exploited by their employers and subsist on the verge of starvation unless they rise against their exploiters and abolish private property in the means of production, that is, the capitalistic system.

Most of the young European intellectuals were swayed by Marxist ideas made respectable especially by the "Socialists of the Chair," the university professors. The only European scholar who in time answered Marx was an eminent Austrian professor, Eugen von Böhm-Bawerk (1851–1914). He refuted Marx in a chapter called "The Exploitation Theory" in his *History and Critique of Interest Theories,* first published in 1884, and again in a special essay titled "Karl Marx and the Close of His System," published in 1896. He first disposed of one of Adam Smith's casual remarks on which Marx had built his structure. According to Smith, "what every article is really worth to the man who acquired it and wishes to sell it or to exchange it for something else, is the effort and difficulty which it enables him to avoid and to unload on others."[1] Böhm-Bawerk answered conclusively that everyday experience clearly contradicts the proposition that effort and difficulty are the principle of the value of goods. Every day individuals waste much effort on valueless results, quite regardless of whether the cause be ineptitude, misguided speculation, or merely bad luck. And there are many instances in which slight effort is rewarded with high value.

Marx rested his "logical proof" of labor value and exploitation on Aristotle's thesis that "there can be no exchange without equality, there can be no equality without commensurability."[2] Böhm-Bawerk exploded this ancient fallacy: All exchanges of goods and services actually spring from inequality of valuation rather than equality. People engage in exchanges because they hope to improve their well-being. To build a labor theory of value and exploitation theory on such reasoning, Böhm-Bawerk concluded, is to rest it on an abundance of errors, on frivolous assumptions, specious dialecticism, inner contradictions, and blindness to the facts of reality.

By the time of Böhm-Bawerk's passing in 1914, his adverse criticism had reached academia throughout most of the Western world, and the theories of subjectivism and marginalism had become an integral part of economic thought everywhere. He had built on Carl Menger's cornerstone of subjective valuation, had elaborated it, and had used it to explode the Marxian doctrines. In England, Professors PhilipWicksteed, Francis Edgeworth, and William Smart were influenced by this Austrian thought; in America, Professors William Patterson, John Bates Clark, and Frank A. Fetter were in sympathy. But while the Austrians had succeeded in sharing their doctrines with the academic world, they had failed completely to win the support of the "progressive" parties, which preferred to inaugurate "social policies," such as labor legislation, social security, pro-union policies, progressive taxation, protective tariffs, and cartels. The generation that fought World War I learned to rely on authoritarianism, government omnipotence, and "welfare" policies. It rejected Austrian thought for being too "abstract" and instead advocated a "humane" and "social" mode of dealing with problems at hand, all of which meant regulation and distribution of income by political discretion and force. Some critics even asserted that the nations differ so significantly that they require different economic reasoning. Others added that economic principles differ fundamentally in various periods of history. In the fury of the war and the frustrations of the postwar, Austrian economic thought disappeared entirely not only from the European political stage but even from the universities.

When Ludwig von Mises appeared on the scene after World War I, there was no intellectual opposition to socialism in all its forms from guild socialism to Christian socialism, military socialism, national socialism, and communism. The Marxian doctrines of class conflict and of the "ideological" impregnation of thought by the thinker's class membership were guiding the policies of both the defeated nations and the European victors. In this situation, in which men of courage always seem odd and sinister to the rest, Professor Mises' decision to speak and write about what he knew to be true was an act of great courage. In 1920 he launched a counteroffensive against socialism at its most vulnerable point: He published in German a 35-page essay on "Economic Calculation in the Socialist Commonwealth." And two years later, in his book *Socialism: An Economic and Sociological Analysis,* he elaborated his thesis that without market prices and free markets, rational economic calculation is impossible. Unfortunately, an English translation of the book appeared only fourteen years later, in 1936. By that time the government of Great Britain had already developed its social services—unemployment insurance in 1921 and old-age and widows' pensions in 1926. In the United States, the Roosevelt New Deal was busily initiating the social policies Professor Mises had called to account—labor legislation, social security, pro-union policies, progressive taxation, and government regulation and control.

Absolutely certain of his perception and teaching, Professor Mises was impervious to the machinations and expedients of the world. Without consideration for his own position and well-being, he built a powerful fortification of capitalism and its material civilization. His book *Socialism* repelled all the charges made against capitalism—the alleged exploitation of labor and responsibility for unemployment, for depressions and monopolies, for wars and slavery. It stunned the academic world, which brushed it aside as a vain attempt at rehabilitation and rectification of an evil system. A few of Mises students who were surprised by the sudden appearance of the magnum opus began to study it in utter disbelief. His most famous student, the Nobel laureate Friedrich von Hayek, wrote about the shattering impact that the book had on his beliefs and those of his contemporaries. On the occasion of the presentation of my wife's *Festschrift* in honor of Professor Mises, Professor Hayek reflected:

> *Die Gemeinwirtschaft,* later translated as *Socialism,* appeared in 1922. Much as we had come to admire Mises' achievements in economic theory, this was something of much broader scope and significance. It was a work on political economy in

> the tradition of the great moral philosophers, a Montesquieu or Adam Smith, containing both acute knowledge and profound wisdom. I have little doubt that it will retain the position it has achieved in the history of political ideas. But there can be no doubt whatever about the effect on us who have been in our most impressible age. To none of us young men who read the book when it appeared was the world ever the same again. If Röpke stood here, or Robbins, or Ohlin (to mention only those of exactly the same age as myself), they would tell you the same story. Not that we at once swallowed it all. For that it was much too strong a medicine and too bitter a pill. But to arouse contradiction, to force others to think out for themselves the ideas which have led him, is the main function of the innovator. And though we might try to resist, even strive hard to get the disquieting considerations out of our system, we did not succeed. The logic of the argument was inexorable.
>
> It was not easy. Professor Mises' teachings seemed directed against all we had been brought up to believe. It was a time when all the fashionable intellectual arguments seemed to point to socialism and when nearly all "good men" among the intellectuals were socialists. Though the immediate influence of the book may not have been as great as one might have wished, it is in some ways surprising that it had as great an influence as it did. Because for the young idealist of the time, it meant the dashing of all his hopes, and since it was clear that the world was bent on the cause whose destructive nature the work pointed out, it left us little but black despair. And to those of us who knew Professor Mises personally, it became, of course, soon clear that his own view about the future of Europe and the world was one of deep pessimism.[3]

Wilhelm Röpke, a noted German economist and leading architect of German revival after World War II, congratulating Mises on his eightieth birthday, expressed a similar thought;

> I would like to stress, on this occasion, how immense is my debt to Ludwig von Mises for having rendered me immune, at a very early date, from the virus of socialism with which most of us came back from World War I.[4]

With great courage and endeavor Professor Mises actually engaged the enemy on two fronts. He fought Marxian socialism, which had grown roots throughout the world, and simultaneously engaged radical interventionism, the road that leads to socialism. The most ominous manifestation of interventionism in those years was inflation. In central and eastern Europe it largely destroyed productive capacity as the calls for social services and economic rehabilitation led governments to resort to the printing presses. Once started, the widespread disruption of business, the general loss of confidence, and the breakdown of tax collection caused the printing presses to accelerate. In the great German inflation the circulation of marks reached astronomical figures when, by the end of 1923, the sending of a local letter required a postage of one hundred billion marks.

During the war the government of the Austrian Empire had increased the quantity of paper money thirteenfold, and goods prices had risen sixteenfold. After the war the Austrian Republic increased it by more than 14,000 times, which caused a rapid depreciation of the Austrian crown, which hampered and depressed economic output and caused goods prices to accelerate immensely. The crown was finally stabilized toward the end of 1922, which inevitably led to a "stabilization crisis," a painful period of readjustment and recession.[5]

Throughout these months of political turmoil and economic darkness, Professor Mises wrote poignant essays about the follies of monetary depreciation. In 1918 he published three essays building on his 1912 magnum opus, *Theory of Money and Credit.* In 1919, he penned four; in 1920, two; in 1921, two; and three in 1922. His persuasive writing probably contributed to the fact that Austrian inflation was halted one year before the Germans managed to halt theirs. But the net effect of the inflation ravages was similar: the complete destruction and expropriation of monetary wealth. To reduce the purchasing power of 14,000 Austrian crowns to one is to destroy monetary wealth as effectively as the reduction of one trillion German marks to one.

Mises was not just a careful and logical theorist. Driven by a sense of duty and calling, he was a tireless defender of individual freedom and the private property order. In 1927 he published a book titled *Liberalism*, which he defined as the great political and intellectual movement of the eighteenth and nineteenth centuries, giving birth to free market economies, limited government, and individual freedom. He did not mean what Americans have learned to view as "liberalism": government regulation, control, and welfare. It is a book about the free society and about the obstacles and problems lying in the way of creating and defending such a society. He closed the book with a stirring definition of the true meaning of liberty and liberalism:

> Liberalism is no religion, no world view, no party of special interests. It is no religion because it demands neither faith nor devotion, because there is nothing mystical about it, and because it has no dogmas. It is no world view because it does not try to explain the cosmos and because it says nothing and does not seek to say anything about the meaning and purpose of human existence. It is no party of special interests because it does not provide or seek to provide any special advantage whatsoever to any individual or any group. It is something entirely different. It is an ideology, a doctrine of the mutual relationship among the members of society and, at the same time, the application of this doctrine to the conduct of men in actual society. It promises nothing that exceeds what can be accomplished in society and through society. It seeks to give men only one thing, the peaceful, undisturbed development of material well-being for all, in order thereby to shield them from the external causes of pain and suffering as far as it lies within the power of social institutions to do so at all. To diminish suffering, to increase happiness: that is its aim.[6]

Professor Mises labored not only to restore and defend the ramparts of capitalism but also to reveal the destructive effects of socialism in all its forms. In 1929 he published an anthology of several articles under the title *A Critique of Interventionism,* which meant to warn its readers about the road to socialism. Interventionism preserves private property in the means of production in a legalistic sense, but actually is socialism in the economic sense. Legislators and regulations guide and direct economic production.

The six essays of the anthology were directed primarily at readers in Europe where socialistic doctrines permeated the programs of most political parties. In Germany, various coalition governments drawn from the Social Democrats, the Catholic Center party, and the conservative German People's Party pursued "moderate" programs of socialization. In France, the Popular Front, a coalition of Socialists, Radical Socialists, and Communists, would soon win the election and enact harsh social and labor reforms. In Italy, Mussolini, who had seized power in 1922, imposed stringent controls on industry and labor and created a Corporative State directed by the Fascist Party and the militia. In Great Britain, the Labour Party had come to power briefly in 1924. It returned in 1931 in a coalition that took the country off the gold standard and supplanted free trade with protective tariffs modified by preferential treatment for members of the British Empire. In the United States, the Republican administrations enjoyed a spectacular financial bubble; but as soon as it began to deflate, the Hoover Administration fell in step with European governments by closing the borders; boosting its income, estate, corporate, and excise taxes; embarking upon a large public works program; and creating the Reconstruction Finance Corporation to stimulate industry by offering loans unobtainable elsewhere. The Roosevelt Administration followed suit with the New Deal, which differed little from the Hoover Deal and earlier European programs. It created several agencies that were to guide and direct economic activity: the National Recovery Administration, the Agricultural Adjustment Administration, the Works Progress Administration, the Civilian Conservation Corps, the Tennessee Valley Authority, and many more. It seized the people's gold and devalued the dollar by 40 percent. It adopted a Social Security system similar to German Chancellor Bismarck's system of 1889 and reformed labor relations, just as European governments had done long before.

Professor Mises failed to stem the socialistic tide in Europe and probably would have fallen short also in the United States even if all his writings had been translated into English and been available to the discerning reader. Actually, the anthology *A Critique of Interventionism* was translated by this writer and published by Arlington House only in 1977, forty-eight years after it had first appeared. There had been no demand for a Mises book that rebutted the exhortations of the Democratic and Republican Deals.

In 1933, when National Socialism came to power in Germany and the New Deal in the United States, Professor Mises published an anthology of essays dealing primarily with the very meaning and essence of economics. *Basic Problems of Economics: Inquiries into Method, Task and Content of Economics and Social Science* was published in Jena, Germany, at a time when the Nazis already were in power. They permitted its publication either because they had not yet solidified their hold over education and the media or they were unaware of its confrontational content. Their allies in the academic world were aware of its message and, therefore, sought to banish all theoretical knowledge of social phenomena and deny the validity of economic principles valid in all times and places. They rejected economics proper so that they could justify and guard their own socialistic doctrines. Their great adversary, Professor Mises in turn sought to defend the logical legitimacy of economics, just as Carl Menger had done in the *Methodenstreit* during the 1880s and 1890s. Unfortunately, Mises failed as the darkness of National Socialism was about to descend over Germany. In the English-speaking world, progressive governments were reshaping economic activity along interventionistic lines, just as Chancellor Bismarck had done during the 1880s. Students of epistemology had to wait until 1960, when Professor George Reisman translated the essays into English and D. Van Nostrand published them under the title *Epistemological Problems of Economics.* The world had to wait until the 1990s before many governments around the globe began to dismantle their socialistic structures and grant greater measures of freedom to their citizenry.

Mises penned and published his magnum opus, a comprehensive treatise on economics titled *Nationalökonomie,* while at the Institut Universitaire des Hautes Etudes Internationales in Geneva, Switzerland. The book was written in German and published in war-torn Europe in the tragic year 1940, when the intellectual community paid little notice to literary events, being preoccupied with the shocking military news of the year: the German defeat of France and the German occupation of Denmark, Norway, and the Low Countries. With most of the German-speaking world then under the reign of Nazism, the book was completely ignored. But nine years later, after the war, when it appeared translated, recast, and enlarged in English under the title *Human Action,* it was an instant success. In America, numerous students of economics and disciples of the "Austrian School" welcomed a monumental work presenting a profound and wide-ranging discussion of the nature of human action.

The book reveals the great knowledge and wisdom of a philosopher, sociologist, historian, and economist. It presents a general theory of human action of which economic behavior merely is a special case. It analyzes the fundamental epistemological problems of the social sciences and describes the role of economics within the realm of theoretical thought. It is one of the most complete works of economics ever published, touching upon every subject in economics. In a letter to his publisher, Professor Mises himself described the purpose and content of his work as follows:

> My objective in writing the treatise *Nationalökonomie, Theorie des Handelns und Wirtschaftens* was to provide a comprehensive theory of economic behavior which would include not only the economics of a market economy (free enterprise system) but no less the economics of any other thinkable system of social cooperation, viz., socialism, interventionism, corporativism and so on. Furthermore I deemed it necessary to deal with all those objections which, from various points of view—for instance, of ethics, psychology, history, anthropology, ethnography, biology—have been raised against the soundness of economic reasoning and the validity of the methods hitherto applied by the economists of all schools and lines of thought. Only such an exhaustive treatment of all critical objections can satisfy the exacting reader and convince him that economics is a science both conveying knowledge and able to guide conduct.[7]

Within just a few years of its publication *Human Action* was translated and published in the French, Italian, Spanish, Japanese, and Chinese languages; a new German edition of *Nationalökonomie* appeared in 1980. By 1989, when the Soviet Empire began to disintegrate, both *Human Action* and *Nationalökonomie* were found to have been studied widely by many intellectuals behind the Iron Curtain. Mises had helped them understand the causes of their economic inefficiency and the poverty surrounding them. Several Marxian scholars had tried to deal with the Misesian charges that a socialistic system does not permit rational economic planning because of its lack of market prices. Oskar Lange, professor of economics at the University of Chicago during World War II and the first ambassador of the Polish People's Republic in Washington after the war,[8] had made several attempts at a major synthesis of both the capitalist and centrally planned Eastern European socialist countries, at grafting Marxist and Austrian economics. Committed to the socialistic reconstruction of his native Poland, he had sought to build a system which would be different from the Soviet model of polity and economy, preserving markets, market prices, and competition, but no private property in the means of production.

Professor Mises rejected such blueprints for being utopian and contradictory, for playing markets and competition, just as children play their make-believe games. In the world of reality, he asserted, the socialistic managers of the means of production would be working in the dark as there would be no capital and money markets, no stock and commodity exchanges, no trading in futures, and no independent financial institutions. "One cannot play speculation and investment," Mises retorted. Production is directed either by a profit-seeking businessman or by an all-powerful supreme director. There can only be one master: either the consumer who is guiding businessmen or the commissar director who exerts absolute authority over the economic lives of the people.

A steady stream of books and articles revealing the chaotic nature of socialism in all its ramifications flowed from the Mises pen. His *Omnipotent Government* (1944) described the rise of the total state and total war. *Bureaucracy* (1944) warned his readers about the rise of bureaucratism, which is the avant garde of a political command system and the socialistic state. After *Human Action* (1949), there soon followed *Planning for Freedom* (1952), *The Anti-Capitalistic Mentality* (1956), *Theory and History* (1957), and *The Ultimate Foundation of Economics* (1962), all important books in epistemology and economic theory. Every year his pen also produced a number of scholarly articles, some of which were translated into foreign languages—Dutch, French, Hungarian, Italian,

Japanese, Portuguese, Spanish, and Swedish—and read eagerly by the friends and defenders of capitalism everywhere. Mises provided the intellectual ordnance which his students and admirers used vigorously in defense of the market order

The crucial test of an intellectual pioneer and great scholar is that he instill in other men the conviction and the will to carry on. Ludwig von Mises was such a man; he taught two generations of scholars who in turn enlightened more generations of students about the inadequacies of socialism and interventionism. For more than half a century, at first in Austria and Switzerland and then in the United States, he was the dean of liberalism who confronted worldwide socialism, never wavering or compromising, unaffected by the scorn and ridicule of his adversaries, or by the temptations of this world.

Notes

[1]Adam Smith, *The Wealth of Nations* (New York: Modern Library, 1937), p. 30.

[2]Quoted in Eugen von Böhm-Bawerk, *Capital and Interest,* Vol. I (South Holland, IL: Libertarian Press, 1959), p. 291.

[3]Margit von Mises, *My Years with Ludwig von Mises,* 2nd ed. (Grove City, PA: Libertarian Press, 1984), pp. 220–21.

[4]Ibid., p. 167.

[5]See J. van Walré de Bordes, *The Austrian Crown: Its Depreciation and Stabilization* (London: P. S. King & Son, 1924).

[6]Ludwig von Mises, *Liberalism,* 3rd English ed. (Irvington, NY: The Foundation for Economic Education, 1985), pp. 192–93.

[7]Margit von Mises, *My Years with Ludwig von Mises,* pp. 101–2.

[8]Oskar Lange, *On the Economic Theory of Socialism* (Minneapolis: University of Minnesota Press, 1938); Oskar Lange, *Political Economy* (London: Pergamon Press, 1963). Cf. also A. Bergson, "Market Socialism Revisited," *Journal of Political Economy* (October 1967): 655–73; A. Chilosi, "Self-managed Market Socialism with Free Mobility of Labor," *Journal of Comparative Economics* (September 1986): 237–54.

ROBERT W. POOLE, JR.

Human Action as a Guidebook to Modern Public Policy

For those of us who have been laboring in the vineyards of liberty for many years, reading Mises' works at the time we were in college or shortly thereafter was part of the critical information that formed our thinking. It helped us understand the role of government in a free society and the problems of government intervention.

I recently revisited *Human Action* and skimmed Part Six, "The Hampered Market Economy." As you may recall, this set of chapters critiques interventionism by government into the market economy; it examines taxation, restrictions on production of goods and services, restrictions on prices and wages, currency and credit manipulation, confiscation, redistribution, and so forth. It is a devastating critique. Mises, in this work and also in his wonderful book *Bureaucracy,* lays out nearly all of the policy areas in which we need to work to undo the consequences of government intervention.

However, what Mises did not address is how to go about making the changes for freedom. I am surprised, in going through the book and recalling others of his that I have read, that he did not really seem to pay that much attention to the problems of transition. How do you get from here to there? Indeed, in the beginning of Part Six, he talks about a market system versus a socialist system, and he says, "No gradual transition leads from one of them to the other."[1] And then when wrapping up the ten factors that make up Part Six, he says, "We have no knowledge whatsoever about those things which would give our side victory in this clash of ideologies."[2] From the standpoint of someone who set up a think tank, as I did twenty years ago, in attempt to move us from a condition of a seriously interventionist state to as free a society as possible, that really isn't much help. What we need to do is discover precisely those things that will get us over the hump to make the transition and undo this massive complex of interventionism.

Several of Mises' colleagues and students did address this question. One was Murray Rothbard, who took a polar point on this issue in the late 1970s and early 1980s, when he was associated with the Cato Institute and the Libertarian Party. Rothbard maintained that one cannot and must not even attempt to specify how to bring about the transition from a mixed economy of interventionism to a free society. He said that "any particular order of destabilization must be rejected, as should presentations of anything like an alternative budget."[3] For Rothbard, apparently it was all or nothing. Throw a switch (as he sometimes used to say), and there is a free society; we cannot propose anything in-between. Again, I find that very unsatisfying. By contrast I want to call your attention to Hayek, who, I believe, was more interested in the development of ideas that can move society in the direction of freedom. He believed, as did Ayn Rand, that the first important step is to develop a critical mass of intellectual support for the idea of a free society and an understanding of the problems of interventionism, as Mises laid out in *Human Action.* But then, the critical second step is to develop institutions devoted to marketing those ideas and making the proposals to move us step-by-step toward a freer society. That basically was the purpose in creating think tanks.

Hayek, in fact, inspired the creation of the very first think tank of the modern era, the Institute of Economic Affairs in London. He wrote obliquely about some of these ideas in *The Road to Serfdom,* and he said on many occasions, "We have to win the war of ideas. We have to project the vision of a free society. We have to make the building of a free society once more an intellectual adventure, a deed of courage."[4] I took these words to heart a long time ago. He continued, "Once the more active part of intellectuals had been converted to a set of beliefs, the process by which these become generally accepted is almost automatic and irrelevant." Now, I don't think it is quite that easy, but the critical point is that once you have created a critical mass of intellectual support, you then have a basis on which to develop specific policy proposals. And then you have something for political candidates to grab onto, to go out and implement.

It is interesting that Hayek did talk about a step-by-step agenda, although he never laid one out, to the best of my knowledge. In so doing, he clearly had in mind a predecessor movement. Just as I don't believe that a free society is going to be brought about by "throwing a switch," neither did full-fledged socialism in Britain come about all at once. It was built very gradually, with the key role played by the Fabian Society. There had been, in the latter part of the nineteenth century, a slow decay of liberalism and a slow drift into collectivism. The *Times of London* called this "the silent revolution" of increasing government intervention into industrial relations, housing, and education, but the drift became a deliberate, motivated action once the Fabian Society was created in 1884 by George Bernard Shaw and Beatrice and Sydney Webb. Their purpose was explicitly to develop a coherent intellectual justification for a massive expansion of the role of the state—basically to create the welfare state and to develop the tactics and strategy to bring it about step-by-step-by-step-by-step. They adopted two key tactics, which you can read about in a wonderful book called *This Little Band of Prophets* by Anne Freemantle. The two key tactics the Fabians decided on were, first of all, gradualism—small, but systematic step-by-step movements in the direction of the welfare state and socialism. Second was permeation—placing people in key positions in the important institutions of society: that is, people who shared the vision and were committed to both the step-by-step approach and nonpartisanship. This meant being willing to work with any and every politician or party or ideology that could somehow serve the purpose of moving your agenda forward.

Bernard Shaw said, "The Fabian policy was to support and take advantage of every legislative step toward collectivism no matter what order it came from, no matter how little its promoters dreamt that what they were advocating was an installment of socialism."[5] This policy had amazing results—not ones we wanted, but results that changed the world. First, the Fabian ideas really took over and became the views of the Liberal Party. The once proud, once Liberal Party became "New Liberal" under Lloyd George and put in place the first old-age pensions (equivalent to our Social Security), school meals, other welfare programs, and reintroduced protectionism—protectionism from the Liberal Party that had abolished the Corn Laws under Cobdon and Bright. Then came World War I with central economic planning and quasi-nationalizations, and these moves were supported by all parties in Britain at the time.

After World War I, the Fabians persuaded the up-and-coming Labour Party to adopt a new, explicitly socialist constitution, including a commitment to large-scale nationalization of the commanding heights of the economy—the famous Clause IV of the party constitution that committed them to the nationalization of the means of production. Up to and through the Great Depression the Liberals continued to implement collectivism (including the creation of the BBC), while the Labour Party advocated a stronger version of it. By 1940, at the beginning of World War II, the government controled 60 percent of the GDP of Great Britain. Of course, after World War II came the first Labour government and a wave of nationalizations, expanding the national health service and so forth. Full-fledged collectivism came to pass in a span of fifty years due to the implementation of the Fabian design of step-by-step control.

With this background, Hayek talked about first creating the critical mass of ideas and then creating institutions to bring them about and put them into practice. The good news for the cause of liberty is that the undoing of Fabianism, the undoing of collectivism to the significant extent that this has happened in the U.K., did not just happen either. It too is an outgrowth of a similar process of development that was really launched by Hayek and Mises.

In 1944, Hayek published *The Road to Serfdom,* and it caused a sensation. It was the first serious intellectual opposition to the collectivist vision of the Fabians. The U.S. edition, published by the University of Chicago Press, was far more popular than the original British version. Even more influential was the *Reader's Digest* condensed version of this relatively short book. It sold millions. Hayek did a book tour throughout the United States supported by business people. That led the remnant of classical liberalism, including Mises and a young Milton Friedman, to respond to Hayek's call for an international meeting in 1947 on a mountain in Switzerland—Mont Pèlerin. Thirty-eight classical liberal economists and other thinkers gathered and decided to form a global networking organization. You must realize the importance of this. After World War II, everyone assumed that socialism, collectivism, and interventionism would be the wave of the future. It was everywhere; it was the "intellectual" approach. Although Europe had been practically destroyed by the war, there remained a handful of people who still carried the flame of liberal ideas. The idea of networking—in those days before inexpensive international flights and trans-Atlantic phone service, and long before the Internet—was absolutely critical. It was crucially important to build the core of intellectual support.

Then the Institute of Economic Affairs (IEA) was created, the first free market think tank. Again Hayek played a key role. Antony Fisher, who started the IEA, was a former RAF pilot who had read the *Reader's Digest* condensed version of *The Road to Serfdom.* He was excited by its wonderful intellectual challenge, and his immediate reaction was to contribute money to politicians who would implement his vision. So Fisher sought out Hayek, who was at the London School of Economics at the time, and asked him: "What should I do? Which politicians should I support?" Hayek replied, "No. No. No. No. No. It's not time for that yet. What you've got to do is first build the intellectual base. We need to create an institution to nurture these ideas and to discredit collectivist ideas . . . to develop a body of information and specific policy ideas that will be persuasive. If we do it right, politicians will start paying attention. Then you go to the next stage of politics."[6]

It took Antony Fisher a few years to accomplish this. First, he had to make his fortune (he was one of the first in Britain to raise chickens in cages, which proved efficient and productive). In 1955, he had the funds to start IEA, which was very consciously modeled on the Fabian Society. Ralph Harris and Arthur Seldon, who ran the IEA for much of its existence, laid out three basic principles of operation—three steps to a free society—at the 1959 meeting of the Mont Pèlerin Society. First, develop a philosophy of the market economy and build its acceptance among intellectuals—build the intellectual base, just as Hayek had said. Second, develop politically acceptable transition steps: This might well involve devising ways to compensate those who would lose in the short term in the transition from collectivism to freedom. Third, design policies that undercut the pleas of special interests; that is, those who would want to be protected forever from the consequences of the change.

As it turned out, IEA has spent most of its energy over the forty or so years since its inception in building the intellectual core. It has made some progress on the other two, but its main work has been the extremely valuable task of critiquing interventionism and laying out the merits of a free society and free institutions. The work of IEA provided the intellectual framework for Margaret Thatcher's successful campaign for Prime Minister, which resulted in three remarkable terms that led to the turnaround of the welfare state in the U.K.

The Adam Smith Institute was instrumental in developing the tools to figure out how to make the necessary step-by-step transitions, the very thing Mises said we have no knowledge whatsoever of how to do. The Adam Smith Institute was the first think tank in Europe to address head-on the challenge of designing public policies to move us toward freedom. IEA and others worked out the underlying principles that tell us how things work. But the next step is to take these principles and apply them to solve specific problems. That is the challenge that the Adam Smith Institute took up under the leadership of Madsen Pirie. I recommend that you read his book *Micro-Politics*. It outlines the task of designing policies to move us past the huge obstacle of the interest groups that benefit from collectivism, from the welfare state, from massive government intervention. Let me give you three examples from the privatization program of Margaret Thatcher's government, which were designed with help from the Adam Smith Institute.

The first involved public housing. During Margaret Thatcher's three terms some two million units of public housing were privatized. Because the purpose of selling public housing was not to raise revenue for the government—the purpose was to transform welfare recipients into homeowners—the selling prices were nominal. The longer the residents had lived in a public housing unit, the larger their discount from the so-called fair market price. The program started in a small way, and the first few hundred thousand units were readily accepted by tenants—even though the Labour Party viciously denounced it as an assault on the poor and an attack on the cherished principles of public support. What happened next was nothing short of amazing. Driving around London during Thatcher's first term, it was easy to see which housing had been privatized and which had not. As soon as a unit became the private property of the people who lived in it, they had an incentive to take care of it in a way that they never had before.

And think about what happens when people who have voted Labour all their lives suddenly become homeowners. What happens to their political image of themselves and to their future voting behavior? Most of them turned into Conservative Party voters, not Labour voters. This action proved to be very smart politically.

The second example also concerns privatization. Large state-owned enterprises that have all sorts of featherbedding work rules and subsidies become very inefficient and noncompetitive. You can replace the top management, as Thatcher did, because they are not civil servants, but you still have a mass of unionized workers who are going to be very worried about competing in the marketplace with no protection from the state. What the Thatcher government did was to give shares of stock—that is, give ownership—to the workers in every privatized enterprise. While this did not remove all problems or resistance, it made a remarkable difference. First, it gave compensation in exchange for eliminating the security of being an employee of the state. The employees, as shareholders, would get dividends to the extent that the company was profitable. This gave them an incentive to rethink the featherbedding practices and to redesign the workload to be more efficient. If the company makes a profit, the workers/shareholders will get dividends, and the value of their stock will go up. This transformed wasteful government enterprises into world-class companies: An example is British Airways.

A third example, similar but with a slightly different purpose, involved designing the method of privatization. Previous Conservative governments had sold off state enterprises, which had usually involved a sale to a large corporate entity. Thatcher insisted, with advice from the Adam Smith Institute, that in nearly every privatization the rule should be massive widespread stock offerings targeted to individual investors. As a result, in Thatcher's years in office, the percentage of people who owned shares in companies tripled or quadrupled. Her vision was to create a shareholding democracy. Instead of selling the government-owned enterprises by auction to huge industrial bidders from overseas, they were sold through massive stock offerings, making it easy for individual investors to buy shares. Politically this insulates against future Labour governments having a serious chance of renationalizing those companies once they return to power. In fact, not only has Tony Blair's New Labour government not proposed renationalizing anything, even before he was Prime Minister, he bulldozed the absolute repeal of Clause IV through the party conference The historic Clause IV that called for nationalizing the economy is no longer part of the party's platform. Not only that, New Labour has about $10 billion worth of additional privatizations on the agenda, including the air traffic control system, the London Underground, and possibly even the British post office. Margaret Thatcher did more than make privatization irreversible; she institutionalized it and made it the accepted way of doing business.

The good news is that the United States today has a welcome profusion of free market think tanks that are applying these same lessons. The first generation of free market think tanks included the Foundation for Economic Education, created in 1946 by Leonard Reed, and the American Enterprise Institute, created a few years earlier in Washington, D.C. The second generation came in the late 1970s: the Heritage Foundation in 1976, the Cato Institute in 1977, the Reason Foundation in 1978, and the Manhattan Institute in 1979. These four national organizations were founded by people with basically libertarian, free market views, all of them highly influenced by Mises, Hayek, and Friedman. A third generation of state-oriented, state-level free market think tanks began to appear in the mid-1980s: the James Madison Institute in Florida, the Pioneer Institute in Massachusetts, and the Heartland Institute in Chicago. And of course there are specialized libertarian lobbying groups, such as Citizens for a Sound Economy and the Competitive Enterprise Institute, which research, lobby, and perform legal-action work. This wealth of resources simply did not exist in those dark days after World War II, when *The Road to Serfdom* and *Human Action* were first published.

The step-by-step approach has grown over the years and has had an increasing impact. An example is an effort the Reason Foundation has been forwarding over its twenty years of existence —the idea of privatizing municipal services. This may seem mundane, but in fact municipal socialism is rampant in the United

States. Our city and county governments operate all sorts of business enterprises, usually inefficiently and poorly. But how do you get these governments out of businesses they are ill-suited for and back to the business of government? It takes time. Before starting the Reason Foundation, I wrote a book called *Cutting Back City Hall*, which helped disseminate the idea to city managers and mayors during the 1980s. We started a newsletter that is now called *Privatization Watch*. It has never had a circulation of more than 1,000, but its readership is fairly influential. Every month the newsletter reports on new developments in the competitive contracting of municipal services. It concentrates on the important first step of shifting from in-house provision to buying services on a competitive basis from the marketplace—not on getting government out altogether. Everything from ambulance service to zoo operation to garbage pickup can be, and is being, done by the private sector. But in the 1970s and early 1980s this was a pretty controversial concept in most communities, and it was fiercely opposed by public employee unions. It caught on initially in the South and Southwest, primarily in right-to-work states where the unions weren't quite so powerful, and usually on an issue-by-issue basis. Not very many cities embraced it as an overall agenda, and so we were continually frustrated. We had yet to find a real champion.

In the summer of 1991 I was invited to Indianapolis to meet with Steve Goldsmith, a young aggressive prosecutor who was running for mayor. We had a long lunch and talked privatization for over two hours. I followed up with a packet of the materials we had produced over the years. Goldsmith latched onto the idea and decided this was to be the key theme of his campaign, even though, interestingly enough, Indianapolis was not a city in trouble. Usually cities are backed into privatizing because of budgetary concerns: When they absolutely have to cut costs, they are willing to go head-to-head with the unions. Indianapolis, however, had been reasonably well run by a succession of Republican mayors, and its budget was balanced. But Goldsmith's vision was long-term, as he stated:

> Cities no longer compete against each other for businesses and families. They compete against their suburbs, and they are

> losing badly. . . . Every time a family moves out, every time a business relocates . . . the central city loses a little bit of its tax base. This creates pressure for more revenue and increases the temptation to raise tax rates, driving more businesses and homeowners away. It is an ugly downward spiral, and cities all across the country are caught in it. . . . These factors converge to force government officials to become better managers. . . . An emerging solution for many policymakers is to turn over the delivery of many services to private sector firms.[7]

He adopted a number of our ideas and over the course of his years in office managed to privatize over seventy services, including the airport and two large, complex wastewater plants. He saved some $400 million and has received national awards from numerous organizations, including some in the liberal mainstream. He has made it respectable for big-city mayors in the industrial heartland to privatize.

Twenty-five years ago, Milwaukee had a socialist mayor. A year or so ago, it became the largest city to privatize its wastewater system. I was in Atlanta the day its Democratic mayor signed the deal to privatize its water system, which will save 40 percent over the next twenty years. Birmingham, Alabama, went the next step when its Democratic mayor put a proposal on the ballot to sell the city's waterworks and use the proceeds to build needed new schools. For various local political reasons it was a very tough battle, and the mayor lost by a slight margin, but it showed that privatization has become an issue that a Democratic mayor can run on. Times have really changed.

Summary

First, Hayek was right. Developing the intellectual groundwork and influencing opinion leaders does produce major gains for liberty. Second, we can see the "engineering approach" to designing public policies move us toward freedom, to undo the influence of special interests that benefit from the status quo, from the privileges and protections of the state. In *Bringing the Market Back*

In The Political Revitalization of Market Liberalism, John Kelley writes, "Those Libertarians who have been most influential have been those who, forgoing revolutionary rhetoric, have taken a leaf from the Fabian socialists in advocating specific reforms rather than grand visions witness"—and here is the commercial—"the Reason Foundation and the Cato Institute's promotion of privatization, school choice and social security reform."[8] Third, I want to emphasize that initial small successes make it possible to take larger steps later. You build on previous successes to go further and do more.

Clearly we could not have gone so far without the pioneering work of Ludwig von Mises, without the theoretical base he set forth so beautifully in *Human Action* for questioning the enormous role of government intervention in our society. But equally clearly, were it not for the critical role played by his student and colleague, F. A. Hayek, we might not have rolled back the state to the extent that we have, not just in the United States and the United Kingdom, but all over the world.

Notes

[1]Ludwig von Mises, *Human Action: A Treatise on Economics* (Irvington-on-Hudson, NY: Foundation for Economic Education, 1996), p. 716.

[2]Ibid., p. 861.

[3]"LP Natcom Buys Controversial Resolutions," *Frontlines* 1(1) (September, 1978): 1.

[4]F. A. Hayek, *The Intellectuals and Socialism* (London: Institute of Economic Affairs, 1998), p. 26.

[5]Quoted in Richard Cockett, *Thinking the Unthinkable: Think Tanks and the Economic Counter Revolution, 1931–1983* (New York: HarperCollins Publishers, 1994), p. 15.

[6]See John Blundell, new introduction to the *Reader's Digest Condensed Version of The Road to Serfdom* by F. A. Hayek (London: Institute of Economic Affairs, 1999), pp. xv–xvi.

[7]Stephen Goldsmith, *The Twenty-First Century City* (Washington, DC: Regnery Publishing, Inc., 1997), pp. 13, 15.

[8]John L. Kelley, *Bringing the Market Back In: The Political Revitalization of Market Liberalism* (New York: New York University Press, 1997), p. 213.

Israel M. Kirzner

Misesian Economics and the Path to Prosperity

Everyone knows that for Mises the path to prosperity is mapped through the establishment and preservation of free markets both domestically and internationally. While this is indeed well-known and true, it fails to convey the complexity of Mises' case for the process by which the free market generates prosperity. In particular, to say that Mises believed that prosperity arises from the free market fails to emphasis Mises' own insistence on the importance of the role, albeit limited, of government. Mises believed in free markets, but he saw a role for government. I would like to discuss some of the subtle nuances of that interface—the tensions and complexities that suffused Mises' position on the appropriate interface between the free market on the one hand and that monopoly of coercion that we call government on the other. That interface has not been sufficiently explored in the standard expositions of Misesian economics.

Prosperity is a rather vague term, perhaps deliberately so. Mises himself used it in the English version of his book *Liberalism*, which in the English edition has the subtitle *The Free and Prosperous Economy*. What did Mises mean by it? If you ask people what prosperity means, you will receive a variety of answers. Some will define prosperity as a high standard of living, but what precisely does that mean? When you try to pin it down, you run into all kinds of difficulties: index-number problems, problems in differences in taste, differences in preferences. It is difficult to observe two societies and be unambiguously certain that one society has a higher standard of living than another. If, for example, a lot of

Russian books but very few English books are published in one economy, and in another economy there are many English books but very few Russian books, it is difficult to say which is more prosperous. Presumably one can say that they are equally prosperous because they speak different languages. Certainly with other commodities it is difficult to be sure from an empirical point of view what a higher standard of living means. Sometimes prosperity is identified with full employment. Full employment is good, but is it what we really want? Everybody should be working? The purpose of life is not to work; presumably the purpose of life is to be able to enjoy the higher standard of living that having a good job makes possible. So prosperity is not full employment per se, and we are left again with the unacceptably vague "high standard of living." Sometimes prosperity is identified in a loose way with rapid economic growth. But what does rapid economic growth mean? Presumably it means rapid growth in the standard of living. So we are back again to standard of living. Perhaps output should be the gauge. How does one measure aggregate output—high increases in production volumes and rates of business profit? Well, business profits are good if you are in business, but that is only a symbol rather than the definition of prosperity and success. So the very word "prosperity" needs careful definition.

I think the meaning of prosperity, what perhaps Mises meant when he used it in his subtitle for the English version of *Liberalism,* has a great deal to do with the title of the book *Human Action.* The name *Human Action* has become very familiar to us; yet precisely because it has become so familiar, we do not often realize how remarkable, how almost bizarre a title this is for an economics book. The German version, published nine years earlier, carried a more conventional title for an economics treatise, *Nationalökonomie.* But *Human Action*? What does that mean? Human action is the analytical unit of Misesian economics, and it differs drastically and importantly from the analytical unit in mainstream economics today, which is the individual maximizing decision. In standard economics the analytical unit, the unit for analysis, is the decision, and the analysis proceeds by spinning out the implications of the insight that people make decisions in maximizing fashion. According to mainstream economics, people are programmed in such a way that they cannot avoid maximizing what it is they want to maximize. They are maximizers—of utility, profits, and so on, and the decision is the mathematical manipulation of means in order to achieve what is impossible for them not to achieve, namely maximization. Human action is different.

Human action emphasizes human purposefulness in an open-ended world of utter uncertainty. It is purposefulness shared perhaps by the analytical unit of the decision—decisions are presumably made in order to achieve purposes, to maximize achievement of purposes. But *Human Action* speaks of purposefulness in an open-ended world of complete uncertainty, meaning that at the moment of action, the individual is not choosing among options that are laid out clearly before him or her but is choosing *what the options are.* At the moment of action the human agent is identifying what the options are and identifying for himself or herself what purposes are worth pursuing. All of that occurs at the moment of action, and the subtlety with which Mises understood, appreciated, and developed the implications of the phenomenon of human action sets *Human Action* apart from all other treatises on economics. Surely this is what Mises had in mind by giving his book such a strange but musical title.

Prosperity must mean the fulfillment of human purposes, whatever they may be: not making money per se, not eating a lot of food per se, not having big houses or big cars per se, but achieving purposes, whatever they may be, as these purposes are identified by the human agents in an open-ended world of utter uncertainty. For many of us prosperity is indeed measured by the size of a car or the number of calories consumed, but that simply refers to the purposes that many of us pursue. But purposefulness is a wide concept that can cover many dimensions. Economics is neutral. As Mises used to emphasize, the economist is value-free. The concrete purposes that different individuals bring to bear in their decisions, in their actions, vary greatly among cultures and human beings. The economist finds a commonality among them: purposeful behavior in an open-ended, uncertain world. Prosperity must consist in enabling these purposes to be fulfilled to the greatest possible degree that we can imagine. These purposes may be selfish or altruistic. They may be mundane or sublime. "Prosperity" is a word sufficiently vague to enable us to encompass all of these purposes. The successful achievement of these purposes is a single idea—prosperity—and when Mises claimed that free markets promote prosperity, he was talking not about the size of cars, the size of houses, or the standard of living in a material sense, but about the fulfillment of human purposes, whatever they may be.

Mises attached, as all economists do, enormous importance to social cooperation achieved impersonally through the exchange process, through free exchange. A statement that hardly ever leaves my mind is, "The market is a process." It is a process of social cooperation without deliberate undertaking of such cooperation. It is a process that operates through free exchange, but this free exchange achieves social cooperation. Mises saw this social cooperation as vital to the survival of the human race. One need only read the concluding passage in *Human Action* to realize how passionate Mises was, how passionately he felt about the importance of free exchange. Throughout the book Mises is the dispassionate "value-free" scientist. In that final passage Mises reveals how his pursuit of the dispassionate scientific inquiry of the economist is driven by his passion as a human being concerned with the survival of the human race. That has to do with prosperity in the broadest sense. Social cooperation is a grand notion that takes the specific form of coordination of activities. Free exchange can achieve the coordination of activities such that activities can be undertaken with a reasonable assurance that the activities of others, upon which one's own activities depend, will indeed be forthcoming. Coordination of activities is required, as Hayek pointed out, by the dispersed character of human knowledge and the necessity of different agents somehow being made correctly aware of what other agents are doing and what other agents are about to do. Social cooperation—the cooperation that is required for the achievement of human prosperity—takes form through the impersonal forces of free exchange and free markets, through these forces articulating prices that transmit the information that makes it possible for coordination to take place. This cooperation and this coordination constitute the path to prosperity.

When Mises used to criticize interventionist policies in his classes, he had a rather curious way of making his point. He would talk about rent control in New York City, and he would point out how simple analysis shows that rent control leads to housing shortages. Then he said, "This is bad." Why is it bad? Not because I, Mises, say that it is bad but because those who voted for the legislation think it bad. These policies are mistaken because they bring about consequences that the initiators of these policies did not intend. That is a rather unique approach to policy assessment—not a welfare approach, but an approach that asks a very simple question: "Is this really what you wanted?" Of course, no one wants consequences such as housing shortages, because no one defines prosperity in terms of housing shortages or the unemployment that results from minimum wages. Therefore, these policies are bad.

Mises applied the same kinds of analysis to broader questions. When Mises, both in *Human Action* and in one of his earlier really great books, *Socialism*, criticized the possibility of socialist economic calculation, what was he doing? He was pointing out that socialist planning is an impossibility in the sense that the different parts of the plan will necessarily be uncoordinated. They will necessarily be internally incoherent, and the attempted plan must fail as a result. It must fail because the individuals who are making the plans cannot know the true values of the resources they are allocating. So again it is social cooperation and coordination that provide the criteria of the achievement of prosperity. To the extent that cooperation and coordination are achieved, prosperity is achieved and human purposes can be promoted and expanded. To the extent that cooperation and coordination are frustrated, to that extent prosperity must also be frustrated.

Now let us explore some of the interface between the roles of the market and government. Mises was emphatic in his rejection of anarchy. Invariably in his seminar one of the younger members would raise the question, "Well, who needs a government at all? Let the market do everything." And Mises used to shake his head and say softly, "Write a book about it and show me." Mises never accepted the idea that the market can replace government in its legitimate role.

I would like to explore what Mises meant by the legitimate role of government. We emphasize the role of free markets in Misesian economics and their ability to achieve prosperity so much that we fail to understand and appreciate the subtlety of Mises' position on government. For Mises the institutions that set up a market are themselves outside the market. A market requires institutions: the institution of private property, the institution of the freedom of contract, and the enforcement of contracts. These are the primordial elements that a market needs in order to work, to exist, to fulfill its function of permitting prosperity to emerge. These institutions consist of establishing and protecting inviolate individual rights. Prominent among these individual rights is, of course, the right to own property. Property rights are not, as some fashionable writers would have us believe, something separate from individual rights or human rights; property rights are, of course, one variety of human right. Individual rights are the core of the institutions necessary to set up a market and permit it to operate. A market can operate only within the institutional framework that identifies and protects individual rights and holds them absolutely inviolate. In order to achieve this identification and protection of individual rights, it is necessary to have a government. Of course the necessity of government raises all those profound problems that make up the history of political philosophy and political science: How can one have government without tyranny? The problem is there, but that does not diminish in any way the fundamental insight that a government is necessary; monopoly of coercion is necessary in order to establish, identify, and protect the inviolability of individual rights. Only on the basis of such protection, only within the institutional framework within which rights are in this way protected, can a free market do what a free market can do: promote the achievement of prosperity in the broad sense in which we have defined it.

This role of government must be contrasted drastically with a statement which I have read in the name of an eminent economist, the late Frank Knight. Knight, a great University of Chicago economist, was one of the few big names in the economics profession that Mises used to mention with respect. Knight is said to have argued that Madison's statement in *Federalist 51*, "If men were angels, no government would be necessary," was incorrect because even angels would need governmental organization. There could not be a sharper contrast with the Misesian approach. Mises would say that Knight, not Madison, was wrong. Mises would say that if men were angels, no government would be necessary, because government is made necessary only by the fact that there is a tendency for individual rights, property rights, and other human rights to be violated in society. This understanding of government explains why, when Mises was confronted with certain examples of alleged market failure, he would point out that they were nothing but a failure of the legal framework to do its job properly.

The statement that even angels would need an organization for making decisions and expressing priorities is something that Mises would have found bizarre. We do not need the government to make decisions and express our priorities. The priorities that we seek to fulfill, that constitute prosperity, are priorities of individuals. It is individuals who express their priorities within a framework of inviolate individual rights. Within the scope of those rights individuals can articulate their priorities by exploiting the availability of others with whom they can exchange. They can seek to advance their priorities. In other words, they can seek to achieve prosperity. We do not need an organization for making decisions. We need a governmental organization to set up the framework, and once that framework is set up, the government has nothing else to do in a Misesian world. The government has to make sure that rights are protected and respected. If there is a dispute, it may be the role of government to adjudicate that dispute, to make sure that rights are protected. If there is crime, it is the role of government to combat that crime to ensure that individual rights are respected and protected. But once the individual human rights, including most importantly property rights, are in place, then everything else will occur as an expression of the priorities of individual human agents. Any interference with these exchanges will frustrate the achievement of these priorities, will frustrate the achievement of prosperity.

Mises had no doubt of the need for a government. He understood the need for government, and he understood the need more deeply for limited government, for government that does not make decisions, for government that does not set priorities. A government has only one priority, one function, one objective: to protect rights. That function is of primary importance, but it requires that the government refrain from interfering, from intervening, from hampering, as Mises would say, the free exchange in which individuals make their decisions with respect for each other by taking advantage of what others are able to do. Mises considered government regulation of prices, production, and working con-ditions unfortunate and illegitimate. One can attack such regulations on ethical and moral bases. One can attack them on the basis of political philosophy. One can see them as wrong for many reasons. Mises and the economists saw that government regulation—the attempt by government to overstep its legitimate function—disrupts those subtle webs of cause and effect arising out of the mutually advantageous exchange opportunities that govern the possibilities for fruitful social cooperation and coordination. Mises and his book demonstrated that free exchange by individuals within a framework of secure, protected rights will achieve prosperity in the sense of permitting and inspiring the utmost fulfillment of human purposes, because human purposes can most of the time be fulfilled only by the simultaneous fulfillment of the purposes of others. An act of free exchange simultaneously fulfills the purposes of both parties to the exchange. It achieves prosperity. The successful achievement of human purposes depends on one's ability to take advantage of the actions that others are taking or might be inspired to take by an action of one's own. To permit that to happen, to recognize the subtlety, the cobweb nature, the delicacy of those webs of human relationships that permit this to occur, is the message of Ludwig von Mises in *Human Action.*

Leland B. Yeager

The Moral Element in Mises' *Human Action*

Science and Values

Israel Kirzner recently asked how Ludwig von Mises could claim to be pursuing value-free science while at the same time showing "enormous *passion*" to communicate its truths.[1] "Passion" in that context implies moral judgment, a concern for truth over falsehood and right over wrong. I will embroider a bit on how Kirzner answered his own question, which, by the way, recognizes the fact/value or is/ought distinction. Further, I will review Mises' insights into the basis of morality.

As Kirzner argued, the passionate pursuit of value-free truths involves no contradiction. Mises wanted people to have the opportunity to pursue happiness successfully. That opportunity presupposes what he called "social cooperation," meaning a secure and peaceful society in which people can interact to their mutual benefit while pursuing their own diverse specializations, projects, and kinds of excellence. Such a society presupposes policies that serve, rather than undercut, social cooperation; and they in turn presuppose that policymakers and the public have some understanding of economics—value-free science. It is too much to expect that most people should actively understand economics; perhaps it suffices if they have the humility to recognize their ignorance and refrain from destructively imposing its consequences.

Still, it is important that enough people do get economics straight and disseminate its teachings. That requires subtle insights and a perspective different from those of the layperson. Its conclusions are counterintuitive, and fallacies pervade public opinion. Most do not understand the law of unintended consequences. Economic ignorance is so widespread and its consequences so frightening that, as Kirzner said, reducing it "becomes a goal invested with independent moral worth." Economic education serves a human goal of such importance that "passionate concern becomes . . . a morally natural phenomenon." Kirzner insists on "a fundamental difference between economic education" and promoting "'libertarian' ideology or rhetoric." Passion need not and dare not "compromise the detachment and objectivity of the *content* of . . . economic education."[2]

I will make one clarification. We cannot expect the whole of any science to be value-free and expect researchers to pursue their work with no heed to values. Values guide scientists toward questions that they find interesting and worth investigating. Values guide the application of scientific findings. What *can* be value-free is the *content* of scientific propositions. The distinction between value-free and value-loaded pertains not to whole fields of study or to professional careers but to propositions, to sentences. Some value-free propositions are that snow is white, that demand curves slope downward, that expanding the quantity of money beyond what people are willing to hold at existing prices causes price inflation, and that private property and genuine markets are necessary (as Mises and Hayek explained) for economic calculation.

Does insisting on a distinction between normative and positive propositions disparage ethics? No. Normative propositions can be argued for and against. All value judgments have descriptive as well as normative content, except only for fundamental value judgments. Examples of relatively specific judgments are that lying, cheating, and stealing are wrong. A fundamental judgment, in contrast and by definition, is one that one cannot argue for because one has reached the end of arguing and must appeal to direct observation or intuition instead. Probably the most familiar example is the judgment that misery is bad and happiness is good; scarcely anyone would try to *demonstrate* that judgment.

Utilitarianism

Utilitarianism rests on that one fundamental intuition or, in other words, on approval of human flourishing, of people's success in making good lives for themselves, and disapproval of the opposite conditions. This is a tame value judgment, to be sure; but combined with positive knowledge of the world and human affairs, it goes a long way in ethics. What fundamental value judgment or criterion could be more plausible?

One great insight of Mises, following David Hume and elaborated by Henry Hazlitt,[3] is that direct appeal to the criterion of happiness over misery is seldom necessary. A surrogate criterion is more tractable. Actions, institutions, rules, principles, customs, ideals, dispositions, and character traits count as good or bad according to whether they support or undercut social cooperation, which is prerequisite to the happiness of a society's members. Economics and the other social and natural sciences have much to say about what does support or undercut it.

Hazlitt gives powerful reasons for repudiating the variety of utilitarianism that calls for whatever action seems most likely, on each particular occasion, to contribute most to the sum total of happiness. That brand, called "act-utilitarianism," has now sunk almost to the status of a mere strawman. Even so, it remains the favorite target of superficial critics. Hazlitt advocates "rules-utilitarianism" instead, which might better be named "indirect utilitarianism." I won't spell out his reasons for espousing this version of utilitarianism here. Suffice it to say that he rejects case-by-case expediency and calls for adherence, almost without exception, to traditional precepts of morality, ethical principles that do satisfy the utilitarian criterion. Utilitarian philosophers can give reasons, grounded in reality, for respecting cherished values.

Ethics in *Human Action*

Henry Hazlitt, and Mises before him, forthrightly and courageously avowed utilitarian ethics in a hostile intellectual atmosphere. Let us look more closely at what Mises wrote. He identifies ethical doctrines as normative disciplines concerned with what ought to be. Praxeology and economics, in contrast, recognize that ultimate ends are purely subjective. They judge means by whether or not they are suitable to attain the desired ends.[4]

Does Mises say that a widely accepted ethical code is essential to a decently functioning economy? I do not find that he says so explicitly—perhaps because the point is almost too obvious to need saying. He says so implicitly, however, when he emphasizes that social cooperation, including market relations, is essential to prosperity and happiness and when he expounds the ethics of social cooperation.

Chapter VIII of *Human Action* explains that the moral rules necessary for social cooperation constitute an autonomous, rationalistic, and voluntaristic ethic. They stand in contrast with the heteronomous doctrines both of intuitionism and of revealed commandments.[5] Earlier we read, "Society and the state are . . . the primary means for all people to attain the ends that they aim at of their own accord." Society is the great means for attainment of all the individual's ends.[6] The division of labor and the exchange of people's specialized outputs enhance productivity. The principle of comparative advantage, which Mises calls the Ricardian Law of Association, goes far toward explaining how. In a world without this enhancement of productivity, there would be no sentiments of benevolence and good will.[7]

The operation of the market coordinates individuals' actions. No special orders or prohibitions are necessary. Noncooperation penalizes itself. The market economy does not ask anybody to deviate from those lines of conduct that best serve his own interests.[8]

Beyond the sphere of private property and the market, organized society has built dams to protect private property and the market against violence, malice, and fraud.[9] Such misbehavior does occur because some persons are too narrow-minded or too weak in moral strength and willpower to adjust themselves on their own to the conditions of social life. They yield to temptations; they seek fleeting advantage by actions harmful to the smooth functioning of the social system. Society could not exist if the majority were not ready to apply or threaten force to keep these others from destroying the social order. Although anarchists overlook this regrettable truth, the state is essential to crush the onslaughts of peace-breakers.[10] "[T]he only purpose of the laws and the social apparatus of coercion and compulsion is to safeguard the smooth functioning of social cooperation."[11]

In some passages Mises is quite explicit about his utilitarianism. The theory of social cooperation elaborated by British political economy from Hume to Ricardo extended the Epicurean philosophy. "It substituted an autonomous rational morality for the heteronomous and intuitionist ethics of older days." The only yardstick to be applied to law, the moral code, and social institutions is expediency with regard to human welfare. God endowed "his creatures with reason and the urge toward the pursuit of happiness."[12]

Mises presents a utilitarian case for democracy and classical liberalism. Liberalism is not itself a theory, he says, but an application of economic and other theories to policy. It attaches a concrete—not purely formal—meaning to happiness and removal of uneasiness. It supposes that people prefer life, health, nourishment, and abundance to their opposites; and it teaches how to act in accordance with these valuations.[13]

If an economist states that a certain policy measure is bad, he is not pronouncing a value judgment; he is simply saying that it is inappropriate for the desired goal.[14]

Reformers want to replace what they call selfishness, acquisitiveness, and profit-seeking, Mises observes, with altruism, charity, and fear of God. But in urging people to substitute considerations of public welfare for those of private profit, one does not create a working and satisfactory social order. How should the "altruistic" entrepreneur proceed?[15]

Flexibility of prices and wages is the vehicle of adjustment, improvement, and progress. Those who condemn price and wage changes as unjust are working against endeavors to make economic conditions more satisfactory.[16]

Is profit to be morally condemned? "The marvelous economic improvements of the last two hundred years were an achievement of the capitalists who provided the capital goods required and of the elite of technologists and entrepreneurs. The masses of the manual workers were benefited by changes which they not only did not generate but which, more often than not, they tried to cut short."[17]

Mises identifies connections between interventionism and the corruption of government officials. In administering many interventionist measures, for example, import licenses, favoritism simply cannot be avoided. Whether or not money changes hands does not matter; licenses can be awarded to people who supply campaign help. "Corruption is a regular effect of interventionism." Mises also identifies the mindset of redistributionists. "They reject all traditional notions of law and legality in the name of a 'higher and nobler' idea of justice. Whatever they themselves do is always right because it hurts those who selfishly want to retain for themselves what, from the point of view of this higher concept of justice, ought to belong to others."[18]

Ethics in Mises' Other Writings

Beyond *Human Action,* Mises wrote on ethics elsewhere. In *Theory and History* we read:

> The ultimate yardstick of justice is conduciveness to the preservation of social cooperation. . . . [S]ocial cooperation is for man a means for the attainment of all his ends. . . . As social cooperation is . . . a means and not an end, no unanimity with regard to value judgments is required to make it work. . . . The characteristic feature of a free society is that it can function in spite of the fact that its members disagree in many judgments of value.[19]

Utilitarianism "dispels the notion that society, the state, the nation, or any other social entity is an ultimate end and that individual men are the slaves of that entity. It rejects the philosophies of universalism, collectivism, and totalitarianism. In this sense it is meaningful to call utilitarianism a philosophy of individualism."[20]

In an essay of 1950 Mises wrote:

> Social cooperation under the division of labor is the ultimate and sole source of man's success in his struggle for survival and his endeavors to improve as much as possible the material conditions of his well-being. But as human nature is, society cannot exist if there is no provision for preventing unruly people from actions incompatible with community life. In order to preserve peaceful cooperation, one must be ready to resort to violent suppression of those disturbing the peace.[21]

The following comes from an essay of 1945:

> The sacrifice that a man or a group makes in renouncing some short-run gains, lest they endanger the peaceful operation of the apparatus of social cooperation, is merely temporary. It amounts to an abandonment of a small immediate profit for the sake of incomparably greater advantages in the long run.
>
> Such is the core of the moral teachings of nineteenth-century utilitarianism. Observe the moral law for your own sake, neither out of fear of hell nor for the sake of other groups, but for your own benefit. Renounce economic nationalism and conquest, nor for the sake of foreigners and aliens, but for the benefit of your own nation and state.
>
> It was the partial victory of this philosophy that resulted in the marvelous economic and political achievements of modern capitalism. . . .
>
> The scientific basis of this utilitarian ethics was the teachings of economics. Utilitarian ethics stands and falls with economics.
>
> [But our age witnesses a] revolt against rationalism, economics, and utilitarian social philosophy; it is at the same time a revolt against freedom, democracy, and representative government.
>
> [The anti-liberals call their adversaries names.] Rationalism is called superficial and unhistoric. Utilitarianism is branded as a mean system of stockjobber ethics . . . "peddler mentality," "dollar philosophy." [Economics is scorned.][22]

Writing probably in 1949 or 1950, Mises recognizes that science does not have the duty to tell people what to seek as their chief good. In assessing a doctrine, we have to ask only whether it is logically coherent or self-contradictory and whether its practical application will help people attain their desired ends. We have to consider doctrines as recipes for action and apply no other standard than that of whether they will work.[23]

> Utilitarianism has rejected all standards of a heteronomous moral law, which has to be accepted and obeyed regardless of the consequences arising therefrom. For [sic] the utilitarian point of view a deed is a crime because its results are detri-

> mental to society and not because some people believe that they hear in their soul a mystical voice which calls it a crime. We do not talk about problems of ethics.[24]

In various writings Mises disavows hedonism in the narrow sense. Notwithstanding superficial critics, "happiness" does not mean mere material, bodily pleasures. Advanced utilitarians, he says, interpret pleasure and pain, utility and disutility in "purely formal" senses, referring to whatever individuals in fact try to achieve or avoid.[25]

Mises recognizes that many people, especially creative workers, are not driven by material desires or narrow self-interest alone. They may also be expressing competence and strength and even heroism.[26] Besides people concerned only with their own egos, there are "people with whom awareness of the troubles of their fellow men causes as much uneasiness as or even more uneasiness than their own wants."[27]

Mises occasionally slipped into repeating slogans about "the greatest happiness for the greatest number."[28] Such a formulation has no precise meaning, of course. All that Mises presumably meant by it is that the happiness to be furthered by morality and other social institutions and practices is the happiness of people in general—of the random member of society—rather than the differential happiness of specific persons or classes at the expense of others. Mises specifically repudiated any idea—such as critics enjoy attacking—of trying to maximize any numerical aggregate of measurable individual utilities.[29]

Some passages from his *Nation, State, and Economy* document Mises' rejection of slogans and intuitions as a basis for policy and his focus on likely consequences.

> Rationalist utilitarianism rules out neither socialism nor imperialism on principle. Accepting it provides only a standpoint from which one can compare and evaluate the advantages and disadvantages of the various possibilities of social order; one could conceivably become a socialist or even an imperialist from the utilitarian standpoint. But whoever has once adopted this standpoint is compelled to present his program rationally.[30]

Utilitarianism has been reproached for aiming only to satisfy material interests and for neglecting higher human goals. It is true that liberalism and utilitarianism aim at the highest possible productivity of labor. But they know "that human existence does not exhaust itself in material pleasures. They strive for welfare and for wealth not because they see the highest value in them but because they know that all higher and inner culture presupposes outward welfare. . . . Utilitarian policy is indeed policy for this earth. But that is true of all policy."[31]

It is an absurd confusion of values and positive knowledge, Mises wrote, when insistence on the economics relevant to some policy issue is criticized as "insensitive." If dispelling economic fallacies "is inhuman, then so is every expression of truth. If to say this is inhuman, then the physicians who exploded the myth of the healing power of mandrake were inhuman, too, because they hurt the people employed in gathering mandrake."[32]

Mises used to say that various interventionist measures could be rejected on the basis of economic analysis and the value judgments of their advocates.

> [A]ll the methods of interventionism are doomed to failure. This means: the interventionist measures must needs result in conditions which *from the point of view of their own advocates* are more unsatisfactory than the previous state of affairs they were designed to alter. These policies are therefore contrary to purpose.[33]

Criticism of Mises' Position

For many decades, utilitarian ethics has had a bad press, not least in libertarian circles. It draws scorn as the mindset of crass, grasping, unprincipled people. It supposedly invites government hyperactivity aimed at maximizing some misconceived aggregate welfare. Ethics and policy must be grounded instead in noble and intuitively obvious principles such as unswerving respect for human dignity and human rights.

Mises the utilitarian has drawn his share of criticism, even from some of his own disciples. I do not maintain that Mises expounded the subtlest version of the doctrine, distinguishing between act utilitarianism and rules or indirect utilitarianism. He wrote mostly before detailed philosophical treatments of these subtleties were published, and, anyway, they were not central to his main concerns. Still, his basic philosophical stance is worth defending. Confronting it with the arguments of critics and would-be reinterpreters helps clarify it and, I think, strengthen its appeal.

Murray Rothbard called Mises "an opponent of objective ethics."[34] This charge is scarcely fair. Certainly Mises was not an ethical relativist or nihilist, scorning all judgments of right and wrong and complacent even when some individuals violate others' rights in pursuit of narrow and short-run self-interest. On the contrary, he was concerned with whether behavior and precepts and character traits tend to serve or subvert social cooperation and people's happiness.

According to Rothbard, Mises made one fundamental value judgment: He hoped that the bulk of the population would get whatever it wanted or thought it wanted. But what if the great majority wants to murder redheads or wants to see innocent persons suffer for its own amusement? A utilitarian such as Mises would include such preferences "fully as much as the most innocuous or altruistic preferences, . . . in the quantitative reckoning."[35] Instead of citing specific statements by Mises, Rothbard criticizes what he supposes Mises, as a utilitarian, must believe.

But whatever even halfway sophisticated utilitarian maintains that preferences and attitudes and character traits must be immune from appraisal? Mises, to my knowledge, never said any such thing. A rules or indirect utilitarianism is indeed concerned with how attitudes and character traits, so far as they are open to influence, tend to affect the health of a society and the happiness of its individual members. For fear of adverse side effects and for other reasons, a utilitarian does not want to enlist the state's coercive powers in suppressing all unfortunate preferences and attitudes and traits; but this in no way means that he considers all of them equally worthy of respect and of influence on policy.

Other criticism is policy-oriented. Rothbard objected that the utilitarian will rarely apply an absolute principle to real-world situations. The utilitarian regards principle as no more than a vague and overridable guideline. He "cannot be 'trusted' to maintain libertarian principle in every specific application."[36] Karen Vaughn regretted that Mises accepted the collectivists' and authoritarians' terms of debate by stressing how efficiently the free market provides well-being. Such a defense of freedom is doubly dangerous. "First, it is open to empirical refutation." Second, the utilitarian calculus might tip in favor of a nonliberal system if it counted the bureaucrats' enjoyment from controlling and regulating. A less risky course simply postulates freedom as supremely "desirable for its own sake" and as "a moral value that, as a bonus, also happen[s] to lead to the well-being of society."[37]

But it seems backward to criticize ethical systems according to whether they unswervingly support preconceived policy positions. It is more sensible to appraise policies according to how they accord with a well-grounded ethics. Furthermore, such criticisms distinguish sharply, if sometimes only implicitly, between ethically principled and utilitarian approaches to policy. They interpret the latter as unprincipled, case-by-case direct calculation of gains and losses of utility. Actually, far from rejecting principles, utilitarianism seeks their sound basis.

On the charge that utilitarians cannot be trusted to hew to the libertarian line in absolutely all cases, compare Mises' remark:

> It may be that socialism represents a better form of organization of human labor. Let whoever asserts this try to prove it rationally. If the proof should succeed, then the world, democratically united by liberalism, will not hesitate to implement the communist community. In a democratic state, who could oppose a reform that would be bound to bring the greatest gain to by far the overwhelming majority? Political rationalism does not reject socialism on principle. But it does reject in advance the socialism that hinges not on cool understanding but rather on unclear feelings, that works not with logic but rather with the mysticism of a gospel of salvation, the socialism that does not proceed from the free will of the majority of the people but rather from the terrorism of wild fanatics.[38]

Mises means that rationalism does reject socialism, yes, but from the scientific comparison of alternative systems.

Natural Law and Natural Rights

One widely admired doctrine in the supposed rivalry with utilitarianism insists on adherence to natural law and natural rights. Rothbard tries to derive many detailed propositions about ethics and law from his conception of rights, purportedly derived in turn from John Locke's axioms of self-ownership and homesteading.[39] (Yet even for these he offers utilitarian arguments, without acknowledging the label.) John J. Piderit, a Georgetown University economist, argues for what he calls a natural-law approach: correct reason ascertains what actions are "natural" and therefore ethically acceptable by reflecting on the nature of human beings, their shared aspirations and fundamental values, and their interactions in community.[40] Yet Piderit can scarcely mean that whatever is natural is right and good. Civilization is largely an exercise in taming natural behavior. Of course, any acceptable doctrine must conform to nature in the sense of not requiring impossible actions or behavior enforceable only at excessive cost. Respecting the facts of nature and human interaction does not distinguish the natural-law approach from utilitarianism.

Natural-law doctrine does make sense if it means merely that all sorts of behavior and precepts, notably including laws made by legislatures and judges, are open to appraisal on moral grounds. Nothing becomes ethically acceptable merely by enactment into positive law. That interpretation of natural law does not rule out a utilitarian grounding of morality. But if the doctrine says that whatever is morally right (or wrong) has all (or none) of the force of positive law. For that reason alone, it fatuously denies a live distinction.

As for natural (or human or individual) rights, the meaning that seems to fit the typical context is this: A right is a person's entitlement to others' treatment of him that is binding on those others with compelling moral force. Some rights are positive entitlements, like a child's right to support by his parents or each party's right to performance by the other party to a contract. The rights mentioned in the Declaration of Independence are negative rights, rights to forbearances, rights not to be coerced or victimized by other persons, notably including agents of the state. One reason why negative rights are especially stringent is that they are relatively easy to honor—simply by not interfering.

Rights, being moral entitlements, *presuppose* an ethical system or tradition and cannot provide its very grounding. On what principles or intuitions provide the basis of rights, "the rhetoric of rights sheds no light whatever."[41] Richard Epstein finds a utilitarian grounding for natural law and natural rights, sensibly interpreted, and even for the Lockean axioms of self-ownership or personal autonomy and homesteading or first possession.[42]

Making natural rights the very foundation of ethics substitutes intuition for factual research and reasoning. Furthermore, some strands of "rights talk" debase political discussion, making absolutistic and moralistic demands, and subverting a creative search for mutually beneficial accommodations.

In the words of Donald Livingston, interpreting David Hume, corrupt modes of philosophizing are undercutting whatever fragments of *sensus communis* could discipline radical self-determination. Philosophical resentment spawns

> an endless stream of self-created victims. Someone's self determination is met with the violent protest that someone else's rights have been violated. Ever more numerous rights are generated to protect ever more numerous desires. . . . "I want" . . . has become an argument of practical reason. . . . Thus a form of the Hobbesian state of nature is renewed in the most advanced civilization, and society is held together not by the enjoyment and cultivation of an inherited *sensus communis* but by *legalism* enforced by an increasingly consolidated and bureaucratic modern state. Consolidation must occur as power is transferred from dismantled, independent social authorities to the center in order to service an ever-increasing number of antinomic individual rights.[43]

As Mises says, declarations about disagreements hinging on irreconcilably and unnegotiably different worldviews

> describe the antagonism as more pointed than it really is. In fact, for all parties committed to pursuit of the people's earthly welfare and thus approving social cooperation, questions of social organization and the conduct of social action are not problems of ultimate principles and of world views, but ideo-

> logical issues. They are technical problems with regard to which some arrangement is always possible. No party would wittingly prefer social disintegration, anarchy, and a return to primitive barbarism to a solution which must be bought at the price of the sacrifice of some ideological points.[44]

Mises and Natural Rights

Mises' own position on natural law and rights is an embarrassment for some of his disciples. Nature is alien to the idea of right and wrong, he observes, questioning the notion of an eternally established standard. Right and wrong are utilitarian judgments. As for natural law, people deduce clashing implications from their arbitrary notions of it. "*De lege ferenda* there is no such a thing as justice. The notion of justice can logically only be resorted to *de lege lata.*" In enacting or changing laws, the issue is not justice but social expediency and social welfare. "There is neither right nor wrong outside the social nexus. . . . The idea of justice always refers to social cooperation."[45]

Utilitarian philosophy and classical economics have nothing to do with the doctrine of natural rights, says Mises. All that matters for them is social utility. Mises even quotes Bentham on the "nonsense" of natural rights. Utilitarians recommend democratic government, private property, freedom, and equality under the law not on illusory grounds of natural law and human equality but because they are beneficial.[46]

Elsewhere, Mises insisted, "Utilitarian Liberalism had nothing to do with these natural rights fictions. The Utilitarians themselves must be credited with the merit of having once and for all refuted them."[47]

To quote Henry Hazlitt, who wrote largely under Mises' inspiration, the inviolability of rights rests "not . . . on some mystical yet self-evident 'law of nature'. . . [but] ultimately (though it will shock many to hear this) on utilitarian considerations."[48]

Some of the formulations quoted above are sharper than I myself would have expressed them, but Mises was nothing if not forthright. Precisely because human rights and human dignity are important values, they deserve a more solid grounding than mere intuitions reported in noble-sounding language. Mises of course did not reject natural law in the scientific sense; and he did not reject natural law and human rights as ethical precepts if they are interpreted in the tame sense that I sketched out earlier, the sense compatible with utilitarianism. What Mises rejected was the exaggerated, foundationalist, almost mystical status that some writers have accorded to them.

Eshelman's Interpretation

Still, some of his disciples sense an embarrassment and try to wriggle away from it. Larry J. Eshelman tries to reinterpret Mises and rescue him from the supposed utilitarian taint by distinguishing, almost explicitly, between utilitarianism and concern for principle.[49] Trying to be fair to Eshelman's position, I will review it in some detail. If it seems to rely too much on hair-splitting and woolly abstractions, Mises' actual position comes across looking all the better.

Mises rejected natural law and natural rights, says Eshelman, because he equated them with intuitionism. However, "he did not reject the categorical moral framework that underlies much of that tradition." Mises took a principled stance on social issues, much as if he believed in natural rights. His moral utilitarianism "owes more to the principled, categorical moral framework of [Herbert] Spencer and [Auberon] Herbert, than to the maximizing, comparative moral framework of Bentham and Mill."[50]

This implied contrast between utilitarianism and morality is familiar but mistaken. Mises takes a principled moral stance, yes—and on utilitarian grounds. Utilitarianism is a doctrine about the grounding of morality.

Eshelman applies the label "harmonist" to doctrines focusing on arrangements, principles, and attitudes that serve social cooperation. He distinguishes between "comparative" and "categorical" harmonists. The comparativists come in different varieties, some wanting to maximize happiness or minimize pain or maximize liberty, others wanting to maximize the expectations of anyone selected at random. Some suppose that happiness can be quantified and summed; others resort to devices like the veil of ignorance or the impartial spectator. But all comparative harmonists are maximizers: Morality means choosing the best from among the alternatives.

Eshelman rejects the maximizing view in favor of categorical harmonism. That doctrine sees only two moral alternatives: "social harmony or social chaos, the way of reason or the way of beasts." For him the primary moral relation is reciprocity. People fall into two classes: those who are and those who are not willing and able to live in harmony with others. The moral world of the categorical harmonist is more black-and-white than that of the comparativist, who creates the illusion of being more humane and tolerant. The categorical harmonist views punishment primarily as restitutional and retributive, while the comparativist views it primarily as a way to deter crime and reform criminals. The categorical harmonist measures justice against the law and the need to preserve social harmony, while the comparative harmonist measures it against the goal of maximum utility.[51]

Eshelman's distinction is contrived and unsuccessful. On most of his supposedly distinguishing points, I would count as a categorical harmonist myself; yet, with Mises, I reject natural-law/natural-rights doctrines except as understood in accord with utilitarianism. On the question of punishment, Rothbard, with his conception of crime as a private transaction between offender and victim, seems not to fit into either of the harmonist camps. Furthermore, Eshelman's rejection of comparative harmonism seems to imply rejecting the comparative-institutions approach to policy. Yet no categorical or absolutist alternative is available. Absolute laissez-faire would mean anarchy, and Mises was no anarchist (he thought government force justified to defend society against its enemies).[52] Government interventions come in various kinds and degrees of desirability or expediency. As long as any government at all exists, it must make decisions. What alternative is there to appraising—comparing—alternative courses of action, with due regard, of course, to moral principle?

Yet Eshelman presses his attack. The comparative harmonist, he says, is always a tinkerer who sees preserving society as only a first step toward the more ambitious goal of increasing social welfare. The comparativist insists on weighing the evidence in each case of possible action; he dismisses any claim to a priori knowledge of the right action as an appeal to intuition or "an infallible pipeline to the truth."[53] Cleared of all euphemisms, the comparative approach boils down to saying that the decision rests with whoever can gain control of government.[54]

Again, Eshelman draws too sharp a distinction. I, no absolutist, certainly do not suppose that every proposal for government intervention must be judged on the separate merits of the particular case. Utilitarianism takes principle seriously.

Mises was no comparativist, Eshelman insists, but rather an astute critic of any maximizing moral framework. (That remark tacitly recognizes, by the way, that a utilitarian need not be a maximizer of some supposed aggregate utility.) Mises' categorical approach shows up in his claim that "freedom is indivisible" and in his rejection of any middle way between socialism and capitalism.[55] The basis for his principled stance is the same as that developed by John Locke (and others before him) and generalized by Herbert Spencer and Auberon Herbert.[56] How then, Eshelman asks, could Mises have been both a principled defender of laissez faire and a defender of the doctrine of social expediency? Passages defending expediency can be interpreted as defending the functionalist doctrine that morality is concerned with preserving society and attacking any appeal to mysteriously intuited principles.[57]

Unfortunately, Eshelman says, Mises insisted that all values are arbitrary. When Mises attacks holding absolute values, however, he almost always has in mind the belief that such values are handed down from Providence and are independent of society. His target is the righteous nihilist or "theocrat." He speaks sarcastically of "those individuals to whom, by the mysterious decrees of some mysterious agency, the task of determining the collective will and directing the actions of the collective has been entrusted." Fortunately, Mises' argument for a principled, categorical approach to social harmony in no way depends upon his rejection of absolute values, says Eshelman, and would be strengthened without it.[58]

But Mises is right about values, and without adhering to them only weakly. He is right, anyway, if he means that fundamental value judgments, being fundamental, cannot be established by positive argument alone. Eshelman himself reads Mises as believing "that it is impossible to give any ultimate reason why one should be committed to peaceful cooperation. Instead, he treats this commitment as a hypothetical imperative."[59] I would make one slight clarification: Peaceful cooperation need not be taken as the utterly ultimate value, since it is instrumental to a more truly ultimate (and in that sense arbitrary) value—human happiness.

Eshelman's scholarly documentation and style foster the illusion that he is rescuing Rothbard's position from the embarrassment posed by Mises, the hard-boiled utilitarian critic of natural rights. Eshelman's main device in this effort, however, his distinction between comparative and categorical harmonists, just does not work. Furthermore, he scarcely even tries to lay out a case for a natural rights approach distinct from utilitarianism; perhaps he expects the reader to know such a case already.

Hoppe's Supposedly Value-Free Approach to Libertarianism

Hans-Hermann Hoppe presents another supposed alternative to utilitarian ethics.[60] He purportedly dispenses with any appeal to value judgments at all, even such a tame one as wishing people happy rather than miserable lives. He does not have to try to get an "ought" from an "is" because the libertarian policy position rests entirely on logic and facts and not at all on value judgments.

Reason, Hoppe says, can prove moral laws valid a priori. It makes explicit what the sheer fact of discussion already implies. The libertarian private property ethic can be justified morally and by argumentation and without invoking any value judgments. Proposing any alternative ethic contradicts what inheres in the very act of engaging in argumentation; nonlibertarian proposals are falsified by the very act of making them.

Argumentation—discussion—is a form of action requiring the employment of scarce means, privately owned. Argumentation presupposes that the participants recognize each one's exclusive control over one's own body. Furthermore, argumentation could not be sustained for any length of time without private property in things beyond one's own body, property ultimately tracing to Lockean homesteading. Without private property defined in objective, physical terms, life, acting, and proposition-making would be impossible. "By being alive and formulating any proposition, then, one demonstrates that any ethic except the libertarian ethic is invalid." Hoppe further says he has proved "that it is impossible to propositionally justify nonlibertarian property principles without falling into contradictions. Empirical evidence has absolutely no bearing on it." He explicitly rejects utilitarianism; his approach is an alternative.[61]

Murray Rothbard had been preaching for over thirty years that economists cannot arrive at any policy conclusion in a strictly value-free way; they have to come up with some kind of ethical system. Then Rothbard said that Hoppe had proven him wrong. "[H]e has deduced an anarcho-Lockean rights ethic from self-evident axioms. . . . Hoppe has managed to establish the case for anarcho-capitalist-Lockean rights in an unprecedentedly hard-core manner, one that makes my own natural law/natural rights position seem almost wimpy in comparison. . . . [I]t is impossible to disagree with the anarcho-Lockean rights ethic without falling immediately into self-contradiction and self-refutation." Hoppe appeals to the concept of the "ethics of argumentation." "*[A]ny* argument whatsoever . . . must imply self-ownership of the body of both the arguer and the listeners, as well as a homesteading of property right so that the arguers and listeners will be alive to listen to the argument and carry it on."[62]

Hoppe seems to say that espousing nonlibertarian policy positions commits self-refutation in the same sense that I would be refuting myself if I wrote a letter saying that it is impossible to write a letter or made an oral statement saying it is impossible for anybody to speak. The self-contradiction of a nonlibertarian may be more complicated and require more attention to expose, but it still is a self-contradiction, and of the same general type. The exposure of self-contradiction is a neat kind of argument and has great appeal—when it works.

In the present case, it just does not work. Hoppe simply asserts, but does not demonstrate, a logical contradiction. Being emphatic and repetitious is not enough. A slaveowner and his slave might conceivably engage in an intellectual discussion, even about the moral status of slavery itself, without either necessarily falling into self-contradiction. I hope it is not necessary to spend time on this point.

The Significance of Rival Doctrines

One reason for mentioning Hoppe's and other alternatives to Mises' utilitarianism (and, more broadly, to the indirect utilitarianism of David Hume, Mises, and Henry Hazlitt) is to show that utilitarianism is not so plastic and all-encompassing as to be vacuous. The existence of rival positions defuses that charge. One envisages a just society in the sense of John Rawls, who rejects viewing justice as a mere means to happiness.[63] Other rival doctrines center on duty or religion. Still others posit conformity to traditional ethical precepts, even if only intuition, rather than analysis of consequences, has tested the precepts; or respect for individual rights that have simply been postulated rather than argued for; or conduciveness to the special flourishing of the few highest and noblest specimens of the human race. One might also conceivably make the criterion the happiness not of people in general but of oneself discriminatorily or of some other specific person or class.

Some of these ostensibly rival doctrines, and perhaps others that do not now come to mind, may turn out, on examination, not to be truly *rival* doctrines. The criteria they appeal to either may not be as ultimate as happiness or may be equivalent to it after all. (In putting forth his axioms of self-ownership and Lockean homesteading, even Rothbard introduces utilitarian considerations.) Some of these doctrines, on the other hand, really are different. Their very existence shows that utilitarianism is not vacuous. If they are too unattractive to be realistic contenders, that fact further supports utilitarianism.

Intuitionism

The most urged alternatives to utilitarianism turn out to be varieties of intuitionism, which Mises quite properly spoke out against. Let me quote and paraphrase from his *Socialism.* (First I should explain a term that Mises uses. Eudaemonistic ethics is, loosely speaking, a system that applies the criterion of happiness.) Philosophers had been arguing about the ultimate Good for a long time, Mises wrote, before modern investigation settled it. All the arguments used in favor of an anti-eudaemonistic ethics were unable to dissociate the concept of Morality from that of Happiness. The vain efforts of these philosophers

> were necessary to expose the problem in all its wide ramifications and so enable a conclusive solution to be reached. . . . [T]he tenets of intuitionist ethics . . . are irreconcilable with scientific method [and] have been deprived of their very foundations. . . . [E]udaemonistic ideas lie concealed in every train of aprioristic-intuitive ethical thought. . . . Every ethical system built up on the idea of duty . . . is finally obliged to yield so much to Eudaemonism that its principles can no longer be maintained. In the same way every single requirement of aprioristic-intuitive ethics displays ultimately an eudaemonistic character.[64]

Conclusion

The fact/value or is/ought distinction, which I introduced at the beginning, is indeed a sound one. Nevertheless, "ought" judgments can be discussed and soundly made (except only for fundamental value judgments, and even for them, considerations can be adduced that incline people to accept them).[65] The soundest, most appealing approach to value judgments and to their use, as in policy recommendations, has been shown by Hume, Mises, Hazlitt, and other writers in their tradition (or in parallel, as R. M. Hare). This approach is indirect utilitarianism.

Mises was forthright, even courageous, in espousing utilitarianism and repudiating intuitionist alternatives. For this his reputation continues to suffer even among disciples who otherwise are carrying on his work. I urge them to reconsider. I am not saying that Mises developed the distinction between the act version and the rules or indirect version of utilitarianism and fully articulated the latter. I am not saying that he anticipated and demolished in advance the axiomatic or intuitionist rights approach that some of his disciples would urge. Doing all that was not possible in his time and was not necessary for his work in economics. However, a sophisticated utilitarianism does fit in with and extend his philosophical framework. Henry Hazlitt, for one, extended it. Mises was on the right track.

Notes

[1]Israel Kirzner, "The Nature and Significance of Economic Education," *The Freeman* 48(October 1998): 582–86.
[2]Ibid.
[3]Henry Hazlitt, *The Foundations of Morality* (Princeton: Van Nostrand, 1964).
[4]Ludwig von Mises, *Human Action,* 2d ed. (New Haven: Yale University Press, 1963); 3d ed., Regnery, 1966. Reprinted San Francisco: Fox & Wilkes, n.d. [Note: page numbers will refer to the third edition; page numbers in the second edition are the same or differ by only one page.)
[5]Ibid., p. 833.
[6]Ibid., pp, 148, 165.
[7]Ibid., pp. 144, 159–64.
[8]Ibid., p. 725.
[9]Ibid.
[10]Ibid., p. 149.
[11]Ibid., p 722.
[12]Ibid., p. 147.
[13]Ibid., p 149–50, 153–54.
[14]Ibid., p. 883.
[15]Ibid., pp. 725–26.
[16]Ibid., p. 728.
[17]Ibid., p. 301.
[18]Ibid., pp. 734–36.
[19]Ibid., pp. 54–61.
[20]Ludwig von Mises, *Theory and History,* (Auburn, AL: Ludwig von Mises Institute, [1979] 1985 reprint), p. 28.
[21]Ludwig von Mises, "The Idea of Liberty is Western," in Richard M. Ebeling, ed., *Money, Method, and the Market Process; Essays by Ludwig von Mises* (Norwell, MA: Kluwer Academic Press, 1990), p. 303.
[22]Ludwig von Mises, "The Clash of Group Interests," in ibid., pp. 209–10.
[23]Ludwig von Mises, "The Role of Doctrines in Human History," in ibid., pp. 300-301.
[24]Ludwig von Mises, "The Role of Doctrines in Human History," in ibid., p. 301.
[25]Ludwig von Mises, *Epistemological Problems of Economics* (in German, 1933), translated by George Reisman (Princeton: Van Nostrand, 1960) (, pp. 52, 151; Mises, *Theory and History,* 12–13; Mises, *Human Action,* p. 21.

[26]———, *Nation, State, and Economy,* translated by Leland B. Yeager from the German of 1919 (New York: New York University Press, 1983), pp. 193, 213.
[27]———, *Human Action,* p. 14.
[28]———, *Nation, State, and Economy,* p. 183.
[29]———, *Human Action,* p. 242.
[30]———, *Nation, State, and Economy,* p. 211.
[31]Ibid., pp. 214–15.
[32]———, *Money, Method, and the Market Process,* p. 234.
[33]Ludwig von Mises, *Socialism: An Economic and Sociological Analysis* (1922, 1936), translated by J. Kahane (Indianapolis: Liberty Classics, 1981), p. 486, from the "Epilogue," published in 1947 as *Planned Chaos.*
[34]Murray Rothbard, "Praxeology, Value Judgments, and Public Policy," in *The Foundations of Modern Austrian Economics,* edited by E. G. Dolan (Kansas City, KS: Sheed and Ward, 1976), p. 105.
[35]Ibid., pp. 105, 108, 182, 210, 213.
[36]Murray N. Rothbard, *For a New Liberty* (New York: Macmillan, 1973), p. 24.
[37]Karen Vaughn, "Critical Discussion of the Four Papers," in *The Economics of Ludwig von Mises,* edited by L. S. Moss. (Kansas City, KS: Sheed and Ward, 1976), pp. 108–9.
[38]Mises, *Nation, State, and Economy,* p. 221.
[39]Rothbard, *For a New Liberty*; Murray N. Rothbard, *The Ethics of Liberty* (Atlantic Highlands, NJ: Humanities Press, 1982).
[40]John J. Piderit, *The Ethical Foundations of Economics* (Washington, D.C.: Georgetown University Press, 1993).
[41]R. M. Hare, *Essays on Political Morality* (Oxford: Clarendon Press, 1989), p. 194, chapters 7–9.
[42]Richard A. Epstein, "The Utilitarian Foundations of Natural Law" and "Postscript: Subjective Utilitarianism," *Harvard Journal of Law & Public Policy* 12 (1989): 713–51, 769–73; Richard A. Epstein, *Simple Rules for a Complex World* (Cambridge: Harvard University Press, 1995), pp. 30, 55, 68, 311–13 & passim.
[43]Donald W. Livingston, *Philosophical Melancholy and Delirium: Hume's Pathology of Philosophy* (Chicago: University of Chicago Press, 1998), pp. 398–99.
[44]Mises, *Human Action,* p. 181.
[45]Ibid., pp. 720–21.
[46]Ibid., p. 475.
[47]Mises, *Money, Method, and the Market Process,* p. 228. 1945 essay commenting on ideas not only of natural law, but also of government by social contract.
[48]Henry Hazlitt, *The Foundations of Morality,* p. 264.
[49]Larry J. Eshelman, "Ludwig von Mises on Principle," *Review of Austrian Economics* 6(2): 3–41.
[50]Ibid., p. 38.

[51]Ibid., pp. 12–14.
[52]Ibid., p. 21.
[53]Ibid., pp. 16, 24.
[54]Ibid., p. 24.
[55]Ibid., p. 22.
[56]Ibid., p. 22.
[57]Ibid., p. 20.
[58]Ibid., pp. 31–33; quoting from Ludwig von Mises, *The Ultimate Foundation of Economic Science* (1962), 2d ed. (Kansas City, KS: Sheed Andrews and McMeel, 1977), p. 107.
[59]Ibid., p. 33.
[60]Hans-Hermann Hoppe, "From the Economics of Laissez Faire to the Ethics of Libertarianism," in *Man, Economy, and Liberty: Essays in Honor of Murray N. Rothbard,* edited by Walter Block and Llewellyn H. Rockwell, Jr. (Auburn, AL: Ludwig von Mises Institute, 1988), pp. 56–76;"The Ultimate Justification of the Private Property Ethic," *Liberty* 2 (September 1988): 20–22;"Hoppe's Rights Theory: Breakthrough or Buncombe?" A symposium by various authors, with a response by Hoppe, *Liberty* 2(November 1988): 4–53, 53–54.
[61]"Hoppe's Rights Theory," 4–53, 53–54.
[62]Ibid.
[63]John Rawls, *A Theory of Justice* (Cambridge: Belknap Press of Harvard University Press, 1971).
[64]Mises, *Socialism,* p. 360.
[65]John Stuart Mill, *Utilitarianism* (1863), edited by Maurice Cowling (New York: New American Library, 1968), chapter 1.

References

Richard A. Epstein. "The Utilitarian Foundations of Natural Law" and "Postscript: Subjective Utilitarianism." *Harvard Journal of Law & Public Policy* 12 (1989): 713–51, 769–73.

__________.*Simple Rules for a Complex World.* Cambridge: Harvard University Press, 1995.

Larry J. Eshelman. "Ludwig von Mises on Principle." *Review of Austrian Economics* 6 (2): 3–41.

R. M. Hare. *Essays on Political Morality.* Oxford: Clarendon Press, 1989.

Henry Hazlitt. *The Foundations of Morality.* Princeton: Van Nostrand, 1964.

Hans-Hermann Hoppe. "From the Economics of Laissez Faire to the Ethics of Libertarianism." In *Man, Economy, and Liberty: Essays in Honor of Murray N. Rothbard,* pp. 56–76. Edited by Walter Block and Llewellyn H. Rockwell, Jr. Auburn, AL: Ludwig von Mises Institute, 1988.

__________. "The Ultimate Justification of the Private Property Ethic." *Liberty* 2 (September 1988): 20–22.

"Hoppe's Rights Theory: Breakthrough or Buncombe?" A symposium by various authors, with a response by Hoppe. *Liberty* 2 (November 1988): 4–53, 53–54.

Israel Kirzner. "The Nature and Significance of Economic Education." *The Freeman* 48 (October 1998): 582–86.

Donald W. Livingston. *Philosophical Melancholy and Delirium: Hume's Pathology of Philosophy*. Chicago: University of Chicago Press, 1998.John Stuart Mill. *Utilitarianism*. 1863. Reprinted in, for example, *Selected Writings*, pp. 243–304. Edited by Maurice Cowling. New York: New American Library, 1968.

Ludwig von Mises. *Epistemological Problems of Economics*. In German, 1933. Translated by George Reisman. Princeton: Van Nostrand, 1960.

__________. *Human Action*. 2d ed. New Haven: Yale University Press, 1963. 3d ed., Regnery, 1966. Reprinted San Francisco: Fox & Wilkes, n.d.

__________. *Money, Method, and the Market Process*. Essays selected by Margit von Mises. Edited and with an introduction by Richard M. Ebeling. Norwell, MA: Kluwer, 1990.

__________. *Nation, State, and Economy*. Translated by Leland B. Yeager from the German of 1919. New York: New York University Press, 1983.

__________. *Socialism: An Economic and Sociological Analysis*. 1922, 1936. Translated by J. Kahane. Indianapolis: Liberty Classics, 1981.

__________. *Theory and History*. 1979. Reprinted Auburn, AL: Ludwig von Mises Institute, 1985.

__________. *The Ultimate Foundation of Economic Science*. 1962. 2d ed. Kansas City, KS: Sheed Andrews and McMeel, 1977.

John J. Piderit. *The Ethical Foundations of Economics*. Washington, D.C.: Georgetown University Press, 1993.

John Rawls. *A Theory of Justice*. Cambridge: Belknap Press of Harvard University Press, 1971.

Murray N. Rothbard. *For a New Liberty*. New York: Macmillan, 1973.

__________. "Praxeology, Value Judgments, and Public Policy." In *The Foundations of Modern Austrian Economics*. Edited by E. G. Dolan. Kansas City, KS: Sheed and Ward, 1976.

__________. *The Ethics of Liberty*. Atlantic Highlands, NJ: Humanities Press, 1982.

Karen Vaughn. "Critical Discussion of the Four Papers." In *The Economics of Ludwig von Mises*, pp. 101–10. Edited by L. S. Moss. Kansas City, KS: Sheed and Ward, 1976.

Ethan O. Waters (pseudonym of R.W. Bradford). "The Two Libertarianisms." *Liberty* 1(5) May 1988: 7ff. (Substantially reprinted in *Liberty* 6 (1) September 1992: 62–67.)

Roberto Salinas-León

A Moratorium on "Neo-Liberalism"

To the memory of Edgard Mason, 1943–1996

It is popular to claim that the "neo-liberal" agenda of reform has occasioned a backlash by angry voices opposed to the "social costs" of market-based transformation—to wit, poverty, black markets, unemployment, and social disunity. A story has to sell, and, across Latin America, the idea that "neo-liberalism" is the root of all evil sells a lot. This problem has magnified since the peso collapse of 1994 and subsequent bouts with financial volatility in the region, as the intellectual corollaries of the so-called "tequila" and "samba" effects, in light of the pervasive antimarket view that the drive toward a free economy has been responsible for the dramatic loss of well-being in the region. My claim is that the debate is rigged by design: The term "neo-liberalism" is devoid of substance, an ad hoc concept that trivializes an important issue via slander, name-calling and pure intellectual default. The term deserves a moratorium.

The real concern is whether the emerging economies of Latin America should move in the direction of an open society—a free enterprise system based on well-defined property rights, sound currencies, the rule of law, and an institutional system that fosters productive uses of limited resources. This issue is not merely clouded by the semantic misuse of terms like "neo-liberalism," but also

An earlier version of this essay was presented at the Regional Meeting of the Mont Pèlerin Society, "Fifty Years of Liberalism in Europe," Barcelona, Spain, September 10, 1997.

by complacency in some contemporary liberal circles that assume the academic validity of the classical market doctrines without the need to package them in ideas that embody wide popular appeal. In a recent interesting attempt to define modern liberalism, *The Economist* warns about the perils of complacency and underscores the danger of presuming that "we are all liberals now"—for not recognizing and reaffirming that our situation involves a grave risk, the risk that "it one day might no longer be true."[1]

A similar sentiment was expressed in April 1997 at the remarkable gathering of the Mont Pèlerin Society in Mont Pèlerin on the occasion of its fiftieth anniversary. The greatest threat to liberty, according to the consensus at the celebration, is the systematic misunderstanding of a liberal market order and the ethical institutions that underpin an open society. In Latin America, reform fatigue and the fear of living without what the celebrated Mexican poet Octavio Paz called the "philanthropic ogre" (the welfare state, unemployment subsidies, redistribution policies) lead to a deliberate misreading of the nature of voluntary exchange, of life in an open society. The problem surrounding the concept of "neoliberalism" constitutes a revealing example of this threat: It is now seen as the source of all social ills, even while any attempt to define what critics mean when they invoke such a pejorative term exposes a strawman argument, a deliberate misunderstanding. This problem is as much the product of ignorance as it is of our own failure to communicate the nature of a market order.

To be sure, Latin America has experienced significant strides in economic reform in the past two decades. The process of reform can be characterized as a four-dimensional program of fiscal and monetary discipline, aggressive deregulation, a broad-based program of privatization and multilateral liberalization of trade and investment. This fits the fashionable description of reform in accordance with the so-called "Washington consensus." The shifts in administration have all expressed commitment to continue structural reform and liberalization despite the changes in the political scenarios. The key priorities that target transformation are reform of the pension system, labor market flexibility, greater deregulation, and a "second wave" of privatization.

Nonetheless, the dramatic crisis engendered by the financial devaluations experienced in the period 1994–1999, beginning with the peso collapse of December 1994, undermined the region's image as an attractive market regime and sparked acute criticism of the entire program of reform through guilt by association. Unfortunately, the association between market reform and currency devaluation generated a widespread counterattack by forces opposed to the transformation process. This has trapped reform in a state of indecision and unpopularity. Consequently, enemies of reform, both inside and outside the body politic, have wielded the prevalence of antimarket sentiment to defend state ownership.

Unfortunately, the emphasis on macroeconomic adjustment has failed to heed the principles of an institutional approach, namely, an emphasis on secure property rights, competitive markets, a stable monetary system, and strong judicial institutions. These are essential features of long-run growth. So, despite the official commitment to market-based transformation, reform has failed to observe required changes in this rubric. In short, much has been done to strengthen liberalization, but much more remains to be done to meet the institutional requirements of a free and prosperous Latin America. The antiliberalization fallout of the currency collapses has led to the phenomenon known as reform fatigue. Indeed, the failure to effect institutional reform entails a moral hazard: If people continue to expect government to bail them out, via subsidies and state-sponsored protection, more of them will continue to engage in risky behavior, thereby making the shift to a free economy more difficult. It is arguable that reform has been partial and preferential. This is especially true of the program of privatization, where failure to expand property to a large community of owners in the interest of reaping the fiscal rewards of highly priced assets has won the initiative a very negative image. Not surprisingly, suspicions of crony capitalism and corruption associated with the sale of state-owned enterprises has inhibited progress in the second wave of privatization.

In general, there is an important idiosyncrasy surrounding the nature of Latin American liberalism: the definition of a liberal as an individual explicitly concerned with the Comtean goal of "how to end poverty and foster progress" through the preconceived design of a social blueprint. In countries like Mexico, the intellectual and historical origins of modern liberalism seek an impossible task—namely, a coherent reconciliation between the essential tenets of classical liberalism (rule of law, private property, civic responsibility, negative liberty, and the like) with a strong participation of the nation state in civil society. This presumption informs the idea of "liberalism with social orientation" and constitutes the basis of the doctrine of social liberalism, which is enshrined in Mexico's Constitution of 1917. Indeed, in its most contemporary versions, Latin American liberal doctrine is centered on the need to develop a *via media* between institutional guarantees of individual rights and the strong positive influence of the nation state as a mechanism to guarantee "social rights" (e.g., the right to free education, the right to a fair wage, the right to housing, and others). The tension between these two objectives is evident. It is a special case of the contradiction embodied in the Estados Justicieros, the heroic attempt to force society to be free, a contradiction that today finds expression in the post-Comtean figure of the modern technocrat, the new champion of "neo-liberalism": the idea that a liberal order can be intelligibly combined with the goals of "social justice," land redistribution, and the right to labor protection.

A clear consequence for the future of liberty in Latin America is that there is a great deal of "homework" for the next generation. The conceptual problem with Latin American liberalism is not merely historical. Indeed, it is either defended by ill-suited figures (the modern technocrat, who presumes to know so much more about society than anyone else) or inadequately defended by its main protagonists. Surely, the hope for a civilized debate is prostituted in the interest of flashy sentimentalism (e.g., soak the rich in order to help the poor) and the abject protagonism of a cause opposed to illusory horrors such as "savage capitalism" or "the heartlessness of the market." The main protagonists of classical liberalism in the Latin American region are all too aware of this problem. Carlos Alberto Montaner, for instance, often asks whether the conceptual opposition ever contemplates viable alternatives, and this question is self-answering. Yet guilt by association has been powerful in sustaining the image of the market as a manifestation of an order that merely serves the interests of a powerful few. The current debates are fraught with distortions of what a liberal society purports to accomplish. The fashion, it seems, is to attack the market with no regard for what it is, what it stands for, the means and the ends of an open society. This is the nonsense of "neo-liberalism," a fallacy that leads to spilt ink and wasted effort. It is the economic analogue of the "bogeyman" tale.

A recent editorial in Mexico's daily newspaper *Reforma* illustrates this practice: After attacking Adam Smith as the intellectual author of laissez faire, the editorial proceeds to designate the free market as no more than cold social Darwinism, devoid of moral content, responsible for the informal economy, the ultimate destroyer of good will among men and women. The same editorial blames "neo-liberalism" for, among other things, the tragic death of Princess Diana. With a definition like this, by all means, let us all proclaim the beauty of antiliberalism! And let us not exclude the common flu from the gamut of demonstrably brutish effects that the free market engenders on the human race!

Without markets, there would be no consumers to sell such cheap shots. Still, a fundamental problem with the liberal doctrines of free market and free trade is that, despite the salient failure of central planning in the twentieth century, proposals for market-based reform lack acceptability among intellectuals. In essence, there is a small market for market views—certainly much smaller than for the views proposed by academics and policymakers of an interventionist bent. The obvious question for proponents of a market order is whether classical liberals can learn from their own views and sell the ideas of the market philosophy in the social and intellectual marketplace. Ideas, after all, have consequences.

As Madsen Pirie warned at the 1994 General Meeting of the Mont Pèlerin Society in Cannes, modern intellectuals tend to shield their esoteric practice behind the coziness of statist and interventionist doctrines—and the subsidies that invariably attend their expression in classrooms and the Ivory Tower. F. A. Hayek himself, the great enemy of the fatal conceit of central planning, urged, "Show no mercy," to demonstrate the overwhelming superiority of the market as a social arrangement to the counterparts proposed by the statist faith of social engineering. With a few exceptions, this goal has not been met. On the ideological front, it should prove standard, but the point is that selling the market is very difficult.

Pirie is right that the liberal alternative should learn more about the principles of marketing. The intellectual task has been generally focused on expressing disagreement with proponents of the statist orientation, not on explaining the benefits derived from the establishment of open markets and open trade per se. In turn, this has engendered criticism that is ill-grounded, but nonetheless invited by the failure to "market the market," for instance, adjectival shots of "supermarket intellectuals," quasi-thinkers swayed by emotion, self-serving analysts corrupted by the forces of financial gain. In the majority of cases, this is an expression of bad faith—or, as Pirie says, lack of marketing the proper perspective. Notwithstanding the utter collapse of socialism and the moral and intellectual bankruptcy of statism, many academics will not assign the title of "intellectual" unless one endorses a state-friendly view.

This underscores what is fundamentally right about Pirie's analysis. The promotion of the market order as the best institutional alternative for a better standard of living entails disassociating it from the image of markets as static entities that are unable to solve "externalities" (the informal economy, environmental degradation, income inequality, business cycles of boom and bust). This is a complex task. Hayek was right in claiming that the origin of wealth and well-being is the consequence of a framework that guarantees private ownership rights and open markets in an atmosphere of competition and freedom. Yet, an ancillary post-Hayekian task involves marketing this idea, with its multiple ramifications, in a manner that can gain public acceptance and influence the current body politic.

Consider, for instance, the critical topic of competition. The market-based tradition that runs from Adam Smith to Robert Barro stresses the dangers involved in alliances of businessmen with political power as a way to secure captive markets and other privileges at the expense of everyone else. This danger is often associated with the market, while it is precisely the lack of open markets that engenders cronyism and the abuse of the political process to gain market share. When liberal intellectuals like Smith, Mises, Friedman, or Stigler talk of competition, and the institutional need for open competition, such discourse is often conflated with another concept, that of perfect competition. This is a standard mistake, but is arguably more attributable to the lack of explanation by classical market economists than to a deliberate misunderstanding by market critics.

A salient example of this phenomenon in Mexico is exemplified by Sergio Sarmiento, a prominent political journalist, who declares that while he characterizes himself as one of the "liberal" persuasion, he is far more attracted by the intellectual left than by the "profoundly boring" intellectual right. Never mind the dubious basis of the distinction between "right" and "left" (a distinction that breeds far more misunderstanding and confusion than is necessary). The point Sarmiento makes is clear: The opponents of market-based ideas are far more captivating and curiously enjoy a greater degree of acceptability than do proponents of the liberal point of view.

So be it. But, to paraphrase Sarmiento, such accusations have become "boring" and predictable. But the point is that much opposition to market views relies on dubious grounds, where name-calling, ad hominem arguments, and adjectival shots are the rule, not the exception. Characteristically, markets are condemned as "savage capitalism," as always leading to an intolerable concentration of wealth, and as enriching the rich at the expense of the poor.

This self-styled view of "social justice" reflects an obscene interpretation of how markets work and of the institutions of property, competition, and individual freedom that sustain them. Yet, despite the collapse of the socialist fantasy in 1989, the advocates of free markets in Mexico and Latin America are accused of right-wing extremism, of being clandestine agents of the CIA, of technocratic elitism and other illogical nonsense. The unbridled faith in government and the welfare state, representative of the vast majority of the establishment, constitutes an exercise in intellectual and moral naiveté. But as Pirie says, the ideals of the free market cannot be settled on the basis of pure reason. The task is to market them in a manner that can gain public acceptance and influence the policymakers of the current political structure.

One who is attempting to market the market is Carlos Alberto Montaner, co-author (with Alvaro Vargas Ilosa and Plinio Apuleyo

Mendoza) of a tract provocatively titled *Manual of a Perfect Latin-American Idiot.* This polemical work is the outcome of exasperation with the blatant fallacies and conceptual abuse of economic language that characterize extant "revolucionario" movements everywhere from Sao Paulo to Chiapas, the very same antagonists that blame all global wrongs on "neo-liberalism": narcotics, poverty, the informal economy, delinquent debts, the "tyranny of money," fiscal inequity, cultural imperialism, and the like.

Indeed, what a gallant cause, to oppose the ineffable ghost of neo-liberalism, described with the sentimental loveliness that characterizes the rhetoric of culture critics who relish the superficial allure of conceptual trendiness. For instance, members of the current literati like Carlos Monsivaís, the Mexican writer who lashes out with such sophistical nonsense with articulate passion: "Neo-liberalism, one of the most odious and oppressive realities of the planet. . . ." Surely, words of beauty and concern, but words which never fail to violate the most elementary principles of logic, which flagrantly beg the question by not taking the time to reflect the content of liberal proposals.

The antiliberal tirades are, according to the criteria in the *Manual of a Perfect Latin-American Idiot,* expressions of contemporary idiocy—the fashionable rhetoric of the semantically adept but conceptually illiterate actor who collects political points by opposing the "tyranny of money," but who fails to reflect on the real consequences of a society without a medium of exchange or store of value. Imagine! No food or toilet paper for resilient structuralists who chant in unison against the evils of foreign investment! This is the mark of a "perfect idiot": the failure to recognize that money is a spontaneous and universal tool required to mediate the needs and desires of agents who demand and agents who supply. As long as scarcity exists, money becomes an elementary tool of economic survival.

There are three traits that define the anatomy of a perfect idiot, and all three manifest themselves in the myriad of statements expressed in contemporary antiliberalism. The first trait is a predictable "anti-gringo" stance: the USA as the source of all socioeconomic evils in the Latin region. A second characteristic of the antiliberal idiot is the belief in fatalism: the idea that the nation's problems are products of forces beyond our control, superimposed by exogenous factors that have perpetuated underdevelopment. It is always "something else": large foreign debts, falling oil prices, financial globalization, speculative capital, rising imports, U.S. interest rates, embargoes, Alan Greenspan, and much more. It is curious, then, that the antiliberal idiot never reflects on the obvious question: Why? In particular, why is it that Singapore and Taiwan produce so much with so little in natural resources, yet Mexico and Brazil suffer such backwardness even though they have the wherewithal to become economic giants?

The answer is found in two fundamental concepts: institutions and confidence. A society with secure property ownership rights, with access to contracts and dispute-solving mechanisms, as well as a reliable currency, will accumulate investment in human capital and generate wealth. The easy way out, proffered by the perfect idiot, is to blame an external factor and indulge in political martyrdom. Indeed, the third characteristic of the antiliberal idiot, the activist who performs gargles with the word "social," is the "pie" theory of wealth: the idea that wealth is a given, preconceived and accomplished beforehand, and that it merely needs to be equitably distributed by a select group of social engineers—a matter of slicing up the pie. This breeds the policy that a solution to the problem of poverty (a very serious problem) can be accomplished via fiscal policies of greater spending and handouts to all (a very superficial and counterproductive solution).

In this age of rapid capital mobility and open, integrated economies, a sharp deviation from proper public policy is immediately castigated with capital outflow shocks. In turn, such developments engender political repercussions. This suggests an immense political risk associated with sticking to a statist agenda of populism and protectionism (an agenda that includes disastrous recipes, such as using monetary expansion as a tool for economic growth). Clearly, however, the worst enemy of liberty and classical liberalism in Latin America would be complacency.

Ludwig von Mises often contemplated a key question: What can we do? To be sure, we can continue to stress the civilizing influence of the market, of the principle that exchange of goods and services enables everyday people to coexist in accordance with implicit norms (contracts) and communications (typically via the system of prices). We can continue to dissociate the market order from the practices of crony capitalism, special favors, concessions, corruption, bureaucratic discretion, permits for everything, and other products of a tradition of mercantilism that will take enterprise and forceful imagination to deconstruct. We can declare a moratorium on the word "neo-liberalism." And, more importantly, we can heed Pirie's advice to market the market in popular and accessible terms. This was a crucial principle of the late Edgard Mason, a brilliant Mexican liberal, who grasped the simplicity and fundamental importance of free markets, and who is best remembered for the following memorable proposition: Only a system like Soviet-style socialism was able to erect the Berlin Wall; but only a system like the free market was able to allocate its entire remains throughout the globe. QED.

Note

[1]"The Perils of Complacency," *The Economist* (December 21, 1996).

Sanford Ikeda

Two Cheers for Government Failure

There are two responses to my title, and they define the respondent's political ideology. One is, "Why cheer for government failure?" The other, "Why not three cheers for government failure?"

What is government failure? In simple language, government fails when those who are ultimately responsible for making policy decisions fail to achieve their objectives. Those decisionmakers—politicians, bureaucrats, and voters—are often referred to in public choice literature and political economy as "public choosers." Government failure occurs when public choosers fail to achieve their objectives or, in other words, when interventions do not succeed in producing the expected outcomes.

When government fails, what is there to cheer about? This depends on what it is that the government has failed to do. Ludwig von Mises believed that government has a legitimate function to fulfill in providing goods and services, such as national defense, that the market would have trouble providing on its own. Government, according to Mises, must exist as a body with a monopoly over violent aggression. The government can beat, imprison, and kill. We give it that authority to achieve an objective: preventing the chaos that would arise if everyone could beat, imprison, and kill. There is no reason to cheer when the government fails at the task of chaos prevention.

But why two cheers? The first cheer has to do with a passage from *Human Action*:

> As soon as something happens in the economy that any of the various bureaucratic institutions does not like or that arouses the anger of a pressure group, people clamor for new interventions, controls, and restrictions. But for the inefficiency of the lawgivers and the laxity, carelessness, and corruption of many of the functionaries, the last vestiges of the market economy would have long since disappeared.[1]

I found this passage intriguing because some political economists would regard "inefficiency, laxity, carelessness, and corruption" as what constitutes government failure. It is common sense: These are vices, but Mises is proposing that they can serve as a defense of the free market.

In his inaugural address as president of the Foundation of Economic Education, Don Boudreaux told an interesting story. Don is from Louisiana, where they catch a lot of shrimp and sell them from the back of station wagons and trucks. The State of Louisiana tried to regulate that practice, requiring vendors to follow certain sanitary procedures and to sell in particular locations. The police in the New Orleans area, who are noted for their corruption, turned a blind eye to this. In his address Boudreaux said, "Rah, rah for corruption," because in this case it was protecting an exchange that should be protected under a legitimate free market regime. It thwarted a statist regime's attempt to stamp out this creative way of doing business. And that is what I think Mises had in mind here.

Many political economists would regard inefficiency as a form of government failure. Probably the most popular approach to political economy among conservatives, public choice theory, tends in most cases to look at this kind of government activity as a form of government failure. Mises is saying that in certain instances we should cheer, not criticize, policymakers' failure to achieve the ends they want to achieve. Inefficiency, carelessness, and so on represent a line of defense for the free market in these instances when the state has overstepped its bounds. So, one cheer for government failure.

The second cheer is a bit harder to explain, but the following three stories should help. In 1929 Mises published *Critique of Inter-*

ventionism. An essay in that book, "A Theory of Price Controls," contains one of Mises' first descriptions of the dynamics of regulation—that is, whereby one regulation produces another. To paraphrase: Suppose the state thinks that the price of milk is too high, that poor mothers need to buy milk for their children, and that if the price of milk could be suppressed below the market level, milk would be more available to these young mothers. Mises warned that such suppression would create shortages after the initial stock runs out, because producers would not be able to cover their costs of production when the price is so low. The quantity demanded will exceed the quantity supplied at a price below the free market price. So what should be done? The state has already created an unintended consequence. It wanted to make milk more available by controlling the price, but instead it has been made less available. The state has created a problem as a result of an intervention that was meant to address a perceived problem. At this point, Mises says the state has two choices. One is to remove the price control, which will allow the price to rise to its free market level, and they will have eliminated the shortage. The other option is to somehow reduce the providers' cost of producing milk. For example, dairy farmers have to buy electricity to operate the machinery that milks the cows; they have to buy feed for the cows. So a public official might then go in and regulate the price of feed and the price of electricity. Then the cost of producing milk will be lower, enabling the providers to cover their costs even at the lowered price of milk. But, of course, the story will repeat itself at that level. Then there will be shortages of electricity and feed. Now what is the state going to do? It can either remove the regulations on the inputs (electricity, feed) and the output (milk) and give it back to the market, or it can intervene further. This underlying logic drives the interventionist process further and further toward the maximal state, toward full collectivism.

If you think Mises' *Critique of Interventionism* is just a theoretical construct, consider Robert Higgs' description of the United States during World War II.[2] A piece of legislation called the Emergency Price Control Act was enacted to hold down the prices the government had to pay for wartime resources. After a short time, however, a series of shortages, price rationing, and political conflicts led to the more comprehensive Economic Stabilization Act, which in turn led to unforeseen shortages. In April 1943, the president brought all consumer goods within the reach of price controls. What had begun as a program to "protect" only goods and services essential to the war effort gradually extended to almost all consumer goods. The market system remained in suspended animation for the duration of the war. During World War II we saw in practice the interventionist logic that Mises had described years earlier. Capitalism it definitely was not.

Another example having to do with price controls and World War II continues to affect our lives today. Because of price controls and the war effort, there was a labor shortage during World War II. Employers needed to hire more employees, but they couldn't, because many were in the military, and because wage and price controls prohibited employers from offering higher wages to attract what labor there was. So employers began to offer health benefits, just as regulation-era banks gave customers free toasters because they could not provide interest on savings deposits. Employers offered their workers health benefits as an enticement, and so in this way health benefits were tied to occupation. Back in 1994, during the debate about President Clinton's proposal to socialize medicine in the United States, one critique of the current system was, "If you lose your job, you lose your health benefits. Isn't capitalism terrible?" But anyone who looks back at history would know that the very fact that health benefits are tied to occupation is the result of a previous intervention. So we have the logic working out again: Intervention follows previous intervention. Interventions cause problems that public officials think need to be solved by more intervention.

Those are the stories: Now let me offer you two paradoxes in an attempt to figure out why we give a second cheer for government failure. Mises assumed in his writings that public choosers are men and women of good will. People who support interventions have good intentions; they want to help promote the public welfare and are public spirited. The first paradox is, if public choosers are benevolent in this sense, why do they continue to support a system that produces failure time and time again? After the first few failures, why wouldn't they just reverse themselves? Mises never explains this fully. The second paradox is that Mises describes interventionism, which is the policy of mixed economy, as unworkable and illogical. It is like trying to mix oil and water. The market process functions according to a logic that cannot work if policymakers try to impose controls on the adjustments that take place. The interventionist system is unstable and transient. If that is true, why is the interventionist mixed economy the most popular and widespread economic system in the world? Mises does not explain this.

Both paradoxes can be resolved in part by recognizing the astonishing complexity of the market process. The market process and entrepreneurial discovery and coordination produce remarkable results, but they require astonishing complexity because of the amazing amount of knowledge necessary to run the show. An amazing amount of cooperation has to take place, and an amazing amount of knowledge has to be coordinated to produce a desired result. The second thing we recognize is that this knowledge is dispersed among thousands and thousands of people. This is the insight that Friedrich Hayek developed from Mises: the dispersed nature of knowledge. And third, we have to recognize the severe limitations on the human mind in discovering this dispersed knowledge; that is Israel Kirzner's contribution to Austrian theory.

Mises, Hayek, and Kirzner have taught us that the market process and the plans in the market process are coordinated through spontaneously generated social institutions: markets, private property, and especially the price system. The price system is a social institution that coordinates the plans of individuals that have contextual knowledge. Prices that result from the free exchange of private property tend to reflect relative scarcity. We can plan rationally as long as we have market prices based on the exchange of private property. Interventionism hinders the cooperation of these individuals because it hinders the operation of prices in coordinating these plans. Over time, it gets harder and harder to see intervention as the source of negative unintended consequences. Well-intentioned people try to produce a result, but something goes wrong, so they try to fix that, and then see other problems. It is all so complex. The consequences are so far-reaching that they are affected by the consequences of interventions that are taking place elsewhere. After a while it is very difficult to see the source of these negative consequences. Moreover, even if that source could be seen, it gets harder and harder to repair these problems as government grows. As the scope of state activity widens, the state generates more and more problems, more and more chaos, making it harder to pinpoint the sources and increasingly difficult to get at those sources. Early in the process, when the market is almost free, it might be possible to go back. But after decades of regulating and regulating and regulating, it is extremely difficult to reform the system. The sorry state of public education in inner cities is an example. Consider the interactions of these interventions: The drug policy of the United States drives up the price of certain narcotics, which makes it very profitable for youngsters to go into business selling them; the welfare system discourages them from working in the legitimate economy anyway; and housing developments make crime a more viable option than living in poor but flourishing communities. If we were to pass the school voucher system and eliminate public education, making it all private, I am not sure that alone would solve the problem—not as long as welfare, public housing, and certain laws that make criminal activity desirable are in place.

What has to happen is across-the-board reform. That is the second cheer for government failure: When the system fails, we reach a crisis that makes radical, sweeping reform possible. Mises described this as the point at which public choosers can decide to go toward full maximal state collectivism, like communism, or back to the free market. They make a choice: Interventionism has shown its true colors, and its inner contradictions are too obvious to ignore. They must go with collectivism, which in a sense is a more rational, more consistent position than interventionism, or they can go back to the free market. Government failure at that point creates a possibility for significant reform, and that is the second cheer. It is pessimistic, perhaps, but I think it is realistic.

So how do we resolve these paradoxes? Why do men and women of good will continue to pursue intervention? Because they cannot see the consequences of their actions, and this is due to dispersed information and the limitations of the human mind. Why are most economies mixed economies? In part it is because the process of interventionism has to go on for a long time before the inner logic of interventionism and its unworkability become apparent. Only at the end is the need for radical reform clear.

I have tried to make three points. One is pragmatic, one is theoretical, and one is what you might call methodological.

The pragmatic point is simply that with the fall of the Berlin Wall and the fall of what we call communism, the legitimacy of central planning is no longer popular among intellectuals in the West. With that occurrence, the interventionist mixed economy is the model now used in these formerly collectivist societies: It is not the free market. You hear the words "free market" in various Eastern European and other former communist countries, but what they are talking about is a mixed economy. Francis Fukayama, for example, talks about the end of history, and what he means is that we have come to the point at which liberal democracy and the welfare state are the model: There is no more argument. Fascism, communism, and socialism are no longer viable options; the only viable option is liberal democracy with a welfare state. So the pragmatic lesson is that we need to study the mixed economy. We need to understand how it works so that we can have a legitimate argument against this view.

The theoretical point is the interventionist theory that we have examined in this essay: Intervention creates problems because it interferes with the way in which the market process handles knowledge.

The methodological point—in a way the most fitting for this occasion—is that important and interesting questions still need to be resolved in Austrian economics.

Mises did a brilliant job of explaining the core of the logic of the interventionist process, but he did not explain everything. He did not explain why people continue these policies, and he did not explain why the interventionist mixed economy is so widespread. These puzzles still remain in *Human Action* and in Austrian economics. I love *Human Action*: It was one of the first books on economics I had ever read, and for a long time I thought it contained the last word. But one eventually realizes that it is not the last word; it is just the beginning. Read Mises' pages for answers to policy questions and to solve certain problems in your mind, but if you think about those problems deeply enough, you will realize that Mises—brilliant as he was, broad-minded as he was—did not see everything.

Consider *Human Action* a starting point for further research. Look at the whole body of Austrian economics—Mises, Kirzner, Rothbard, Ebeling, Larry White, and others. There is a tremendous amount of work to be done. The methodological point is that we should be inspired by *Human Action*; fifty years after its publication it lives because it does still inspire.

There will continue to be new generations of brilliant Austrian economists who will write books that will criticize my book and show where I am wrong. This is part of the intellectual process. We should always ask questions, because once we stop puzzling, once we decide that any book is "the last word," Austrian economics will be dead.

I urge you to take *Human Action* down from the shelf, look at it, read it, think about it, and question it. That is the true way to celebrate this great book.

Notes

[1]Ludwig von Mises, *Human Action*, 2d ed. (New Haven, CT: Yale University Press, 1963).

[2]Robert Higgs, *Crisis and Leviathan* (New York: Oxford University Press, 1987), pp. 207–11.

Karen I. Vaughn

Mises and the Demise of Socialism

It has dawned on me as I have been teaching my classes in the last few years that a certain piece of recent history that seems so terribly important to me is not well-known to my undergraduates. To my students, who were about ten years old when it happened, it is only a distant memory, if it is a memory at all. I am referring to the events of 1989, the collapse of the Berlin Wall, probably the most remarkable peacetime event in modern Western history. For my entire memory, the Berlin Wall was a stark and imposing symbol of the separation of the communist East and the liberal West, a symbol with such a concrete manifestation that I thought it would never disappear. Yet, in 1989 it came down. But not only did the Wall come down, the entire communist bloc fell apart. First Eastern bloc countries became liberated, and eventually the Soviet Union disappeared onto the ash heap of history.

This remarkable event was started by something that would seem insignificant: the decision of Hungary to open its borders and allow free passage into Austria. This meant that East Germans could not only travel easily to Hungary, another communist country, but from Hungary they could make their way into West Germany without having to pass through the East German border. Consequently, a veritable flood of East Germans made their way into the West. What was so startling was that the Soviet Union did nothing to stop them. This was unprecedented in the history of the Soviet Union. Following World War II, any time a satellite country would make an attempt to separate itself from the Soviet sphere, the Soviet Union did not hesitate to resort to force; yet in 1989 it allowed these events to happen. Why in 1989—and not in 1956 and not in 1968—did the Soviet Union allow its empire to fall apart?

One answer that is often given—and that is partly true—is that the man in charge in 1989 was a different kind of Soviet leader. Mikhail Gorbachev really wanted to change the course of the Soviet Union away from its isolation and oppression and open up its ties with the West. While I believe that is partly true, a deeper reason lies behind it. By 1989 Gorbachev had little recourse but to let it happen, because the Soviet economy was in shambles. To have sent in troops and tanks would have required a massive commitment of resources that the Soviet Union could no longer afford. Its collapsing economy was largely hidden from the West until the archives were opened when the Soviet Union dissolved. Those declassified documents revealed a story about Soviet economic performance that differed greatly from the official story.

Most people in the West had believed that the Soviet Union was a great industrial nation that rivaled the United States; in fact, there were times in our recent history when we worried that they would overtake us. Nikita Khrushchev once bragged that the Soviet Union would bury us through its economic performance. Yet the reality was that by 1989 the Soviet Union had been through two decades of relative stagnation, and by the time the Berlin Wall started to fall, the Soviet gross domestic product (GDP) was probably about one-fourth that of the United States. Rather than a great industrial giant that rivaled the U.S., it turned out that the Soviet Union was more like a Third World country with a big army, which it supported by starving consumers of goods and keeping living standards extremely low. The Soviet military was supported at the expense of consumer welfare. Meanwhile the U.S. actually could afford its large army, navy, Marine Corps, and air force and support an increasing standard of living for all of its citizens at the same time. The official GDP statistics do not begin to tell the story of what it was like to be a citizen in the former Soviet Union. Consumers not only had fewer goods than we had, they also suffered incredible inconveniences in their daily lives. Consumer goods were rationed, there were long lines to buy almost everything, and what could be purchased was likely to be of poor quality. Living conditions were extremely crowded, health care was substandard, life expectancy had been falling for about a decade, and probably most nightmarish of all, bureaucrats were ever-present in all aspects of daily life.

This experience was very different from the expectations of the Marxist revolutionaries who had wanted to create a workers' paradise out of the Russian revolution. Inspired by Karl Marx's critiques of capitalism, they set out to eliminate all of the capitalist institutions that they thought were oppressing the workers: private property, especially private property in the means of production (factories, machines, and the capital goods that enabled employers to hire labor); wage labor; money and monetary exchange. At the end of the revolution and during the first stages of communism, they tried to institute this pure version of the Marxist vision; this led to chaos and starvation. And so a hybrid form of communism was introduced wherein all major decisions about what to produce and how to produce it were turned over to a central planning agency. While not pure communism in the Marxist sense, this approach at least fulfilled the minimum requirements of a Marxist regime: That is, there would be no private ownership of the means of production. All businesses would become directed and owned by the state for the people. There would be no private wage labor: Everyone worked for the good of the state. And there would be no private trades among producers.

After Stalin came to power, the Soviet Union did manage to record high growth rates. It was only after Stalin's death, even as official growth rates remained high, that more discerning calculations seemed to suggest that the Soviets were running into trouble and growth rates were starting to fall. Production was still strong and able to support the military, but all hopes that the USSR could surpass or even match the wealth of the West faded into oblivion by the 1980s. When Gorbachev came to power, there was finally a decision to confront the economic problems of the Soviet Union and reform the system. Unfortunately for the Soviets, the system was unreformable and had to be abolished before a rational economic system could be put into place.

Now as tragic as the story of the Soviet Union is, it is doubly tragic because it could have been avoided had the warnings issued by Ludwig von Mises been heeded. As early as 1920 Ludwig von Mises explained why neither a pure Marxist economy nor the hybrid form that was eventually put into place could ever hope to match the ability of a market economy to create wealth and satisfy consumer demand. In 1920 Mises wrote an article titled "Economic Calculation in the Socialist Commonwealth." Years before, when Mises was a student, he had known several other students who were devoted communists and great admirers of Marx. He wrote his article to disabuse them of their foolish notion that an economy could actually be run on Marxist principles. He put forward two major arguments as to why socialism would not work: First, in any economic system rational decisions could not be made about input use and the distribution of goods without prices; second, it would be unrealistic to expect people to work the same way in a society in which they did not have a stake in the outcome of their decisions as they would if they did have a stake in the outcomes. In other words, people need to have some reward system that will induce them to work efficiently. In sum, Mises argued that in a pure Marxist economy—without money, without private property, without wage labor, without private exchange—you could never generate either prices or the proper incentives that would lead to rational economic outcomes.

Let us consider these two arguments in turn. Why do we need prices? Prices are so second-nature to us that we don't even think about them. When you go into a store to buy something that you are accustomed to buying, you know right away if the price changes, if it is too high or too low, and if you can afford it. You are always making calculations based on your knowledge of prices. You are also making calculations based on knowledge of your own income, but where does your income come from? It comes from your work effort, for which there is a price. Mises was arguing that this mundane calculation is actually one of the most fundamental features of the market economy. Prices enable us to figure out what we have to give up in order to get something that we want. When we talk about what something costs, we are really talking about what we have to give up to get something else, and we know how much we have to give up because we know its price. We know what we have to give in dollars, but we know those dollars could be spent on something else. Prices do this work for us because they are measures of relative scarcity, of how abundant something is compared to something else.

Economists are always making claims about alternatives. We never say anything is worth something; we say it is worth something relative to something else. All economic decisions are made by comparing one thing to another. So if some good that we want is very abundant, it will sell for a lower price than if that same good were scarce. Availability affects price. Price is also affected by how intensely you want the good. If you want it a lot, you are likely to pay a higher price for it than if you don't want it as much. Aggregated over an entire economy, we say that things that are in greater demand command higher prices than things that are less demanded. So when economists talk about demand and supply, they are really talking about how much people want things relative to how much of that thing is available. And we make comparisons based on prices because prices measure the importance of one thing relative to its supply compared to something else relative to its supply. Prices are ways of comparing relative values. For consumers they serve a very important function: They help ration goods. If you don't have prices, you must either have a race based on who gets there first, so the swiftest get the commodity rather than the slowest, or you have to fight about it. We don't fight about who gets what; we don't run foot races to find out who gets what; we have prices, and that helps each of us monitor how much we buy.

Getting to the heart of what Mises had to say about the socialist economy, prices tell us as producers how to produce things cheaply and efficiently. If you are trying to excavate a building site and must decide whether to hire one hundred minimum-wage laborers with shovels or one steam shovel and five people, which would be the cheaper alternative? We live in a rich country where labor costs are high, so we probably would immediately choose the steam shovel and just five people, but that might not be the right answer in a different economic system where labor is cheap. This decision cannot be made without knowing how much the shovels cost, how much the steam shovel hires for, and how much you have to pay the laborers. Those decisions have to be made with the help of prices, and that is what Mises meant when he said that you could not run a system without having economic prices to help you make economic decisions.

Now you might be able to allocate consumer goods. The Soviet Union actually did. The prices that were attached to consumer goods did not have much connection to relative scarcities, but they just let people line up. This followed Armen Alchian's suggestion: Let them run a foot race and see who gets there first or, in this case, who has the most patience. That can be done, but producer inputs in the actual production of goods and services will be chaotic and irrational unless there are prices that help you decide whether to hire one hundred men with one hundred shovels or five men with one piece of machinery. Those decisions are crucial to how much can be produced in an economic system. That is one little example of a problem that businessmen face day after day after day. They all compete for the same inputs, the same kinds of intermediate goods, the same kind of machinery, and labor. How do you know which firm should get which inputs and how much they should use? You cannot make those decisions without prices.

Mises next turned his attention to the source of prices. Many Marxists in the 1920s and 1930s understood his point about prices, but they thought that prices could be derived without markets. They contended that prices could be calculated from statistical data, mathematical models, and constructed indexes of relative scarcities. Mises countered, correctly, that prices can be obtained only by allowing people to trade freely in markets based on their ownership of resources and of their own labor. Prices only mean something when they emerge from what Adam Smith called, in a very colorful way, the "higgling and bargaining" of the market. Higgling and bargaining in microcosm is what happens every day in a market economy. People compare how much something is worth to the seller and how much it is worth to the buyer. They strike trades, and these prices then provide information to other people. Prices are the result of people communicating to each other how much things are worth to them. It gets hidden because we are always trading for money: We don't higgle and bargain at the grocery store; we just pay the price. But underneath that fixed price a higgling and bargaining process has taken place somewhere down the wholesale chain. All prices in market economies come about because people who own goods figure out trades that are mutually beneficial, and they decide on prices that reflect what Thomas Aquinas once called a "common estimate" of the value of a thing. When Mises was telling the socialists back in 1920 that Marxism was not going to work, he was saying that without this free trade based on private ownership, they would never know what things are really worth. He was telling them no more than the absolute truth, but they did not believe him. Not only did the architects of the Soviet system not believe him, but most of the economics profession did not believe him either.

Prices figure in yet another way in the producer market. Businesses need prices to calculate profit and loss. Profit sometimes gets bad press in our society. It is not commonly understood—at least not by the press and among academics anyway—what profits do. Profits signal to producers that they are producing things that consumers want and they are producing them in such a way that the value of the input—all of the machines, all of the raw materials, all of the people hired to produce these goods—is less than the total value of the things produced. They are creating value. That is what people do when they are allowed to trade freely in markets. They take inputs—everything that goes into producing your toasters and automobiles and clothes and shoes—and they produce something that is worth more to consumers than the value of the inputs themselves in some other occupation.

Profits are good. Profits tell you that you are serving consumers. They also encourage increased supply by making the profitable venture known to other producers, who will want to secure some of the profit for themselves. By having a positive profit, you not only know you are on the right track, but you also encourage other people to do likewise. Profits tell you whether you are really serving consumer demand and doing it efficiently. Losses, of course, tell you that you are not: You are doing something wrong. You should either get out of the business or change what you are doing, because your competitors know more than you do. In a Soviet-style system without private property in the means of production, there are no guideposts to tell you whether you are serving consumer demands or even whether you are serving the central planning board's demands efficiently.

Mises' second argument was that people will work efficiently only if they have an incentive to do so. He said that if businessmen do not have a stake of some sort in their enterprise, they are unlikely to do all of the hard work that it takes to keep costs low. This does not mean that they won't work; it just means that they probably won't do all of the things that a real businessman has to do to make a profit. Mises argued that you could not play at a market; it is not a game. Businessmen do not treat their businesses as a game; they really have to work hard to keep costs down and make all the little adjustments and decisions that make their businesses profitable. Mises argued that no one would take those actions if there were no private ownership of business. It is hard work, it is not pleasant, and people often get mad at you. He was arguing that the incentive structure is different when you do not have private ownership of the means of production.

Mises further pointed out that without private ownership, you have to think not only about what you do now but about your plans for the future. Austrian economics has always put a premium on time: Decisions made today come to fruition only in the future, but every businessman has to make decisions now without knowing how they are going to turn out. He makes his best guess, and he has to take some risks. Mises argued that risks taken with one's own money are fundamentally different from those taken with other people's money. If you are in a system in which the property is not yours and you are following orders, you will be much more careful about obeying the rules than about coming up with a profitable bottom line. I think this was one of Mises' really important insights: A socialist system would have to rely on a central planning board, creating an economy run by a vast bureaucracy. It would be entirely different from a market economy, and it would have to be less efficient.

As other economists tried to figure out ways to come up with prices other than by free trade in the markets, they started to devise ways in which a central planning board could run things based on these prices generated by other means. They concluded that Mises was not right and that Mises and his younger colleague,

Friedrich Hayek, who also worked on this problem, were really kind of anachronistic. They convinced themselves that scientific socialism really was possible. The economics profession agreed that while socialism might have problems, they certainly were not truly economic problems.

Then the Wall fell, and we learned more about the Soviet Union. By 1992 the American Economic Association's meeting included a session on the collapse of communism and the transition because all the formerly communist countries wanted to become market economies. All of a sudden papers began to appear with the title "Mises was Right." Confronted with obvious evidence, they finally agreed that it is not possible run a centrally planned economy without market prices. The Soviet Union set up its own method of planning that tried to allocate inputs "efficiently," without relying on economic prices or private property. But it really was a hopeless exercise. They began with how firms were actually producing goods, and they set up a table that related the amount of input they were using to the amount of output they were producing and then extrapolated predictions of increased output from added resources. Such a system might work for a few years because the allocations remain pretty close to the way firms had done business when they were still private. But it does not work in the long run because of a fact that Mises pointed out in 1920, that Hayek pointed out in the 1930s and 1940s, and that economists are still learning about: The world does not stay the same; things change. Not only do demands change, but techniques of production and resources change, and a producer must adjust to meet these changes.

The longer the Soviet experiment went on, the more suboptimal their production became because the world was changing and they were not. East Germany was supposed to be the crown jewel in the Soviet bloc, the most efficient of all the communist countries. It turns out that East Germany, when it was finally united with the West, had a hopelessly obsolete capital stock, so obsolete that it could not be salvaged. Their worker skills were so far below West German standards that this supposedly very advanced communist country with its very advanced economy had to be totally retooled: It simply could not keep up with the West. Under a planning board that has no prices and no ability to judge how to change production, factories will allow their capital stock to wear out and their machines to be overused. Managers won't know how to upgrade them, or if they want to upgrade them, they have to get permission from central planning. That will create a burden for the central planners, so the managers probably will have to put in requisitions and wait for years to get some sort of response. It reminds me of how a state university is run. I was a department chairman for seven years, and I had to requisition everything and wait for approvals. I could not just solve a problem directly facing me: I had to get someone else's permission, and I had to make sure I had a paper trail to cover whatever I did. That is when I really started to understand how a centrally planned economy works.

It turns out that factor pricing was far more of a problem than consumer pricing because the Soviet use of factors was utterly irrational. There were continual problems of mismatches of raw materials and partially finished goods and the need for them. Too much steel might be sent to an automobile factory, while too little was sent to a construction site. The automobile factory and the construction site were not allowed to trade with each other; they were supposed to go back and tell the central planners that there was a problem so that the central planners could reallocate the steel. But that would take forever, so a kind of "gray market" developed in which the two firms would trade with each other illegally, but in a way that was tolerated because it was the only way to set things right. Consumer goods were always supplied in the wrong amounts, either because of underpricing or because of short supply. Incentive structures were totally perverse. Managers were rewarded for fulfilling a plan and punished for underfulfillment, so they would just fulfill a plan any way they could, even if they didn't get the right mix of inputs or made really shoddy products. What mattered was that they could check off "plan fulfilled."

The next two examples are in all the textbooks, but I love them anyway. A nail factory told to produce so many tons of nails turned out a few very big, very heavy nails because it was easy to produce them that way. They had lots of big, heavy nails and not enough small ones, so the next planning period when they were told to produce a certain quantity of nails, they produced lots of really skinny, very weak nails. If told to produce so many feet of windowpane, they would produce very thin windowpane that cracked with the first breeze. If the windowpane target was evaluated in terms of pounds, they would produce very thick, very heavy windowpanes that you could not see through. In the Eastern bloc, it was just one story after another of mistakes, shoddy products, workers who took breaks in the middle of the day to stand in line to buy needed consumer goods, and managers more concerned about where they stood with the party than about turning out useful products.

Mises was right about the inability to run an economy without prices and without the right incentives. He was right about something else, too; that is the last part of the story and not a very happy part either. If we look at what is happening now, over eight years after the Soviet Union dissolved and eleven years since the Eastern bloc countries won their independence, we see a very mixed result of the post-communist era. We see countries like Poland, Hungary, and especially the Czech Republic doing pretty well. These countries had the strongest ties to the West and had more historical memory of having participated in a market economy; their leaders had a pretty good idea of what had to be done. Russia, by contrast, is in as dismal a state as it was 1992: Life expectancy has fallen further, and their statistics are totally unreliable, so no one knows what output is now. There are pockets of abundance, but a lot of widespread poverty in the areas outside Moscow. Russia seems to be at a real crisis point. Why? They claimed that they wanted to become a market economy; they claimed that communism did not work; they claimed to have learned their lesson. Yet they are in a situation so dire that some people are nostalgic for communism. This is because they did not learn one more lesson that Ludwig von Mises had to teach them: A market economy does not exist in a political vacuum. It relies on laws of property and contract, on a sound monetary system, and on a set of attitudes that values honest dealing, does not value bribery, and does not see violence as a way of doing business. Despite their claims to the contrary, Russia has not yet managed to institute laws that protect private property. They do not even know how to register business ownership. A friend who teaches in Moscow tells me that as recently as three years ago they were registering shares of ownership in business by writing them down in pencil in a notebook. That is a pretty flimsy guarantee of your right to collect a dividend. Until those laws are in place, I cannot see that a market economy is going to flourish in Russia, but I do not see how those laws are going to be in place with the old politicians still running the show. Unless they can establish a rule of law that makes property secure, resists unequal taxes, and punishes violence, Russia will continue to be a Third World country—this time, one hopes, a Third World country without a big army.

LUDWIG VON MISES

My Contributions To Economic Theory

Your kind invitation to address you on my contributions to economic theory honors me greatly. It is not an easy task. Looking back on my work, I realize very well that the share of one individual in the total achievements of an epoch is small indeed, that he is indebted not only to his predecessors and teachers, but to all his colleagues and no less to his pupils. I know how much I owe to the economists of this country in particular since the time, many years ago, when my teacher [Eugen von] Böhm-Bawerk directed my attention to the study of the works of John Bates Clark, Frank A. Fetter, and other American scholars. And during all my activities, the recognition of my contributions by American economists encouraged me. Nor can I forget that, when still a student at the University of Vienna, I published a monograph on the development of Austrian Labour Legislation, an American economist was the first who showed an interest in it. And later the first scholar who appreciated my *Theory of Money and Credit* was again an American, my distinguished friend, Professor B. M. Anderson, in his book, *The Value of Money,* published in 1917.

From Ludwig von Mises, *Planning for Freedom,* 4th ed. (Grove City, PA: Libertarian Press, 1980; <www.libertarianpress.com>). This address was delivered before the Economics Faculty of New York University at the Faculty Club on November 20, 1940, a few months after Dr. and Mrs. Mises had arrived in New Jersey (August 2, 1940) as refugees from war-torn Europe. During his early months in America, Mises wrote his intellectual autobiography, *Ludwig von Mises, Notes and Recollections* (Grove City, PA: Libertarian Press, 1978); foreword by Margit von Mises; translation and postscript by Hans F. Sennholz.

I

When I first began to study the problems of monetary theory there was a general belief, namely, that modern marginal utility economics was unable to deal with monetary theory in a satisfactory way. Helfferich was the most outspoken of those who held this opinion. In his *Treatise on Money* he tried to establish that marginal utility analysis must necessarily fail in its attempts to build up a theory of money.

This challenge provided me with the incentive to use the methods of modern marginal utility economics in the study of monetary problems. To do so I had to use an approach radically different from that of the mathematical economists who try to establish the formulas of the so-called equation of exchange.

In dealing with such an equation the mathematical economist assumes that something (obviously, one of the elements of the equation) changes and that corresponding changes in the other values must follow. These elements of the equation are not items in the individual's economy, but categories of the whole economic system, and consequently the changes do not occur with individuals but with the whole system, with the *Volkswirtschaft* as a whole. This way of reasoning is eminently unrealistic and differs radically from the procedure of modern catallactics.* It is a return to the manner of reasoning which doomed to frustration the work of the older Classical economists. Monetary problems are economic problems and have to be dealt with in the same way as all other economic problems. The monetary economist does not have to deal with universal entities like volume of trade meaning total volume of trade, or quantity of money meaning all the money current in the whole economic system. Still less can he make use of the nebulous metaphor "velocity of circulation." He has to realize that the demand for money arises from the preferences of individuals within a market society. Because everybody wishes to have a certain amount of cash, sometimes more, sometimes less, there is a demand for money. Money is

*Catallactics is a name for the science of exchanges, the "branch of knowledge to investigate the market phenomena, that is, the determination of the mutual exchange ratios of the goods and services negotiated on markets, their origin in human action and their effects upon later action." Mises, *Human Action,* p. 232.

never simply in the economic system, money is never simply circulating. All the money available is always in the cash-holdings of somebody. Every piece of money may one day—sometimes more often, sometimes more seldom—pass from one man's cash-holding to another man's. But at every moment it is owned by somebody and is a part of somebody's cash-holdings. The decisions of individuals regarding the magnitude of their cash-holding, their choices between the disutility of holding more cash and its advantages, constitute the ultimate factor in the formation of purchasing power.

Changes in the supply of money or in the demand for it can never occur for all individuals at the same time and to the same extent and they, therefore, never affect their judgments of value and their behavior as buyers and sellers to the same degree. Therefore the changes in prices do not affect all commodities at the same time and to the same degree. The over-simple formula both of the primitive quantity theory and of contemporary mathematical economists according to which prices, that is, all prices, rise or fall in the proportion of the increase or decrease in the quantity of money, is absolutely wrong.

We have to study monetary changes as changes which occur first for some groups of individuals only and slowly spread over the whole economic system to the extent that the additional demand of those first benefited reaches other classes of individuals. Only in this way can we obtain a realistic insight into the social consequences of monetary changes.

II

Taking this as my point of departure I developed a general theory of money and credit and tried to explain the business cycle as a credit phenomenon. This theory, which is today styled the monetary theory or sometimes the Austrian theory of the trade cycle, led me to make some criticism of the continental, especially of the German, credit system. Readers were at first more interested in my pessimistic judgment of the trends of German Central Bank policy and my pessimistic forecast which nobody believed in 1912—until a few years later things turned out much worse even than I had predicted. It is the fate of the economist that people are more interested in his conclusions than in his explanations, and that they are reluctant to abandon a policy whose undesired but inevitable results the economist has demonstrated.

III

From my studies of monetary and credit problems, which later stimulated me to found the Austrian Institute of Business Cycle Research, I came to the study of the problem of economic calculation within a socialist community. In my essay on economic calculation in a socialist world, first published in 1920, and then later in my book on *Socialism,* I have proved that an economic system, where there is no private ownership of the means of production, could not find any criterion for determining the values of the factors of production and therefore could not calculate. Since I first touched upon this point, many dozens of books and many hundreds of articles published in different languages have dealt with the problem; this discussion has left my thesis unshattered. The treatment of the problems connected with planning, of course total planning and socialization, has been given a completely new direction by the indication of this as the crucial point.

IV

From the comparative study of the essential features both of capitalist and socialist economy I came to the related problem of whether, apart from these two thinkable systems of social cooperation, i.e., private ownership of the means of production and public ownership, there is a third possible social system. Such a third solution, a system which its proponents claim is neither socialism nor capitalism, but midway between both and avoiding the disadvantages of each and retaining the advantages of both, has again and again been suggested. I tried to examine the economic implications of these systems of government interference and to demonstrate that they can never attain the ends which people wish to attain with them. I later broadened the field of my research in order to include the problems of the *stato corporativo,* the panacea recommended by fascism.

V

Occupation with all these problems made necessary an approach to the question of the values and ends of human activity. The reproach of sociologists to the effect that economists deal only with an unrealistic "economic man" could no longer be endured. I tried to demonstrate that the economists were never so narrow as their critics believed. The prices whose formation we try to explain are a function of demand and it does not make any difference what kind of motives actuated those involved in the transaction. It is immaterial whether the motives of those who wish to buy are egoistic or altruistic, moral or immoral, patriotic or unpatriotic. Economics deals with the scarce means of attaining ends, irrespective of the quality of the ends. The ends are beyond the scope of rationality, but every action of a conscious being directed toward a specific goal is necessarily rational. It is futile to convict economics because it is rational and deals with rationality. Of course, science is always rational.

In my treatise on Economic Theory, published in the German* language in Geneva a few months ago—an English† edition will be published in the near future [accomplished in 1949]—I have dealt not only with the economic problems of a market society but in the same way with the economics of all other thinkable types of social cooperation. I think that this is indispensable in a world where the fundamental principles of economic organization are at stake.

**Nationalökonomie, Theorie des Handelns und Wirtschaftens* (Geneva, Switzerland: Èditions Union, May 1940), 772 pages.

†*Nationalökonomie* was superseded by *Human Action* (New Haven, CT: Yale University Press, 1949), 927 pages, which English edition first appeared in 1949. Mises' "Foreword to the First Edition" describes *Human Action* as follows: "The present volume is not a translation of this earlier book. Although the general structure has been little changed, all parts have been rewritten."

I try in my treatise to consider the concept of static equilibrium as instrumental only and to make use of this purely hypothetical abstraction only as a means of approaching an understanding of a continuously changing world. It is one of the shortcomings of many economic theorists that they have forgotten the purpose underlying the introduction of this hypothetical concept into our analysis. We cannot do without this notion of a world where there is no change; but we have to use it only for the purpose of studying changes and their consequences, that means for the study of risk and uncertainty and therefore of profits and losses.

VI

The logical result of this view is the disintegration of some mythical interpretations of economic entities. The almost metaphysical use of terms like capital has to be avoided. There is in nature nothing which corresponds to the terms capital or income. There are different commodities, producers' goods, and consumers' goods; it is the intention of the individuals or of acting groups which makes some goods capital and others income. The maintenance of capital or the accumulation of new capital are always the outcome of a conscious action on the part of men who restrict their consumption to limits which do not reduce the value of the stock available. It is a mistake to assume the immutability of the capital stock as something natural which does not require special attention. In this respect I have to disagree with the opinions of one of the most eminent economists of our time, with Professor Knight of Chicago.

VII

The weak point of the Böhm-Bawerkian theory [of Capital and Interest] is not, as Professor Knight believes, the useless introduction of the concept of the period of production. It is a more serious deficiency that Böhm-Bawerk reverts to the errors of the so-called productivity theory. Like Professor Fetter of Princeton I aimed at an elimination of this weakness by basing the explanation of interest on time preference only.

The touchstone of any economic theory is according to an oft-quoted dictum, the treatment of the trade cycle. I have tried not only to restate the monetary theory of the cycle but also to demonstrate that all other explanations cannot avoid using the main argument of this theory. Of course, the boom means an upward movement of prices or at least a compensation for tendencies working toward falling prices and to explain how this requires the postulation of a rising supply of credit or money.

VIII

In every part of my treatise I try to take into account the relative weight to be assigned to different institutional factors and to different economic data. I further discuss the objections raised not only by different theoretical schools but also by those who deny the possibility of any economic science. The economist has to answer those who believe that there is no such thing as a universally valid science of society, who doubt the unity of human logic and experience and try to replace what they call international and, therefore, as they say, vain knowledge with doctrines which represent the peculiar point of view of their own class, nation or race. We do not have the right to let these pretensions pass unchallenged even if we have to assert truths which to us seem obvious. But it is sometimes necessary to repeat truths because we find repeated instances of the old errors.

Ludwig von Mises

Austrian School of Economics

Usually when referring to economics in Vienna and Austria, one speaks of the "Austrian School." Many people misunderstand this term, believing there was a special Austrian school of economics in Vienna, an organized institution like a law school in this country. Now the fact is that the term "school" in connection with Austrian economics refers to a certain trend in doctrines; it is a doctrinal term.

The term "Austrian School" was originally given to a small group of Austrian economists by their adversaries in Germany. When the term was first used against the Austrians in the 1880s, it was used as a pejorative, with a certain amount of contempt. In this respect, it differed greatly from the names of the other two Austrian groups—the Psychoanalytical Movement and the Vienna Circle of Logical Positivism, both of which chose their names themselves. Both these other two groups have become internationally known as scientific groups. As a matter of fact, the so-called Logical Positivists have come to dominate the teaching of philosophy in the Anglo-Saxon universities, first of all in England and in the United States, not so much in France. What all these three groups

From *Austrian Economics: An Anthology,* compiled and edited by Bettina Bien Greaves (Irvington-on-Hudson, NY: Foundation for Economic Education, 1996). This address was given May 2, 1962, at the New York University Faculty Club. Dr. Mises was introduced by Dr. William H. Peterson, then a professor at New York University Graduate School of Business Administration. In the audience was Friedrich A. Hayek, professor of social and moral science of the Committee on Social Thought at the University of Chicago.

had in common is that they were not very popular with the authorities of the official Austrian academic hierarchy.

All the universities in Continental Europe are state universities. Even the idea that a university could be a private institution is foreign to most of these countries. So the universities are operated by the government. But there was a fundamental difference between them and other governmental institutions; the difference was that the professors enjoyed academic freedom.

All government employees, functionaries of the government, are bound, in the exercise of their functions, to obey strictly what they have been told and ordered to do by their supervisors. But although the teachers at the universities, technological universities, and all other schools of the same rank, were government employees, they had no superiors; they enjoyed academic freedom. Nobody, not even a member of the cabinet supervising the duties of the supreme management of instruction, had the right to interfere in any way with their teaching. This was of very great importance because the tendency has prevailed again and again for the government in these countries to influence the teaching of law, also of economics, political science, and the social sciences in general.

Now the important fact was that these three groups—the Austrian School of Economics, the Vienna School of Logical Positivism, and the Psychoanalytical Movement—had one thing in common. In the postwar period, at least, they were represented, not by professors appointed to teach, but by *Privatdozents.* A *Privatdozent* is an institution unknown to the universities of the Anglo-Saxon countries. A *Privatdozent* is a man who is admitted as a private teacher at the university. He does not receive any payment from the government; actually he has only the very unimportant right to receive the fees paid by his students. Most *Privatdozents* made the equivalent from their fees of about $5.00 or $10.00 a year. Therefore they had to find some other means of making a living in whatever way they wanted. As for me I served as economic adviser to the Austrian government's Chamber of Commerce.

I had been admitted to lecture at the University of Vienna as a *Privatdozent* a little over a year before the outbreak of the first World War. The War interrupted my teaching. When I came back from the War many years later, I found that many young men were very much interested in the study of economics; they wanted not only to pass the examinations but to become economists and contribute something to teaching and research in the field.

In regard to the study of modern languages the preparation of students in Austria for economics and legal studies, which were combined at the university, was very unsatisfactory. Instruction was rather good in Greek and Latin at the lower level of the Austrian Gymnasium [high school/junior college], as well as at the Gymnasiums of other European countries, say in France and Germany, but modern languages were neglected. Those who knew French and English had acquired their knowledge privately, which was not so easy to do during the War. And after the War the young men, who came to the seminar that I conducted as a *Privatdozent,* were practically not at all familiar with any foreign language. One of these men, Fritz Machlup, now a professor at one of the best known and biggest American universities, Princeton, tells me every time we meet, "Do you remember you gave me a list of books for a paper I had to prepare for your seminar, and on this list English-language books dominated?" Dismayed, Machlup had told me, "But these are English books!" Machlup reminds me I had then answered, "Certainly. Learn English."

Already at that time, immediately after the war, I had my first American student. This American student came to Vienna not as a private citizen but as a lieutenant in the U.S. army, as the aide-de-camp to another American, an older man, a colonel. The colonel's assignment in Vienna gave him practically nothing to do so he had a lot of leisure time. His young assistant had still less to do, and still more leisure time. He decided to use his leisure time in a way that would make it possible for him to take back to the United States with him, to Harvard University, a ready-made doctoral dissertation. In my seminar he wrote a doctoral dissertation on direct taxation in Austria. In the United States the income tax was at that time very new. Austria, with its 100-year history of income taxes and its corporation tax, had far more experience than the United States, so there was a lot for Americans to learn from Austria about taxes. This young man, John Van Sickle, became a very well-known author of books and is today a retired professor of Wabash College.

I had a two-hour seminar once a week at the University. But very soon that appeared insufficient. There were students in the seminar who had already acquired a very good knowledge of economic problems and who wanted to do serious research work. And then there were beginning students. So very soon I started a *Privatseminar,* which is considered by the German, French, and Austrian systems to be the most important work a professor can do. A *Privatseminar* has practically no official or legal connection with the university; it is simply an institution which permits a member of the faculty to meet regularly with his students to work and discuss problems of economics and history.

Now I started such a *Privatseminar,* and I must say that, looking back today, this *Privatseminar* was a success. In this very room I see one of its earliest members, Professor Hayek. And there are others from my seminar who are now teaching in this country—Gottfried Haberler at Harvard, Fritz Machlup and Oskar Morgenstern at Princeton. At Marquette University, there is Walter Froelich. Then there is a lady, Dr. Ilse Mintz, professor at Columbia University's School of General Studies.

We dealt with all kinds of problems which related economics to the other social sciences, for there were not only economists in my *Privatseminar.* Many of the students were less interested in economics as such than in the general problems of the social sciences and the sciences of human action. One of these was Eric Voegelin, for 20 years a professor at Louisiana State University, Baton Rouge, and now Professor of Philosophy at the University of Munich in Germany. Voegelin's name may perhaps be known to you as he acquired some fame as an author of philosophical books. Then there were two professors who taught at the New School for Social Research, Dr. Alfred Schütz and Dr. Felix Kaufmann. You will be perhaps astonished to learn that one member of my seminar, Dr. Emanuel Winternitz, teaches, or taught, history of art at Yale. You may be still more astonished to hear that Dr. Winternitz was a practicing lawyer and that when he came to this country he was almost immediately appointed by the Metropolitan Museum to a position in his specialty, a very special field dealing with problems in which painting and music come together; he is now head of one of the departments of the Metropolitan Museum of Art.

There were others, foreigners who came to Vienna for a time and attended my seminar not very regularly but often enough. I shall mention only a few. As you know I am not very much in favor of Marxism and similar doctrines, so you will be astonished to hear that one of these foreigners was Hugh Gaitskell, the present chief of the British Labour Party. Again you will be astonished to learn that another was a Japanese professor, Kotari Araki, who, later as a professor at the University of Berlin during the time of the Axis, taught about Japanese economics and Axis economic problems. I want to mention one other foreigner who attended my seminar, François Perroux, the present professor of economics at the Collège de France, the most renowned institution of French learning. There were also many others.

Due to the inflation and the economic conditions in Europe at that time, the problem for European students in general and for young students in Austria in particular was to a great extent financial. The regular study of economics was rather difficult for persons who couldn't afford to buy texts and other books, especially as libraries, even the official libraries, didn't have the money to buy them either. Therefore, it was of very great importance to find the means and the method to give these young men an opportunity to go abroad.

The first student of mine who went to a foreign country in this way was Professor Hayek. A distinguished professor at New York University, Jeremiah Jenks, had written important studies on the gold exchange standard in the Far East; one could say that Jenks was the man who made the gold exchange standard known to economists. Jenks came to Vienna because he wanted to study and write about European conditions and I introduced him to Hayek. Later by special arrangement, Dr. Hayek became Jenks' secretary for some time in New York. This was an exceptional case. Both Jeremiah Jenks and Hayek were exceptional men. To help others, it was necessary to find some other way.

One American institution that did an excellent job in this regard was the Laura Spelman Foundation, better known as the Rockefeller Foundation. Laura Spelman was the wife of the original old Rockefeller. This Laura Spelman Foundation made it possible for young European scholars to spend one or two years in the United States. They could attend universities if they wanted and visit different parts of the country; they could really derive great advantages from the arrangement.

The man who represented the Foundation in Austria was a professor of history, Francis Pribram. Pribram also accepted economists whom I recommended, and in the course of the years Gottfried Haberler, Oskar Morgenstern, Fritz Machlup, and several others came to the United States, spent two years here under the Foundation's auspices, and then went back as, I would say, "perfect" economists. As you know, they later wrote many very interesting and good books. One other Laura Spelman student I might mention was the German, Professor Wilhelm Roepke.

Another thing that developed out of my *Privatseminar* and my activities as economic adviser to the Austrian Chamber of Commerce was that in 1926 in Vienna we started the Institute for Business Cycle Research. Its first manager was again Professor Hayek. When Hayek left Vienna in 1931 to teach at the London School of Economics, Morgenstern, now professor at Princeton, succeeded him. In spite of some "unpleasant" experiences with the Nazis, this Institute still exists in Austria, although it is no longer the Institute for Business Cycle Research but a more general institute, the Austrian Institute for Economic Research.

What is very interesting is that these students, who studied in the 1920s at the Austrian universities and wanted to choose a scientific career and contribute to the development of science, let us say, as researchers in economics, had at that time in Austria very slim chances of making sufficient money or earning a living in this capacity. As students they knew very well that they would have to work in some other field and would only be able to devote their leisure time to their true interest, the study of economics. At that time they couldn't know that, when Austria was invaded by Nazi Germany in 1938, many of them would be able to find teaching positions in foreign countries, especially here in the United States, and that they would find here a much broader field of activity than any they could ever have found in Austria.

Therefore, I must say that I consider the real success of my work as a professor of economics in Vienna was that I made it possible for a number of very gifted and able men to find a way to devote their lives to scientific research. This, of course, was not due to my merit. It was something that developed because of the general attitude in this country that accepted these young European refugees as teachers without regard to the fact that they were not born Americans and that they had been educated and had reached maturity in Europe under very different situations. What this country gained from these former students of mine is not bad; certainly today they now hold very good positions. As teachers of economics in this country, they have contributed to the success of American universities and especially to the departments of the social sciences and economics. Many are also working in other fields and in branches of business, often academic businesses.

There is a lot of talk today about international cooperation and international friendship among nations. In fact, nothing has been done officially in this regard. On the contrary the world is still divided in hostile camps, which is very unfortunate. But what has really developed unofficially in the world is an internationalism of science and teaching. I am proud that I could contribute a little bit to this internationalization. The fact that today there is international cooperation among members of the same field of research is one of the most important developments of recent years. We can all be proud of the fact that we have contributed a little bit to its development.